The Asbury Theological Seminary Series in Christian Revitalization Studies

This volume is published in collaboration with the Asbury Theological Seminary Series in Christian Revitalization Studies. Building on the work of the previous Wesleyan/Holiness Studies Center at the Seminary, the Series provides a focus for research in the Wesleyan Holiness and other related Christian renewal movements, including Pietism and Pentecostal movements, which have had a world impact. The research seeks to develop analytical models of these movements, including their biblical and theological assessment. Using an interdisciplinary approach, the Series bridges relevant discourses in several areas in order to gain insights for effective Christian mission globally. It recognizes the need for conducting research that combines insights from the history of evangelical renewal and revival movements with anthropological and religious studies literature on revitalization movements.

In this study, Patrick Eby demonstrates continuity with the aims of this Series through his careful study of the theme of the restoration of the image of God (*imago Dei*) in humanity, viewed as integrative factor in bringing together diverse issues embodied in the four major developmental phases of the life and theology of Charles Wesley. Special focus is given to the hymns, as well as other important primary sources from the body of Charles Wesley's literary corpus. This reading of his work in relation to this major integrative theme should also offer insight for contemporary movements of revitalization and church renewal, and for that reason the volume is offered as an appropriate contribution to this Series.

J. Steven O'Malley
General Editor
The Asbury Theological Seminary Studies in World Christian Revitalization

The Heart of Charles Wesley's Theology

Patrick A. Eby

Asbury Theological Seminary Series:
The Study of World Christian Revitalization Movements in
Pietist/Wesleyan Studies

EMETH PRESS
www.emethpress.com

The Heart of Charles Wesley's Theology

Copyright © 2017 Patrick A. Eby
Printed in the United States of America on acid-free paper

All rights reserved. No part of this book may be reproduced, or stored in a retrieval system or transmitted in any form or by any means, electronic, mechanical, photocopying, recording, scanning or otherwise, except as permitted by the 1976 United States Copyright Act, or with the prior written permission of Emeth Press. Requests for permission should be addressed to: Emeth Press, P. O. Box 23961, Lexington, KY 40523-3961. http://www.emethpress.com.

Library of Congress Cataloging-in-Publication Data

Names: Eby, Patrick A., author.
Title: The heart of Charles Wesley's theology / Patrick A. Eby.
Description: Lexington : Emeth Press, 2017. | Series: Asbury Theological Seminary series in Christian revitalization movements in Pietist/Wesleyan studies
Identifiers: LCCN 2017039963 | ISBN 9781609471187 (alk. paper)
Subjects: LCSH: Wesley, Charles, 1707-1788. | Hymns--History and criticism. | Methodist Church--Doctrines.
Classification: LCC BX8495.W4 E29 2017 | DDC 230/.7092--dc23
LC record available at https://lccn.loc.gov/2017039963

Contents

Abbreviations / ix

Preface / 1

Introduction / 5

1. The Rise of Methodism: 1725–1739 / 17

2. Methodist Revival and Theological Challenge: 1739–1749 / 61
    Charles Wesley and the Moravians / 62
    Charles Wesley and the Predestinarians / 68
    Persecution and the Necessity of Suffering / 73
    The Role of Marriage: The Single Life and the 'Single Eye' / 75
    The Theology of Charles Wesley in *Hymns and Sacred Poems* (1749) / 79
    Conclusion / 92

3. Methodism in the Midst of Suffering and Conflict: 1750–1762 / 101
    Charles Wesley and the Lay Preachers / 102
    The Perfectionist Controversy / 110
    Charles Wesley's response to Suffering / 113
    The Theology of "Short Hymns on Select Passages of Scripture" / 121
    Conclusion / 138

4. Methodism in Charles Wesley's Waning Years: 1763–1789 / 151
    Charles Wesley's Continued Emphasis on the 'Single Eye' and Suffering / 152
    Charles Wesley's Continued Support of The Church of England / 158
    Charles Wesley's Continued Rejection of Antinomianism / 160
    Charles Wesley on Dying Well / 161
    The Theology of Charles Wesley in MS Scriptural Hymns / 162
    Conclusion / 170

Conclusion / 177

Select Bibliography / 183

Abbreviations

DDCW	Charles Wesley Papers
DDWES	Wesley Family Papers
EqH (1750)	Hymns Occasioned by the Earthquake, March 8, 1750 (1750)
HSP (1739)	Hymns and Sacred Poems (1739)
HSP (1749)	Hymns and Sacred Poems (1749)
MARC	Methodist Archives and Research Center, John Rylands University Library of Manchester, England
OED	Oxford English Dictionary
SHSPS (1762)	Short Hymns on Select Passages of Scripture (1762)

Preface

Charles Wesley used the language of being restored in the image of God to describe the goal of the Christian life. His definition stressed the importance of faith, purity, humility, love of God, and the love of neighbor; a definition similar to that of Henry Scougal. This book examines Charles Wesley's poetry and other documents from four different time periods to reveal Charles's perception of the situations he faced and how he used being restored in the image of God to respond to these situations.

Chapter one examines the time at Oxford and the early years of Charles's ministry before 1739. Chapter two examines the early years of the revival, from 1739-1749. During this period, Charles responded to the theologies of the Moravians and the Calvinists. Charles responded to their theology by stressing the importance of the means of grace and the universal love of God. Chapter three examines the time period from Charles's marriage until 1762. This was a time filled with much suffering and struggle. Both he and John struggled with personal issues and with issues that would shape the Methodist movement. Charles argued that the Methodists should remain in the Church of England in opposition to some of the lay preachers. During this period, John and Charles also dealt with the perfectionist controversy. Charles's reflections on both the earthquakes that shook England in the 1750's, and on family illnesses and deaths, helped him to clarify the role suffering played in the restoration of the image of God. Chapter four focuses on the final years of Charles's life. During his waning years, Charles continued to resist those who desired to separate from the Church of England. He dealt with complaints that his lifestyle was no longer consistent with the Methodist definition of having a 'single eye'. These complaints dealt mostly with the way he raised his musical sons.

This study argues that Charles Wesley maintained a consistent definition of what it meant to be restored in the image of God, although the way he applied it changed throughout his lifetime.

Any project of this magnitude could not be accomplished without the encouragement, help, and support of several people and organizations. I am grateful for the guidance and feedback I have received from John R. Tyson. His feedback and encouragement helped me not only complete my research, but also showed me areas where my arguments were weak and needed further development. I am also grateful for the feedback I received from Peggy Samuels who provided helpful comments on style, the use of poetry, and areas that would need to be developed for a reader outside of the Methodist tradition.

I would like to thank the faculty, staff, and several of my fellow students at Drew University for their help and friendship. I am thankful for the help of several professors including Charles Yrigogen, Dale Paterson, James Pain, Virginia Burrus, Morrey Davis, Don Dayton, Jill Burnett Comings, and Ken Rowe. Staff at the Library and The United Methodist Library and Archives have helped me in my search for resources. I would especially like to thank Chris Anderson, Jocelyne Rubinetti, Mark Shenise, Jennifer Woodruff Taft, and Robert Williams. Several friends shared my joys and my frustrations in my time at Drew. I will not forget the friendship of Luther Oconer, Paulo Mattos, John McNassor, Matthew Akers, and Kevin Newburg.

There are several people from other institutions whose help was invaluable. Thank you to Duke Divinity School for the opportunity to study and use the resources available at the libraries and archives. A special thanks to Richard Heitzenrater for allowing me to use Frank Baker's transcriptions of Charles Wesley's letters for this project. I would also like to thank Randy Maddox for his feedback and his help in securing some of the more difficult manuscripts. I am thankful for my friendships with Steven Hoskins and Tom Albin which began during my time at Duke. I am also thankful for the resources Tom Albin has shared with me including his transcriptions of several early Methodist manuscripts.

My time at the Methodist Archives and Research Center at John Rylands University was an important part of my manuscript research which would not have been possible without the help of Peter Knockles, Gareth Lloyd, and the archive staff. They were very helpful in finding the manuscripts I was looking for and providing a sense of what is available at Rylands for future research. I would also like to thank Paul Chilcote, S T Kimbrough, and Peter Forsaith for their help in thinking about Charles Wesley.

As important as professional contacts are, some of the most important contacts are personal. This project was enriched by people at Stroudsburg Wesleyan Church who allowed me to share not only the content of my study, but who shared in the joys and the struggles one faces when completing such a project. I especially want to thank those who have been a part of my small groups and Dana Antal who has been both a friend and a fellow inquirer into the life of the Wesleys. Finally, I would like to thank my family. Mom and Dad, you helped instill a passion for learning early in my life. Ruth, Aaron, Nichole, and Benjamin—you have learned more about Charles Wesley than you ever expected. You have listened with grace and interest. You have encouraged me when I struggled and you have been patient with me when I have been under stress. Your presence has been invaluable!

Any acknowledgment is incomplete. There are many more people who could have been named from family, friends, and professional contacts. You know who you are and even though you're not mentioned you know the place you have in my life. Thank you for all you have done.

Introduction

On March 14, 1736, Charles addressed his small congregation about the adventure they were beginning in Frederica. As he spoke to them, he turned to a theme that would continue to be a major focus of his theology; he challenged them to have a 'single eye' that was focused on the "one thing needful, namely the recovery of the image of God."[1] Charles used the language of being restored in the image of God to describe the goal of the Christian life throughout his life, but his experiences and interaction with others changed how Charles defined and applied what it meant to be restored in the image of God. Because Charles's language of restoration was a major focus of his theology throughout his life and because he changed how he defined and applied what this meant, it is important to examine how he used the concept of being restored in the image of God throughout his life. This will help to illustrate how Charles Wesley's presentation of his theology changed throughout his lifetime.

Although there has been no detailed study of how Charles used the idea of being restored in the image of God, there is little or no disagreement that it is an important key to understanding his theology. John Whitehead, Charles's first biographer, pointed out the role this doctrine played in the life and ministry of Charles Wesley: "He possessed the requisites for his office in no small degree: he had a clear view of the state of human nature, and of the doctrines of the Gospel, pointing out God's method of restoring sinners to his favour and image."[2] According to Whitehead, Charles not only understood how people could be restored in the image of God, his ministry included sharing this understanding with others.

On the other hand, although J. Ernest Rattenbury agreed that this was a central emphasis of Charles's theology, he was less confident that Charles's definition was practical. According to Rattenbury, Charles intentionally taught something he thought was the impossible to attain.[3] Rattenbury said the title "Waiting for Full Redemption" was an appropriate description of Charles's theology.[4] The recovery of the image of God was something to wait for, but it was something that would never be realized in this life. It was a process that never would be completed in this life, a process that included the imitation of Christ and his suffering.[5] So, although both Whitehead and Rattenbury agree that being restored in the image of God was an important doctrine for Charles, they seem to define what this meant in different ways. Whitehead suggests Charles was able to guide people to being restored in the image of God, but Rattenbury believes Charles thought it was impossible.

The difference of these two views highlights the difficulty of understanding the writings of Charles Wesley. His theology is difficult to determine for several reasons. First, most of Charles's theology was written in the form of hymns and/or poems. The use of poetry to express theological concepts presents problems of its own. For instance, the use of paradox can be misleading if not understood in its larger context. Sometimes Charles used paradox to work through a theological issue. At other times, he used it to express a sense of mystery. A second problem is the tendency to simplify, categorize, or generalize the thought of an individual. This tendency can be seen in the question, "What was Charles Wesley's theology?" This implies that Charles's theology was consistent and unchanging. These questions or problems are evident in an examination of Charles's theology of what it means to be restored in the image of God. Charles made what seemed to be contradictory statements, sometimes focusing on the impossibility of recovering the image of God, but at other times talking of being recovered now. Why are there these contradictions? Are these differences a result of his poetic method and the use of paradox? Are they an indication of how his theology developed over time? Does it indicate an inconsistency explained by something else? When his poetry is examined over time, with an understanding of his poetic method and within the context which it is written, what seems like a contradiction, both the impossibility of recovering the image of God and the immediate recovery of the image of God, may be more fully understood.

Another feature of Charles's poetic method was to use different words or phrases to express the same idea. For this study, it will be important to be aware of other words or phrases he used to express being restored in the image of God. For instance, in one poem, Charles compared regaining God's image with regaining God's character and nature.

> Away my faithless fear
> That I shall seek in vain!
> I must regain thine image here,
> I must thyself regain;
> Thy nature, and thy mind,
> Thy purity and love
> I shortly upon earth shall find,
> And then my place above.[6]

In another poem, Charles described putting on the image of Christ as being given the meek and lowly mind of Jesus.

> I too, forewarn'd by Jesu's love,
>   Must shortly lay my body down;
> But ere my soul from earth remove,
>   O let me put Thine image on!
> Saviour, Thy meek and lowly mind
>   Be to Thine aged servant given,
> And glad I'll drop this tent, to find
>   Mine everlasting house in heaven.[7]

The understanding of Charles's theology can also be enriched through recognition of his use of parallel language. Not only does it give additional information about how Charles viewed the Christian life, it helps to define what Charles meant by being restored in the image of God. For instance, although not dealing directly with being restored in the image of God, Craig Gallaway notes how Charles used the concept of having the mind of Christ to indicate a concern for the poor and outcasts of society. This concern included both listening to and giving his all to those who were marginalized. For Gallaway this concept was closely linked to "those biblical references concerning Christ's presence among the poor which liberation theology itself has found so central and inspiring."[8] For instance, Charles wrote,

> 2 Thy mind throughout my life be shewn,
>   While listening to the wretch's cry,
> The widow's and the orphan's groan,
>   On mercy's wings I swiftly fly,
> The poor and helpless to relieve,
> My life, my all, for them to give.[9]

John R. Tyson describes another major emphasis in Charles's theology, how Charles used images or phrases that focused on restoring the original righteousness found in Eden. Charles "occasionally defined sin as the loss of original righteousness." According to Tyson, Charles did this in order to highlight his emphasis on "a return to perfection that was lost in the Edenic fall into sin." In other words the counterpoint to a "sinful state was the restoration of the *imago Dei* (image of God) within the Christian."[10] Tyson has also shown how this emphasis in Charles focused on a 'full salvation,' one that dealt with both original and actual sins.[11] Tyson also notes how Charles's development of this doctrine bears a striking resemblance to the Eastern Fathers' ideas of both recapitulation and *theosis*.[12] Specifically, Tyson argued that Irenaeus's theology of being restored in the image of God "became the centerpole of his [Charles Wesley's] theology."[13]

A. M. Allchin agrees with this assessment, arguing that Charles was one of a small group of theologians in the Anglican tradition that believed in *theosis* or in a "Participation in God."[14] Allchin's examination of the theme of *theosis* was partially his attempt to question the way that the Evangelical and Catholic intentions are set in opposition. According to Allchin, "The Evangelical Movement had, in its origins, profoundly Catholic intentions."[15] One of the ways that this can be seen was in the way the Wesleys defined the means of grace. Although they realized that without "a living faith in God in Christ" the means of grace were without value, they at the same time taught that the means of grace were necessary for a person "to grow in maturity and balance, to become firm and sure, and thus be rooted in the shared faith and experience of the Christian centuries."[16] After examining several hymns arguing for a union of the Divine and the human, Allchin qualifies what this language would mean for Charles: "Of course the language of absorption, which Charles Wesley does not hesitate to use, needs to be interpreted in the light of the definition of Chalcedon which both John and Charles Wesley wholeheartedly maintained."[17]

In order to understand Charles's ideas one must understand his context. This not only includes a basic understanding of the theological, political, social, and poetic circumstances of the eighteenth century, it also includes a more detailed understanding of the Evangelical and Methodist movement in the Eighteenth Century. Fortunately, some work has been done on the development of the doctrine of perfection—a concept closely related to being restored in the image of God—in the early Methodist era. One example of this is the meticulous work of M. Robert Fraser, who traces the theological understanding of Christian Perfection chronologically through the lives of John Wesley, Charles Wesley, John Fletcher, and others of the rank and file. He clearly shows how the Methodist movement struggled with the definition of perfection.[18] Allan Coppedge also employs a historical approach in his study of the concepts of predestination and perfection. Both of the themes are addressed in Charles's presentation of what it means to be restored in the image of God. Coppedge's primary focus is John Wesley, but special attention is also given to the influence of Charles Wesley and George Whitefield.[19]

Another important consideration is how this doctrine figured in the theology of John Wesley. This can be used to highlight the part Charles played in the struggle for a Methodist theology, although a detailed comparison of the struggle between John and Charles is beyond the scope of this project. Hoo-Jung Lee argues that John Wesley's emphasis on the recreation of the image of God provides the hermeneutical clue with which to read John Wesley. He believes that by reading Wesley through this lens, one could avoid an overly individualistic approach to salvation.[20] Theodore Runyon in *The New Creation* argues that the heart of Christianity for John Wesley was the renewal of creation through the restoration of humanity in the image of God.[21] Runyon notes that, "The renewal of creation and the creatures through the renewal in humanity of the *image of God* is what Wesley identifies as the very heart of Christianity."[22] For John, this restoration will surpass what was lost in the fall.[23] Like others, Runyon believes salvation for Wesley was more than justification; it includes the renewal of people and creation in the image of God. Runyon argues that John Wesley's view of sanctification "is an important corrective to the evangelical Protestant tendency to equate salvation with justification or conversion, for it points to the divine goal not just of reconciliation and a new status in the eyes of God, but the gracious re-creation of both individuals and the social world through the renewal of the image of God in humanity."[24]

While it seems obvious that being restored in the image of God was a central emphasis, not only of Charles Wesley, but also of early Methodism, what still needs to be addressed is how Charles used this doctrine to express and shape the theology of eighteenth-century Methodists. Some questions to consider include: Is his understanding static or dynamic? Does the way he defined being restored in the image of God change as he struggles to define the theology of Methodism? What, if any, are the catalysts for the changes in the way he expressed his theology?

In order to examine Charles's presentation of this doctrine, I will employ two primary approaches. First, I will determine the issues Charles addressed when he spoke of being restored in the image of God. These issues, which arise out of specific experiences, can be used to examine his corpus as a whole. Some questions arising from these issues include but are not limited to the following. What does it mean to be restored in the image of God? When is one restored in the image of God? How is one restored in the image of God? What are the ethical implications of being restored in the image of God? Second, I will examine the development in Charles's published theology by comparing and contrasting the way Charles expressed the idea of being restored in the image of God at different times in his life. I will do this primarily through an examination of his poetry. Because Charles was a prolific writer of poetry and is believed to have written as many as 9000 hymns and poems, a subsection of his poetry will be selected.[25] The number of poems will be limited by looking primarily at one collection that was written during different periods of his life. Charles Wesley's poems have been divided into three main categories; those published before 1749, those published in and after 1749, and those that remained unpublished during Charles's lifetime.[26] In order to represent Charles Wesley's poetry appropriately, I will examine four major collections of his poetry in their entirety, having at least one come from each of these main categories.

The first collection I will examine will represent the earliest period of Charles's life. For this I will be examining *Hymns and Sacred Poems* (1739).[27] I will look at this collection both to discover Charles's early thought and to examine the influence others may have had on his theology. It will not be used to argue for Charles's theology at this point in his life; instead poems both by him and others will be explored in order to give a context against which Charles's later work can be evaluated. The main reason for using this hymnal as a backdrop, and not as an example of Charles's early theology, is that any composition from this hymnal or any other collection published before 1749 may have been either composed or edited by John. In the case of *HSP* (1739) many of the poems were composed by neither John nor Charles and all of the poems composed by John and Charles lack attribution.[28] Even though this collection is *not* being used to determine Charles Wesley's theology, it still would be beneficial to know which hymns Charles authored, if possible. One way to determine which hymns Charles authored is to examine individual hymns using the internal 'canons' formulated by Henry Bett.[29] These 'canons' attempt to differentiate Charles Wesley's work from that of his brother by dealing with internal evidence such as rhyme, meter, or word usage. Others have modified these 'canons' but Frank Baker's assertion is still valid; "Much study is still necessary before anything like certainty can be achieved on many of these conjectures."[30] These difficulties make examination of the historical setting of a poem and any existing manuscript evidence necessary. On the other hand, one cannot dismiss these early hymns out of hand because they are an important witness to the development of Methodist theology, a theology that Charles helped to shape and a theology that shaped him. During the early days of the revival, until about 1749, John and Charles shared the leadership of the 'Wesleyan' branch of the Methodist movement. One place this can be clearly seen is that many of the early tracts, pamphlets, and hymnals bore either the names of both John and Charles, or the names of neither. The fact that Charles allowed his name to be attached to these publications seems to indicate, at the very least, his acceptance of their publication, and may even indicate his approval of the theology they contain. Even when John and Charles chose to use anonymity, it was intended to present their efforts as joint efforts. Even so, any theology from this period would be just that, a joint theology. It would be directly under the influence of John and, therefore, at the very least it is a theology of Charles seen through the editorial pen of John. Because of these difficulties, in the collections before 1749 I will be looking mainly for the influence these early publications had on Charles's later theology. In other words, these early publications will be used primarily to show some of the ways being restored in the image of God was being used in poetry with which we know Charles was familiar.

The next two collections I will look at are *Hymns and Sacred Poems* (1749) and *Short Hymns on Select Passages of the Holy Scriptures* (1762).[31] John did not edit either of these collections. Instead, we have John's comments, made in his personal copy of the collections, stating he did not approve of all that Charles wrote in these two texts.[32] Because of this, we can be confident these two publications represent a distinctive presentation of Charles Wesley's theology. *HSP* (1749) collected many of the poems written during the early days of the movement. Charles hastily collected these poems to raise money for a 'bride price'. *SHSPS* (1762) includes comments on select scriptures and is representative of the period following 1749 when the difficulties between John and Charles are most evident. It also gives Charles's early response to the perfectionist controversies. In the preface, he said his purpose was both to prove and to guard the doctrine of Christian perfection.[33] The final collection I will look at is a manuscript from 1783 called MS Scriptural Hymns.[34] Charles copied this manuscript between May 11 and May 26 in 1783. This text will be used to examine the mature thought of Charles Wesley.

Rattenbury rightly claimed that the only way to understand the poetry and hymns of Charles Wesley is to understand the context within which they were written. Hints of this context can be seen in Charles's reflections on his personal experience in his journal and letters. The letters and journal contain Charles's personal witness or perspective of the events as he experienced or perceived them.[35] The letters are valuable because they give details that would otherwise be lost. The letters are our main source of Charles's reflections on his daily life. They give a picture of his family life, his relationship with Sally, and the relationship both he and Sarah had with the people of Bristol. As has been noted, Charles did not write for a wider audience. Charles's tendency to be more direct in the way he writes may be one result of his plan to leave his letters and his journal unpublished, unlike his brother John who used both his letters and journal to promote Methodism.[36] Gareth Lloyd argued that this more private use of his letters meant he felt no need to promote the party line like John. At times, the letters give examples of how Charles Wesley put his theology into practice. For instance, the advice he gave to individuals, especially about spiritual matters, probably reflect those things that were most important to him.

The journal of Charles Wesley is another important source for determining the context in which Charles wrote his hymns and poems. For the journal, I will be using the new critical edition recently published by Kenneth G. C. Newport and S T Kimbrough.[37] Although this resource is a critical edition of Charles Wesley's Journal, it is still of limited value because of the uneven nature of Charles's writing. It is also limited in value because the entries only cover a short period of Charles's life. Thomas Albin rightly maintained that the entries before 1738 are relatively full of details, revealing the inner struggle and reflections of Charles Wesley, but after 1738 the entries are much more terse and are primarily concerned with his ministry and travel.[38] The period of time covered by The Manuscript Journal is from 1736 to 1756. There are nine gaps in the journal, and the gaps after August 31, 1751 are "so significant that for all practical purposes the journal ends on this date."[39]

The sermons of Charles Wesley are another possible source for discovering his theology. I will be using Kenneth Newport's critical edition of Charles Wesley's sermons.[40] What value do the sermons have for determining Charles Wesley's theology? For the purpose of this book, they play an important role because they show what type of sermon Charles preached in the early years of his ministry. As we have already seen in our discussion of the poems, the early period of Charles Wesley's theology is difficult to distinguish from his brother's because of their close association until 1749. So like *HSP* (1739), these sermons will be used to provide a foundation on which to examine Charles's later theology. I will look for the language, images, and theology found in these sermons that parallel the later poetry of Charles. I will also look for ideas and language he seems to avoid in his later publications. The value in these sermons is that they show how Charles Wesley presented ideas of being restored in the image of God to his congregation.

This book will examine four time periods from Charles Wesley's life. Each chapter will deal with a specific time period. Chapter one will look at Charles Wesley's time at Oxford and the early years of his ministry up until 1739. It was during this time that the emphasis on being restored in the image of God can first be seen in Charles's life. This chapter will give an overview of how restoration in the image of God was described not only in Charles's life, but also in broader Methodism. One of the reasons for looking at broader Methodism is the scarcity of primary sources and the inability to separate the work of John and Charles Wesley in *HSP* (1739). It will be argued that two of the major influences on Charles's definition of being restored in the image of God were Henry Scougal and William Law.

Chapter two will examine the early years of the revival, from 1739-1749. During this period, Charles faced challenges from both the Moravians and the Calvinists. Charles stressed the importance of the means of grace in opposition to their antinomian tendencies. Charles also stressed the universal love of God in opposition to the Calvinistic doctrines of predestination and reprobation. During this time period, the Methodist movement experienced persecution. This chapter will show how Charles argued that persecution and other forms of suffering were a necessary part of being restored in the image of God. Towards the end of the decade, Charles faced a life-changing decision: would he reject his commitment to remaining single, a commitment of the 'Oxford Methodists', or would he marry Sarah Gwynne. His struggle with this decision will be explored in light of his commitment to having a 'single eye'. As a part of his decision to marry Sarah Gwynne, Charles published *HSP* (1749). This collection will be examined to see how Charles presented his theology of being restored in the image of God.

Chapter three will examine the time period from Charles's marriage until he published *SHSPS* (1762). This was a time filled with much suffering and struggle. He and John struggled with both personal issues, and more importantly with issues dealing with the shape of the Methodist movement. Charles argued for the importance of the Methodists remaining a part of the Church of England in opposition to some of the lay preachers. John and Charles also dealt with a controversy about the nature of perfection during this time period. Charles's response to this controversy shows what he thought were the key elements of being restored in the image of God. The role of suffering in the restoration of the image of God will also be examined through Charles's reflections on both the earthquakes that shook England in the 1750's and his personal reflections on family illnesses and death. SHSPS (1762) will be examined to see how Charles presented his arguments about being restored in the image of God in poetry during this time period.

Chapter four will focus on the final years of Charles's life. During his waning years, Charles continued to resist those who desired to separate from the Church of England. He also had to deal with complaints that his lifestyle was no longer consistent with the Methodist definition of having a 'single eye'. These complaints dealt mostly with the way he raised his musical sons. During this period, Charles collected poems on selected verses of the Old and New Testament in an unpublished manuscript, MS Scriptural Hymns. This manuscript will be examined to show how Charles presented restoration of the image of God in the waning years of his life.

Charles's focus throughout each of these periods was on the importance of being restored in the image of God. How he applied this in his everyday life changed as he married and had children, but the goal of being restored in the image of God continued to guide his definition of the Christian life. How he presented these ideas helped to shape the Methodist definition of the Christian life and was used as a check against those who denied the importance of being restored in the image of God.

Notes

1. Charles Wesley, Sermon 16, "Matthew 6: 22–3," in *The Sermons of Charles Wesley: A Critical Edition, with Introduction and Notes*, ed. Kenneth G. C. Newport (Oxford: Oxford University Press, 2001), 309. Hereafter cited as *Sermons of Charles Wesley*.
2. John Whitehead, *The life of the Rev. John Wesley, M.A. some time Fellow of Lincoln-College, Oxford. Collected from his private papers and printed works; ... With the life of the Rev. Charles Wesley*, vol. 1 (London: Stephen Couchman, 1793), 180.
3. J. Ernest Rattenbury, *The Evangelical Doctrines of Charles Wesley's Hymns* (London: .Epworth Press, 1942), 288.
4. Ibid.; and Charles Wesley, *Hymns and Sacred Poems*, with an editorial introduction by Randy L. Maddox (Bristol: Felix Farley, 1749), The Center for Studies in the Wesleyan Tradition, Duke University, *http://divinity.duke.edu/initiatives/cswt/charles-published-verse*. Hereafter cited as *HSP* (1749). It is worth noting that Charles also has a section called "Waiting for Redemption." For Charles this waiting did not imply that one could not achieve redemption, only that it was a process.
5. Rattenbury, *The Evangelical Doctrines of Charles Wesley's Hymns*, 288-89.
6. Charles Wesley, "'He that seeketh, findeth'—[Matt.] vii. 8," in *Short Hymns on Select Passages of the Holy Scriptures*. 2 vols., with an editorial introduction by Randy L. Maddox (Bristol: Farley, 1762), The Center for Studies in the Wesleyan Tradition, Duke University, *http://divinity.duke.edu/initiatives/cswt/charles-published-verse*, 2:147-48. Hereafter *SHSPS* (1762).
7. Charles Wesley, "[784.] 'Shortly I must put off this my tabernacle, even as our Lord Jesus Christ hath shewed me.'—[2 Pet.] i. 14," in *SHSPS* (1762), 2:397.
8. Craig B. Gallaway, "The Presence of Christ with the Worshipping Community: A Study in the Hymns of John and Charles Wesley" (Ph. D. diss., Emory University, 1988), 222.
9. Charles Wesley, "[739.] 'Pure religion, and undefiled before God and the Father, is this, to visit the fatherless and widows in their affliction, and to keep himself unspotted from the world.'—[James] i. 27," in *SHSPS* (1762) 2:380.
10. John R. Tyson, *Charles Wesley on Sanctification: A Biographical and Theological Study* (Grand Rapids, MI: F. Asbury Press, 1986), 51.
11. Ibid., 54.
12. Ibid., 60.
13. Ibid., 60-61.
14. A. M. Allchin, *Participation in God: A Forgotten Strand in Anglican Tradition* (Wilton, CT: Morehouse-Barlow, 1988).
15. Ibid., 24.
16. Ibid., 35.
17. Ibid., 31.
18. M. Robert Fraser, "Strains in the Understandings of Christian Perfection in Early British Methodism" (Ph. D. diss., Vanderbilt University, 1988).
19. Allan Coppedge, *Shaping the Wesleyan Message: John Wesley in Theological Debate* (Nappanee, IN: Evangel Pub., 2003).
20. Hoo-Jung Lee, "The Doctrine of New Creation in the Theology of John Wesley" (Ph. D. diss., Emory University, 1991).
21. Theodore Runyon, *The New Creation: John Wesley's Theology Today* (Nashville, TN: Abingdon Press, 1998).
22. Ibid., 8.
23. Ibid., 11. This emphasis in John Wesley can be seen most clearly in his sermon

"God's Love to Fallen Man." (John Wesley, Sermon 59, "God's Love to Fallen Man," in *Sermons II,* ed. Albert C. Outler, vol. 2 of The Bicentennial Edition of the Works of John Wesley [Nashville: Abingdon Press, 1985]), 422-435.

24. Runyon, *The New Creation,* 231.

25. Charles Wesley, *Representative Verse of Charles Wesley,* Frank Baker, ed. (London: Epworth Press, 1962), xi. Hereafter cited as *Representative Verse of Charles Wesley*; and Charles Wesley, *Charles Wesley: A Reader,* ed. John R. Tyson (Oxford: Oxford University Press, 2000), 21. Hereafter cited as *Charles Wesley: A Reader.*

26. Joanna Cruickshank, "Charles Wesley and the Construction of Suffering in Early English Methodism" (Ph. D. diss., The University of Melbourne, 2006), 32-33.

27. John Wesley and Charles Wesley, *Hymns and Sacred Poems: A Facsimile of the First Edition, London: William Strahan, 1739,* with a preface by S T Kimbrough Jr. and a Introduction and Notes by Paul Chilcote (Madison, NJ: The Charles Wesley Society, 2007). Hereafter cited as *HSP* (1739).

28. A new database published online by The Center for Studies in the Wesleyan Tradition, Duke Divinity School (*http://divinity.duke.edu/initiatives/cswt*). Resources include a first line index of works contained in the published works thought to be written by Charles Wesley. Also included are a file for each collection of published hymns with a critical introduction, hymns written only by Charles, notes which detail changes from edition to edition, and notes that John made in his copies of Charles' publications. The site also includes a transcript of most of Charles's Manuscript Hymns and Poems. The site defines its purpose as follows: "This online collection is intended to provide a standard source for scholarly study and citation of the poetical works of John and Charles Wesley."

29. Henry Bett, *The Hymns of Methodism in Their Literary Relations* (London: Epworth Press, 1920), 21-33.

30. *Representative Verse of Charles Wesley,* lviii-lx.

31. *HSP* (1749) and *SHSPS* (1762).

32. These notes are included in the new database published online by The Center for Studies in the Wesleyan Tradition, Duke Divinity School.

33. *SHSPS* (1762), 1:i.

34. Charles Wesley, "MS Scriptural Hymns (OT & NT)", MARC, MA 1977/576, Center for Studies in the Wesleyan Tradition, Duke University, *http://divinity.duke.edu/initiatives/cswt/charles-manuscript-verse.* Hereafter cited as "MS Scriptural Hymns." This manuscript has proposal for the *HSP* (1749) glued into front of it. Did Charles place this in the front cover? If so, does it indicate he considered publishing this manuscript?

35. Rattenbury, *The Evangelical Doctrines of Charles Wesley's Hymns,* 15.

36. Lloyd, "The Letters of Charles Wesley," 345.

37. Charles Wesley, *The Manuscript Journal of the Rev. Charles Wesley, M.A.*, Kenneth G. C. Newport and Jr. Kimbrough, S T, eds., 2 vols. (Nashville: Kingswood Books, 2007). Hereafter cited as *Manuscript Journal.*

38. Thomas R. Albin, "Charles Wesley's Other Prose Writings," in *Charles Wesley: Poet and Theologian,* ed. S T Kimbrough Jr. (Nashville, TN: Kingswood Books, 1992), 87.

39. Ibid. Jackson filled these gaps with some of Charles's journal letters in his edition of the journal. There are 18 pages in the Jackson edition of the Journal covering this period of time (*Manuscript Journal,* xxv).

40. *Sermons of Charles Wesley.*

1

The Rise of Methodism: 1725-1739

In 1739, John and Charles Wesley published *Hymns and Sacred Poems* (1739).[1] This collection was their first joint publication. How this publication reflected and shaped the theology of early Methodism is the main focus of this chapter. First, a brief overview of Charles's life from his time at Oxford in 1726 until the beginnings of the Evangelical revival in 1739 will be given. This background will provide a context in which to interpret Charles's hymns and poems. J. Ernest Rattenbury has rightly argued, "The theology of Charles Wesley cannot be properly understood apart from his life and experience."[2] In this chapter Charles's life will be divided into three major periods—periods that roughly correspond to John's three rises of Methodism.[3]

First, Charles's time at Oxford will be described. Information about Charles's time at Oxford comes primarily from his letters and the writings of other 'Oxford Methodists', including John Wesley, Benjamin Ingham, and George Whitefield. It was during this period of his life that Charles formed many of his ideas about the importance of people being restored in the image of God.

The second period explored will be Charles's time in America. Charles's involvement in the mission to Georgia will be considered by examining his letters, journal, and the first sermons he preached, some of which were copied from his brother's manuscripts.

The third period explored is his return to England. It was during this time that he experienced his 'Pentecost'. Again, much can be learned from Charles's letters, journal, and his sermons. An additional source of information for this period is the letters of those who had been impacted by Charles's ministry. These letters supplement Charles's record, and more importantly they show how others viewed his ministry. These letters in particular provide a clue to the ways Charles helped to shape early Methodism.

The final section of this chapter will examine how the theology of early Methodism was presented in *HSP* (1739). Although it is difficult to determine Charles's part in the publication—which hymns he wrote, translated, or paraphrased or how what he had written was edited by John—it is still important to examine this publication because it helped to shape the theology of early Methodism at the beginning of the Evangelical revival.[4] *HSP* (1739) is also important because it includes poems that reflect the theology of the early days of Methodism at Oxford and in America. By 1739, John and Charles had rejected the theology presented by some of these hymns, but they still chose to publish them.[5] It will also be shown how *HSP* (1739) highlighted the new direction Methodism began to take because of their positive interaction with the Moravians and their growing rejection of the English mystics.

The First Rise of Methodism: Beginnings at Oxford

Late in their lives, both John and Charles Wesley remembered their time at Oxford as the place where they were first called Methodists.[6] Seeing this as a beginning did not deny that many people and events had already shaped the life of Charles before he came to Oxford, including his mother and father and his brother Samuel Wesley Jr., but for Charles the move to Oxford in 1726 meant a new beginning, and at first it also meant a new found freedom. It was the first time he was not under the supervision of either his parents or his brother Samuel. By his own admission, he spent his first year in diversions, but this was soon replaced by a turn to a seriousness that would influence the rest of Charles's life.[7] One result of this turn to seriousness was his involvement in and leadership of a group of students who later become known as the 'Oxford Methodists'. For this study, how the group started is less important than the focus of the group and the influence which Charles's participation in the group had on his theology.

To be an 'Oxford Methodist' meant a commitment to meeting with three to six members of the group several times during the week.[8] The group activities included study, devotion, and charity. The goal of these spiritual disciples was the pursuit of both inward and outward holiness.[9] Some devotional practices were mostly private like meditation, self-examination, prayer, and Bible reading. Other practices, though personal, would not go unnoticed by those around them. The observation of the stationary fasts and rising early in the morning attracted the attention of others and was a major source of ridicule. They also regularly attended public services and participated in taking communion as often as possible. Their acts of charity included caring for the poor, disadvantaged, sick, and infirm. This included visits to prisons, workhouses, and the houses of the sick and infirm.[10] Heitzenrater noted that the 'Oxford Methodists' "were, in effect, following the *The Country-Parson's Advice* to unite in friendly societies, 'engaging each other in their several and respective combinations to be helpful and serviceable to one another in all good Christian ways.'"[11]

Their study together included both academic and devotional works. Many of the devotional books they read encouraged them to imitate the life of Christ. These authors included "Thomas á Kempis, Ignatius of Loyola, Lorenzo Scupoli, Francis de Sales, Joseph Hall, Johann Gerhard, Richard Baxter, Jeremy Taylor, Henry Scougal, Madame Guyon, Anthony Horneck, and William Law . . ."[12] Based on the limited evidence we have of what Charles was reading up until 1739, it seems he valued Henry Scougal (1650-1678) and William Law (1686-1761) more than he valued the others. Of these two, it seems likely though, that the most influential author in forming Charles's emphasis of people being restored in the image of God was the work of Henry Scougal. Scougal was a Scottish Episcopalian, but this did not limit his influence as his work "was much admired by both English Puritans and Scottish Presbyterians."[13] The main focus of Scougal's book, *The Life of God in the Soul of Man*,[14] was how to be restored in the image of God. His definition influenced Charles's theology throughout his life.

This book was important not only in Charles's life and in his ministry, but also in the lives of those he influenced. It may be that he first developed his love for the book from his mother. When speaking of his turn to a more serious life, he mentioned the role he felt his mother played. "'Tis owing in great measure to somebody's (my mother's, most likely) that I am come to think as I do, for I can't tell myself how or when I first awoke out of my lethargy—only that 'twas not long after you [John Wesley] went away."[15] Scougal's book had long been a favorite of Susanna Wesley. In a letter to John she said, *"The Life of God in the Soul of Man* is an excellent book, and was an acquaintance of mine many years ago; but I have unfortunately lost it."[16] John's purpose in the letter does not seem to be to get a recommendation from his mother (the 'Oxford Methodists' had been reading the book together as a group in the summer of 1732);[17] instead, he seemed to want her opinion on this specific book. She said it was an excellent book, but also noted that there were others she had found helpful from time to time.[18] Whether or not Charles was exposed to the book before 1731, it is clear that Charles not only read the book while at Oxford, but also recommended it to others. For instance, the group was reading it during the summer of 1732. Charles not only read it, but he also loaned his copy to George Whitefield.[19] George Whitefield recorded his response to the book in his journal, noting the influence it had upon his life. "In a short time he [Charles Wesley] let me have another book, entitled, *The Life of God in the Soul of Man*; [and, though I had fasted, watched and prayed, and received the Sacrament so long, yet I never knew what true religion was, till God sent me that excellent treatise by the hands of my never-to-be-forgotten friend.]"[20] Towards the end of his life, Whitefield reaffirmed the importance of this book in his sermon "All Men's Place," "I must bear testimony to my old friend, Mr Charles Wesley. He put a book into my hands, called, "The Life of God in the Soul of Man," whereby God showed me that I must be born again or be damned. I know the place: it may be superstitious, but whenever I go to Oxford, I cannot help running to the spot where Jesus Christ first revealed Himself to me, and gave me the new birth."[21]

Another 'Oxford Methodist' who reported reading *The Life of God in the Soul of Man* was Benjamin Ingham. He began it on Friday, August 28, 1734, while visiting Epworth with John and Charles and finished it the next day.[22] Heitzenrater has argued that Benjamin Ingham was a part of a group that met primarily with Charles. It seems probable that Charles introduced him to this important book. Charles not only read and recommended Scougal's works at school; he also read them with his sister Mehetabel, whose nickname was Hetty. He noted the good effect they had on her, "I went again to my simple Hetty, to learn some of her humility. Her convictions were much deepened by my reading of *The Life of God in the Soul of Man.*"[23] That this was a focus of Charles during this time is suggested by Charles's sermon on the previous Sunday. Charles had preached "The One Thing Needful" from Luke 10:42, a sermon whose theology was very similar to that found in *The Life of God in the Soul of Man*.

Charles was familiar with other books by Scougal. Later in the same month, Charles recorded reading a sermon by Scougal with Hetty. He wrote,

> Contrary to my expectation, I found Hetty left behind. We passed two hours in conference and prayer.
> Two hours afterwards I was with her again, and read Scougal on "Few Saved." She was quite melted down, and after a prayer for love, said, "God knows my heart. I do desire nothing but him."[24]

From these few references, it seems that *The Life of God in the Soul of Man* in particular and the writings of Scougal in general were important not only in the formation of Charles Wesley's theology, but also in the development of early Methodist theology. The continued importance of *The Life of God in the Soul of Man* for Methodism can be demonstrated by the recommendations made to the lay preachers at the 1746 Annual Conference, where they were encouraged to read it as a part of their morning and evening devotions.[25] Its continued importance to the Methodist movement is also illustrated by John's publication of an extract of it throughout his life. John published five editions of *The Life of God in the Soul of Man* during his lifetime starting in 1744 and ending in 1790. It continued to be published by the Methodists even after John's death.

The primary focus of *The Life of God in the Soul of Man* was how to be restored in the image of God. Scougal defined 'true religion' as a "Union of the Soul with God, a real participation of the Divine Nature, the very Image of God drawn upon the Soul, or in the Apostle's phrase, *it is Christ formed within us*."[26] His definition of the divine life had five main characteristics. "The root of the Divine Life is Faith, the chief branches are Love to God, Charity to Man, Purity, and Humility. . . ."[27] Faith for Scougal was a divine sense. He believed it had "the same place in the Divine Life which Sense hath in the natural. . . ."[28] It was through the divine sense that one experienced the Love of God as "a delightful and affectionate sense of the Divine perfections, which makes the Soul resign and sacrifice it self wholly unto him. . . ."[29] According to Scougal, when someone experienced the love of God, they responded with a love to God, a love marked by a willingness to sacrifice all for God. This definition included both recognition of the character of God and the personal response of sacrifice and resignation. Charity, which was the second branch of religion for Scougal, included "all the parts of Justice, all the Duties we owe to our Neighbor. . . ."[30]

Scougal's definition of purity and humility seem to have had a distinctive impact on Charles's theology. Scougal defined purity as the ability to "despise and abstain from all pleasures and delights of sense or fancy which are sinful in themselves, or tend to extinguish or lessen our relish of more divine and intellectual pleasures; which doth also infer a resoluteness to undergo all those hardships he may meet with in the performance of his duty."[31] In other words, purity meant denying oneself pleasures that were sinful and pleasures that diminished one's love for God. Purity meant being willing to endure hardships associated with showing love to one's neighbor. Scougal illustrated this type of purity by looking at the life of Jesus, who although he did not deny legal pleasures for others—like marriage—chose to live a life without these pleasures. According to Scougal, Jesus' refusal to enjoy the blessings of this life should be the example Christians follow. It was this understanding of the Scriptures and of the life of Christ, which seemed to be accepted by 'Oxford Methodism': Jesus' example was to be followed exactly, even his example of celibacy. John's description of following Christ in "A Plain Account of Christian Perfection" reflected this idea of Christ as the model for the Christian's life.

> 5. In the year 1729, I began not only to read, but to *study*, the Bible, as the one, the only standard of truth, and the only model of pure religion. Hence I saw, in a clearer and clearer light, the indispensable necessity of having 'the mind which was in Christ,' and of 'walking as Christ also walks'; even of having, not *some part* only, but *all* the mind which was in him; and of walking as he walked, not only in *many* or in *most* respects, but in *all* things. And this was the light, wherein at this time I generally considered religion, as an *uniform* following of Christ, an *entire* inward and outward conformity to our Master. Nor was I afraid of anything more, than of *bending* this rule to the experience of myself, or of other men; of allowing myself in any *the least* disconformity to our grand Exemplar.[32]

The final characteristic of the Divine Life according to Scougal was humility. He defined humility as "a deep sense of our own meanness, with a hearty and affectionate acknowledgement of our owing all that we are, to the Divine Bounty, which is always accompanied with a profound submission to the Will of God, and great deadness towards the glory of the world, and the applause of men."[33] Scougal again looked to Jesus as the pattern for the life of humility. He emphasized the "infinite condescension of the Eternal Son of God," and his "lowly and humble deportment while he was in the World."[34] His humility was demonstrated in his ascribing "the honour of all to his Father, telling them, *That of himself he was able to do nothing.*"[35] This God-reliant and self-effacing attitude not only guided Charles's actions, it was also a measure by which he judged the actions of others.

The other author who seems to have significantly influenced Charles during his time at Oxford and the early days of his ministry was William Law. Most of the evidence that Charles read, met, and recommended Law to others is recorded in his Journal, which began in 1736. That Law influenced Charles at an earlier date is suggested by the influence Law had on the 'Oxford Methodists'.[36] Not only did they read his works, the most important being *A Serious Call to a Devout and Holy Life*,[37] they also visited him when they had the opportunity. On one such occasion, while they were in London, John Gambold, Westley Hall, and Benjamin Ingham visited Law "and heard his words again on 'man's fall, and the one thing necessary.'"[38] William Law's importance to Charles can be illustrated by looking at his Journal. The following is but one example among many. "While I was talking at Mr Checkley's on spiritual religion, his wife observed that I seemed to have much the same way of thinking with Mr Law. Glad I was and surprised to hear that good man mentioned, and confessed all I knew of religion was through him."[39]

Eventually, both John and Charles began to question the theology of their spiritual mentor. What this questioning meant will be explored later in this chapter. Even that later questioning does not diminish the influence he had on their view of perfection. Harald Lindström stressed William Law's influence in the formation of John Wesley's view of sanctification through Christian love. Even though this influence was before 1738, he believed Wesley's mature view of Christian love continued to have some affinity with that of William Law.[40] The major source for Lindström's discussion of Law's view of Christian love was *A Practical Treatise upon Perfection*.[41] Law's ideas about being restored in the image of God are similar to Scougal. He believed "the sole end of Christianity is to deliver us from our present misery and disorder and raise us to the blissful enjoyment of the divine nature."[42] This was accomplished by loving God and neighbor. This love involved cooperation "between the divine grace and human obedience and effort."[43] From Lindström's description, it is possible that someone reading Law would mistake human effort as his primary emphasis. It was the responsibility of people to prepare themselves for the grace of God. According to Lindström, Law taught, "Man must fulfil his obligations, for instance that of humility, not merely because it is a 'reasonable Duty' and 'proper to our State' but because it also '*qualifies* and *prepares* us for larger Degrees of Divine Grace, such as may Purify and Perfect our Souls in all Manner of Holiness.'"[44]

If this is the way Charles read William Law, it would help to explain the many activities in which both he and the 'Oxford Methodists' were involved. It also helps to explain the moralistic tone exhibited in most of his earliest sermons. Lindström said that Law believed, "This is why religion 'calls us to a State of *Self-denial, Humility*, and *Mortification,* because it is a State that awakens the Soul into right Apprehensions of Things, and qualifies us to see, and hear, and understand the Doctrines of eternal Truth.'"[45]

Law's emphasis on the love of neighbor can also be seen in the theology of the Wesleys. For Law, love for God only became Christian love when it was extended to all. The reason that love must be extended to all was that it was an imitation of the love of God.[46]

Before turning to one of the most difficult periods in Charles's life, his time in America, it should be noted that even during his time at Oxford he sometimes struggled with the standards set before him. For Charles the decision to become more serious did not come easily. Although it is unclear why he struggled with these commitments, his struggle may have resulted from the resistance he encountered both from the students he was leading and from some of the leaders of the University. In a letter to his father on June 11, 1731, Charles recounted some of these difficulties. He began with a question on taking communion, and then he shared how one student in particular—a student whom people had feared Charles would make into an enthusiast—now received communion only three times a year and had also given up his prayers and studying.[47] Did the doubts and actions of this student raise questions in Charles's mind? A year later Dr. Terry, who was the canon of Christ Church, "was rumored to be prepared along with the censors to 'blow up the Godly Club,' as they were called by some. The complaints directed at John Wesley in particular, focused on the impression that he was singular, whimsical, and formal."[48] These external attacks may have, at least temporarily, weakened Charles's commitment to the lifestyle prescribed by 'Oxford Methodism'. In 1732, when the outside pressure against the group was at its most severe, Charles may have shared his doubts about some of their practices with John. It seems by John's comments, that Charles was having doubts specifically about the necessity of constant communion. Heitzenrater has argued this was Charles's struggle based on comments in John's diary: "When Charles himself began wavering on the question of the Sacrament during the next month, it is likely that the opinion of Clayton was of some weight and value in helping John Wesley 'recover' his brother to their former view."[49]

That Charles was 'recovered' to the singular practices of 'Oxford Methodism' is reflected in a letter he wrote to his brother Samuel the following February in which he argued for the necessity of fasting, one of the most unpopular disciplines practiced by the 'Oxford Methodists'. He wrote, "Since my Last I met with a Remarkable Clause in our Statutes wch not only justifies, but I think requires my pressing the Duty of Fasting on my Pupils."[50]

Samuel Wesley Jr. continued to provide guidance for Charles while he was at Oxford. Charles looked to his brother for help when deciding whether or not to go to America. Although in the end he followed the direction of John, he still valued his brother Samuel's advice. Something of Charles's idea of being renewed in the image of God is revealed in his correspondence with his brother Samuel. It seems that Charles equated being renewed in the image of God with being in a 'state of salvation', or at the very least his brother Samuel understood what he said this way. Samuel rejected this, saying, "By being renewed in the image of God, if you mean to grow still better, 'tis sense and piety; but if you hint at your not being now in a 'state of salvation', I should fear you are distracted."[51] This seems to be an ongoing concern with Charles—his not yet being in a 'state of salvation'. In responding to several letters he had received from Charles while he was in America, Samuel again questioned his brother's doubts: "That you had lived eighteen years without God, I either do not understand, or I absolutely deny."[52] Charles's doubts would not be relieved by his mission to Georgia; they would be exacerbated.

The Second Rise of Methodism: The Mission to Georgia

Charles's decision to join his brother in going to America involved a change in his plans. Until his brother approached him, Charles planned to stay at Oxford. His concern for the spiritual health of others can be seen in the midst of these changes. One example of this concern is found in his correspondence with James Hutton. James Hutton and his sister "had been 'earnestly awakened' by John Wesley's solemn preaching on 'The One Thing Needful' just prior to the Wesleys' departure for Georgia."[53] Charles was concerned his absence might have a negative impact on James's spiritual development. Charles addressed this fear to James: "I fear'd yt as soon as I was gone, you wd fold yr Arms again, & sink down into your Spiritual Lethargy: Yt Nature wd prevail over Grace, and plunge you as deep as ever in that fatal Lukewarmness wch is more abominable with God than even Sin itself."[54] He told James that the only way to be secure in his faith was to continually make progress in his faith. This progress included a hunger and thirst after righteousness, which should have as its goal nothing short of having "the mind wch was in Xt Jesus."[55] Charles also urged James Hutton to move from "a meer State of Nature wholly Alienated from the Life of God."[56] Once again, the goal to which Charles spurred him on was a renewal of the image of his mind. He quoted William Law to argue that a renewal of the mind was a change from a carnal mind to "a Spiritual Mind."[57] Charles also referred to Henry Scougal's argument that in the religious person the "Divine life bears Sway" whereas in the wicked person "the Animal life doth prevail."[58] Charles suggested to James that to progress in the religious life he should read and meditate throughout the year on "The Country Parson, Kempis & Law."[59] The Scriptures Charles quoted in his advice to Hutton included "take up your Cross daily"[60] and "be not conform'd to this World, but be you Transformed by the Renewing of yr Mind."[61] He reminded James not only of the necessity of avoiding the things of the world, but also of the need to suffer. He explained taking up the cross of Christ as follows: "You will not long continue so unacquainted with Sufferings; so unlike yr Master. Only labour faithfully to root out Self, and you will perceive what the *Interna Crux Christi* means."[62]

Two and a half years later, after his return from Georgia, Charles continued to instruct James Hutton. This time he asked a specific question relating to his commitment to God. He asked James, "Do you go to sleep at Ten & rise at Six? Till you thus deny yourself every Night & take up your X every Morning, I cannot be, to any purpose. . . ."[63] Charles's letters to James demonstrate that for Charles being restored in the image of God involved not only a singular purpose and asceticism, but also it included a need to deny oneself by taking up the cross of Christ.

In November of 1735, Charles wrote to his brother Samuel and shared how their trip had been delayed. In the short time he had spent with his fellow travelers just off the coast of southern England he made the following observation: "He

[John] is learning German for ye sake of ye Bohemians we carry with us, who are all pious Xians."[64] Thus began a relationship that would help to redefine, at least in part, the theology of Charles Wesley and early Methodism.

If a letter to Varanese (Charles's pseudonym for Sally Kirkham) is any indication, the voyage to and the prospect of ministry in America had negatively impacted the disposition of Charles. In the first line, he shared his desire to die—a recurring theme in his writings.[65] He began, "God has brought an unhappy unthankful wretch hither through a thousand dangers to renew his complaints and loath the Life which has been preserved by a series of Miracles."[66] He continued to complain to Varanese, who according to Charles was the only person to whom he felt comfortable complaining. After this, he gave a summary of his beliefs, beliefs he struggled to follow himself. In spite of his own struggle to live by these principles, he encouraged Varanese to be single in her desire and devotion to God.

> I cannot follow my own Advice, but yet I advise you—Give GOD your Hearts; Love Him with all yr Souls; Serve Him with all yr Strength. Forget ye things yt are behind; Riches, Pleasure, Honour—in a Word, whatever does not lead to GOD. From this [hour] let yr Eye be single. Whatever ye speak, or think, or do, let GOD be your Aim, and God only! Let your One End be to please and love GOD! In all your Business, all yr Refreshments, all yr Diversions, all Conversations as well all in those, which are commonly call'd Religious Duties let yr Eye look strait forward to GOD. Have One Design, One Desire, One Hope! . . . His H. Spirit shall dwell in you & shine more and more upon yr Souls unto ye Perfect Day. He shall purify Hearts by Faith from every Earthly Thought, every Unholy Affection. He shall stablish yr Souls with so lively a Hope as already lays hold on ye Prize of your High Calling. He shall fill you with Peace & Joy & Love. Love, the Brightness of His Glory, ye Express Image of H[is] Person! Love wch never rests never faileth, but shall spre[ad] its Flame, still goeth [on] conquering and to conquer, till what was but now a Weak foolish, wavering sinful Creature be filled with all ye Fullness of GOD![67]

A few things are worth highlighting from this passage. First, Charles emphasized having a single focus, having one goal. That goal was to love and serve God. Anything that did not lead to this love of God must be forgotten and left behind. Charles used the image of a 'single eye' to stress the importance of having this single focus. He also used this image of a 'single eye' in some of the sermons he preached during this time. For instance, he began a sermon on Matthew 6:22-23 with the importance of having a 'single eye' because, "The light of the body is the eye." He then contrasted the 'single eye', which is focused only on God, with the 'divided eye', which is evil.[68] Second, Charles described the Image of God as love, a love that would spread and result in a person "being filled with all ye Fulness of GOD."

Charles's last days in America were marked by some of the same concerns noted in this letter to Varanese. His time of leisure in Boston was something Charles could not enjoy because he understood faith as being totally devoted to God. He was treated with honor and respect, his every need was met, and he was meeting with the leaders of Boston, but his time in Boston had not improved his attitude.

Even his illness did not relieve him of the doubts he was abandoning the ascetic lifestyle for a life of pleasures. He wrote to his brother John, "I have lived so long in honours and indulgences that I have almost forgot whereunto I am called, being strongly urged to set up my rest here."[69] In another letter to John, he once again expressed his desire for a short life. "Though I am apt to believe I shall at length arrive in E[ngland] to deliver what I am entrusted with, yet do I not expect or wish for a long life. How strong must that principle of self-preservation be which can make such a wretch as me willing to live at all!—Or rather, unwilling to die; for I know no greater pleasure in life than in considering it cannot last for ever!"[70]

The suffering and persecution he experienced while in America may explain the continued desire for a short life. The only comfort he mentioned in the midst of his suffering in America were the daily readings of Scripture from both the morning and evening lessons. One journal entry will be sufficient to illustrate how the Scripture comforted him.

> I was struck with those words in the evening lesson:
> Thou therefore, my son, be strong in the grace that is in Christ Jesus. . . . Endure hardness, as a good soldier of Jesus Christ. . . . Remember that Jesus Christ was raised from the dead, according to my gospel, wherein I suffer trouble, as an evil-doer, even unto bonds; but the word of God is not bound. Therefore I endure all things for the elect['s] sake. It is a faithful saying, for if we be dead with him, we shall also live with him; if we suffer, we shall also reign with him [2 Tim. 2:1–12].[71]

Charles believed that suffering was a necessary part of the Christian life. In a letter to his brother Samuel he wrote, "I am not sorry to hear of the offense your regulations are likely to give, for I am more and more convinced, that none escape being evil-spoken of, but those that deserve not to escape it."[72]

Charles's sermons during this period support this emphasis on a singleness of intent. The earliest extant sermon written by Charles was based on Philippians 3:13-14 and included the phrase, "but this one thing I do . . ."[73] Charles argued in this sermon that to pursue the "one thing" meant a commitment to strive for Christian perfection. This pursuit included a rejection of worldly pleasures. He argued, "since we are not so secured of our reward, as to be excluded from all possibility of losing it, we are not at liberty to indulge ourselves in a state of ease and security."[74]

Another sermon he preached on his way to America was based on II Kings 18:21. In this sermon, he presented the need to choose between two options. The people Charles seemed to be addressing in this sermon were those who had chosen the things of this life. He asked, "Do we not see many Christians who make loud professions of zeal for religion, still anxious for the good things of this life?"[75] According to Charles, there are three major competitors for our affections, and these competitors lead us away from the most important thing in this life—loving God. These three competitors are the world, the flesh, and the devil. Charles continued emphasis on asceticism can be seen in his definition of 'the world'. He said,

> For who is there among us that may be termed holy in the strict sense of the word as it implies a total renunciation of the world, the flesh, and the devil; an entire and absolute devotion of ourselves to God? . . . There are, God knows, many rivals, who will dispute with him his right to absolute and entire dominion. Theworld with her pomps and vanities, pleasures and delights, entertainments and diversions, has monopolized a large share of our affections.[76]

Later in the sermon, he further emphasized this point.

> The blessed apostle St James saith expressly (Jam 4.4) that the friendship of the world is enmity with God; and whosoever will be a friend of the world is an enemy of God. Here we see that there is no such thing as dividing our love. The love of the world is absolutely inconsistent with the love of God. So that if we afford the world, or anything besides God any part of our love, in such proportion do we become the enemies of God.[77]

This sermon also focused on the danger of voluntary sins. Charles allowed that God forgave some of our sins, specifically our involuntary sins, but he could not forgive those sins that involved the "omissions of duty and commissions of sin which men wilfully live in through a fond and vain persuasion that it is not required of them to be as holy as possibly they can."[78] For Charles this included a total devotion to living a perfect life as far as it was possible: "We say then that a state of voluntary imperfection, a half *course* of piety, a life divided between God and the world, is a state which God has nowhere promised to accept nor yet assured us of a reward for it."[79]

A third sermon written by Charles and preached during the earliest days in Georgia was based on Psalm 126:7. It focused on the role of suffering in the life of the Christian. It highlighted the way that the virtues of humility, faith, hope, and love lead to each other and ultimately to an eternal joy. The need for a heavenly focus can be seen in Charles's explanation of those moments when people are overcome by the cares of the world, when they become in Charles's words "like common men." The call for a singular focus went beyond the common, it was a call to consistent holiness.

> If they have a deep humility, a strong faith, a lively hope, and a fervent love sometimes, do they not at other times droop, and so faint in their minds as to become like common men? If they do, no one can expect their joy should reach farther than the cause of it; they cannot be always happy till they are always holy. When they are always heavenly-minded, they shall then rejoice evermore![80]

During this early period, Charles copied three sermons from his brother John dealing with the pursuit of the 'one thing needful'. The first sermon Charles preached in America was based on Matthew 6:22-23 and was entitled "A Single Intention." Even though this sermon was copied from his brother, it focused on a theme common to all of the sermons looked at above. Matthew 6:22-23 reads, *"The light of the body is the eye: if therefore thine eye be single, thy whole body shall be full of light. But if thine eye be evil, thy whole body shall be full of darkness."*[81] In the first section of the sermon, Charles described what he meant by "the light of the body is the eye." If the eye be single, your whole life will be filled with light, "'but if thine eye be evil', if thy intentions be not single, . . ." then the result was darkness. This singleness was described as a "recovery of the image of God." If one was not pursuing this goal, the result was a life filled with darkness, ignorance, guilt, and misery. Charles wrote,

> 3. 'But if thine eye be evil', if thy intention be not single, if thou hast more ends than one in view; if, besides that of pleasing God, thou hast a design to please thyself, or to do thy own will; if thou aimest at anything beside the one thing needful, namely, a recovery of the image of God: 'thy whole body shall be full of darkness;' thou wilt see no light, which way soever thou turnest.[82]

Charles applied this message to the adventure they were about to begin in Georgia. He argued that to be single in their intentions meant observing their religious duties not to please people, but to please God. It meant seeing everything—their work, their meals, their diversions, and their conversations—as a way to please God. Charles ended this sermon by highlighting the rewards and/or benefits resulting from this commitment. The ultimate goal was to so be filled with peace, joy, and love that one became the "express image of his person!" The result would be a person "filled with the fulness of God!" He said,

> He shall purify your hearts by faith from every earthly thought, every unholy affection. He shall establish your souls with so lively a hope as already lays hold on the prize of your high calling. He shall fill you with peace, and joy, and love! Love, the brightness of his glory, the express image of his person! Love which never rest [sic], never faileth, but still spreads its flame, still goeth on conquering and to conquer, till what was but now a weak, foolish, wavering, sinful creature, be filled with all the fullness of God![83]

Starting in September 1736, Charles preached on the phrase "One thing is needful" from Luke 10:42.[84] This was copied from John's manuscripts and once again emphasized having a singular focus. Many of the ideas already noted are present in this sermon, but in this sermon, some of them have been qualified. This sermon still related singularity to being restored in the image of God, but it also focused on the loss of the image and the resulting problems. Charles argued that people were originally created in the image of God and the great work of this life was to regain that image.

> Now this great work, this one thing needful, is the renewal of a our fallen nature. In the image of God was man made, but a little lower than the angels. His nature was perfect, angelical, divine. He was an incorruptible picture of the God of glory. He bore his stamp on every part of his soul; the brightness of his Creator shone mightily upon him. But sin hath now effaced the image of God. . . . The glory is departed from him! His brightness is swallowed up in utter darkness![85]

To regain what has been lost involved having "our diseases cured, our wounds healed, and our uncleanness done away."[86] At times Charles defined the image of God as love. This love was the desires or affections of an individual. The goal of the Christian life for Charles was for people to acquire and express affection for the same things for which God expressed affection. The only way for someone to have affection for the things of God was by experiencing God's love and responding with a love for God and the things of God. This was at odds with the natural inclinations of people. Charles believed the natural tendency was to love the things of this world, which were at odds with the love of God. Charles stressed that if anyone loved God, then God would come to them and fill them with God's presence.

> For to this end was man created, to love God; and to this end alone, even to love the Lord his God with all his heart, and soul, and mind, and strength. But love is the very image of God: it is the brightness of his glory. By love man is not only made like God, but in some sense one with him. 'If any man love God, God loveth him, and cometh to him, and maketh his abode with him.'[87]

This sermon also addressed the place that pain and pleasure have in the Christian life. "Every pain cries aloud, 'Love not the world, neither the things of the world.' And every pleasure says, with a still small voice, 'Thou shalt love the Lord thy God with all thy heart.'"[88] Charles did not completely condemn the marks of success, instead he conceded that the marks of success could be used in the pursuit of the 'one thing needful'. He continued, however, to deny that they *were* the 'one thing needful'. "Is it [the 'one thing needful'] to obtain honour, power, reputation, or (as the phrase is) to get preferment? Is the one thing to gain a large share in that fairest of the fruits of earth, learning? No. Though any of these may sometimes be conducive to, none of them is, the one thing needful."[89]

In spite of the concession that honor, power, reputation, and learning may be used to obtain the 'one thing needful', the sermon was still primarily ascetic in its focus. The main distraction to being restored in the image of God was still a love of the world and its pleasures. The diseases from which people needed to be healed included "those inbred diseases of our nature, self-love, and the love of the world."[90]

Charles began preaching another sermon copied from John Wesley's manuscripts on Mark 12:30 in October of 1737.[91] The overarching theme of this sermon was how to love God. The emphasis was that the love of everything else should either lead to a love of God, or flow from a love for God. Charles concluded this sermon with the following summary; "The full sense of the first and great commandment is therefore contained in this single sentence: 'Thou shalt love God alone for his own sake, and all things else only so far as they tend to him.'"[92] The major obstruction to fulfilling this commandment according to Charles was once again a divided purpose and the love of the world.

> 3. What wonder is it, then, that the essential wisdom of the Father knew no mean between a single and an evil eye! That his inspired Apostle cries out with such vehemence of affection, 'Purify your hearts, ye double-minded;' that his beloved disciple, after 'This is the true God,' immediately subjoins, 'Little children, keep yourselves from idols.' What idols and what idolatry we are to keep ourselves from

he elsewhere explicitly declares, in those well-known words, 'Love not the world, neither the things of the world: if any man love the world, the love of the Father is not in him.'[93]

It is not only in his sermons that we can see how Charles presented his theology, his journal from this period also shows how he taught and interacted with others. One way Charles used his journal was to record conversations. The reflections written in his journal need to be seen for what they are, Charles's presentation of either the way he saw things or the way he wanted others to understand what he was experiencing. This is true whether or not Charles ever intended to publish his journal.

On July 31, 1736, after the sudden death of Appee's fiancée, Charles had an opportunity to ask him about his loss. Charles recorded the impression of their conversation. "I concluded his heart was right, and its uppermost desire to recover the divine image." Immediately after this, Charles was positively affected by taking the sacrament. "Something of this desire [to be restored in the image of God] I felt myself at the holy Sacrament, and found myself encouraged, by an unusual hope of pardon, to strive against sin."[94] Appee later confessed his lack of faith to Charles. Charles encouraged him to begin immediately to work out his salvation, which would include "the one condition of exchanging this world for the next."[95]

Two conversations Charles had with Appee suggest Charles struggled to live out his theology of pursuing the 'one thing needful'. Appee shared with Charles the perception that others had of both him and John. In one conversation between Charles and Appee, Appee recalled a conversation with Olgethorpe.[96] He shared with Charles that their fasting and other "abstentiousness" was seen as "mere hypocrisy." He also told Charles that it seemed that Charles was either uneasy under the restraints of John, or was more interested in pleasing himself than God. Later, Charles recorded the following observation of Appee. "He frankly replied he took me to be partly in earnest, but I had a much greater mind to please myself than to please God. That as for money, I did not much value it, but in my eagerness for pleasure and praise I was a man after his own heart. That as I could not hold it, he wished I would leave off my strictness, for I should then be much better company."[97] Charles neither affirmed nor denied Appee's observations.

The Third Rise of Methodism: The Return to England

Charles did not intend his return to England in December of 1736 to be permanent. Charles's poor health was what finally kept him from returning to America. He saw the trip to England as a part of his duties as Olgethorpe's secretary. His mission was to deliver the letters he was carrying to Mr. Vernon, which he did during his first week in London. Over the next year, Charles stated his desire to return to Georgia several times. In a letter to his brother Samuel, he noted the reason for the delay in his return to Georgia was his being sick: "One consequence of my sickness you will not be sorry for—its stopping my sudden return to Georgia."⁹⁸ It was not until April of 1738 that Charles wrote his letter of resignation to Olgethorpe (almost two years after he initially offered to resign in Georgia in July of 1736). Even then, Olgethorpe wanted Charles to keep the position and have a deputy fulfill Charles's responsibilities in his absence.⁹⁹ Charles's desire to return to Georgia was probably based on his belief that he could only make progress in his spiritual life where there was suffering and persecution.¹⁰⁰

Charles's view that persecution and suffering were a necessary part of being restored in the image of God at this point in his life can be seen in a letter to his brother John. Charles began by congratulating John on his "late glorious treatment," a treatment that reinforced Charles's desire to return to Georgia. This treatment was mainly to endure the gossip of some of the people to whom Charles and John were ministering in Georgia. The gossip, however, ruined relationships with leaders in the colony and may be one of the main reasons their ministry in Georgia was so short. Charles described the importance of the glorious treatment they received while in Georgia as their willingness to suffer as Christ had suffered. Charles argued that the persecution they experienced was a result of the struggle between the light and the darkness and was a necessary part of being a follower and imitator of Christ. He reminded his brother of three Scriptures among the many he found supporting his understanding of suffering. Charles wrote, "'All that will live godly in Christ Jesus *shall suffer persecution;* [II Timothy 3:12]'—'The disciple is not above his master; [Matthew 10:24, Luke 6:40]'—'If they have persecuted me, they *will also persecute you* [John 15:20];'—and a thousand others."¹⁰¹ He reminded his brother that they should have expected and rejoiced in the treatment they had received. In fact, their suffering was a necessary part of being restored in the image of God. Charles reminded his brother, "You *know* the absolute impossibility of being inwardly conformed to Christ without this outward conformity, this badge of discipleship, these marks of Christ. You marvel not, as if some new thing had happened unto you, but rejoice in tribulation, as knowing that hereunto you are called, and can only be made perfect through these sufferings."¹⁰²

John's experience in Georgia had increased Charles's desire to return to Georgia. Charles noted that suffering produced the fruits of meekness, gentleness, and love. In other words, the only way to become like Christ, to gain the fruits of meekness, gentleness, and love was to be willing to suffer as Christ had suffered. Charles ended this letter by quoting a passage from Thomas á Kempis, which he was reading in Latin at that time. The following is a translation of that passage found in John Wesley's edition of *The Christian's Pattern.*

> Thou oughtest for the love of God willingly to undergo all things, even labours, griefs, temptations, vexations, anxieties, necessities, infirmities, injuries, detractions, reproaches, humblings, shame, corrections, and contempts. These help to virtue; these try a soldier of Christ; these make the heavenly crown.¹⁰³

The necessity of suffering continued to be an emphasis of Charles's theology. For instance, in September of 1739 he observed that taking up the cross was a mark of following Christ. "Christianity flourishes under the cross. None who follow after Christ want [lack] that badge of discipleship."[104] Other 'Oxford Methodists' had a similar view of suffering and encouraged Charles to continue in this understanding. One of the possibilities Charles was considering while back in England involved what Benjamin Ingham referred to as *"worldly Preferment."* Ingham was glad that Charles had been saved from its deceitful, alluring, and bewitching temptations. He also prayed that Charles would continue to have "power to overcome the World the Flesh and the Devil, & like a brave Soldier manfully fight under Xt's Banners."[105] Towards the end of the letter, Ingham recounted the success he was having in his ministry at Ossett. He enjoyed the company of the Christians so much that he felt he was in "need of Suffering to counterbalance it [his pleasure]."[106] These comments reveal the same fears Charles was expressing while at Boston, that the comforts of this life would somehow retard his progress in being restored in the image of God.

One of the people Charles looked to for advice during his time was William Law. Charles often reported reading or hearing Law read. Charles would use those occasions to press or encourage certain behaviors. Recalling one such evening he wrote, "I had the satisfaction of seeing Mr Granville much affected to a chapter he had been reading of Mr Law. He desired his sister might hear it. I read it a second time, and took that opportunity of pressing upon him a daily retirement."[107] There were also occasions when he even sought out the advice of his mentor. After one meeting with William Law, Charles recorded, "I talked at large upon my state with Mr [William] Law at Putney. The sum of his advice was, 'Renounce yourself; and be not impatient.'"[108] The advice Charles received from Law reinforced his acetic tendencies and supported his commitment to suffering as a necessary part of the Christian life.

Another person who was just beginning to influence the theology of Charles was Peter Böhler. Charles first mentioned him in his journal in February of 1738. According to Charles, Böhler talked about faith during most of their time together. Charles's frustration with Böhler's ideas is evident in one of their conversations. Charles wrote,

> He asked me, "Do you hope to be saved?" "Yes." "For what reason do you hope it?" "Because I have used my best endeavours to serve God?" He shook his head, and said no more. I thought him very uncharitable, saying in my heart, "What, are not my endeavours a sufficient ground of hope? Would he rob me of my endeavours? I have nothing else to trust to."[109]

Charles's conversations with Böhler, at least in part led Charles to rethink his understanding of faith. After Böhler had prayed for Charles in the midst of his ongoing illness Charles wrote, "I immediately thought it might be that I should again consider Böhler's doctrine of faith; examine myself whether I was in *the faith*; and if I was not, never cease seeking and longing after it till I attained it."[110] Charles confessed his unbelief and the conviction that his unbelief had kept him from receiving the atonement, but he also believed he would receive the atonement before he died.[111] After Böhler left, Mr. Bray continued to share with Charles this new understanding of faith. One of the books Charles read during this time was Luther's commentary on Galatians.¹¹² While reading about Luther's emphasis on faith alone, Charles discovered that the doctrine of justification by faith alone was also found in the Articles and Homilies of the Church of England.¹¹³ He was astonished he ever thought this a new doctrine and resolved to share this newfound discovery. He wrote, "From this time I endeavoured to ground as many of our friends as came in this fundamental truth, salvation by faith alone, not an idle, dead faith, but a faith which works by love, and is necessarily productive of all good works and all holiness."¹¹⁴ Charles's reading of Luther seemed to invigorate him. He said, "I laboured, waited and prayed to see 'who loved *me*, and gave himself for *me*' [Gal. 1:6-7]."¹¹⁵

It is important to note that his new understanding of faith did not modify his understanding of the goal of the Christian life. Charles's new understanding of faith would still ultimately result in being restored in the image of God. What did change was the means that would be used to achieve that goal. The difficulty in trying to determine what happened on Charles's 'Pentecost' is the imprecise language Charles used and the varying ways he expressed it to different people. One possibility is that Charles experienced what John referred to as justifying faith. Although this is a possibility, it is one that was rejected by those closest to Charles. Immediately after his 'Pentecost', Charles seemed to adopt this as the explanation of what had changed. Charles's mother Susanna asked for his definition of justifying faith in October of 1738, because he had given her the impression that it was something recently experienced. She said, "I would gladly know what your notion is of justifying faith, because you speak of it as a thing you have but lately obtained."¹¹⁶

Whether or not what he experienced was justifying faith, the most important consequence for his understanding of the Christian life seems to be his newfound assurance. The relationship between a faith that brings assurance and a justifying faith was described by John. John said there were three types of faith; one could have a faith that gives assurance or one could have a justifying faith or one could have a faith that was neither a justifying faith nor a faith that brings assurance. What is most important in this definition was the allowance that one could have a justifying faith without sensing an assurance of being justified. John made this clear to Charles. John argued, "a man may have, and frequently has, justifying faith before he has the assurance that he is justified."¹¹⁷ This definition suggests that it is possible that both John and Charles saw the events of May 1738 not as justifying faith, but as the time when they first experienced the assurance of being justified.

Charles also presented his doctrine of assurance in a variety of ways during these early days depending on the person or group he was addressing. About a year after his 'Pentecost' experience, Charles was defending his doctrine of assurance to his brother Samuel. Charles explained to Samuel that they shared the same view of assurance. He wrote,

> My Doctrine of Assurance [(wch I] shall now tell you), it is no more than yours. Th[at there] is such a thing as the πληροφορια της πιστ[ης I] must allow for I find

it in the Scripture: but yt a [man] cannot be a Christian without it I as absolutely [deny as] you do. I have it not myself, yet humbly hope yt [in the] lowest Sense of ye Word, I am a True Christian. [This then] is my belief & my Doctrine of Assurance: how wi[dely] distant from what it has been represented to you![118]

Charles's interaction with his mother and brother in these letters show a little of what Charles was working through in defining his 'Pentecost' experience. When describing the experience to his mother he left the impression that he had recently received justifying faith. After a year of reflection, he was trying to convince his brother Samuel that his understanding of assurance was the same as Samuel's view. Did Charles waver in his understanding of what had happened? If he did, one explanation for Charles's uncertainty may be his tendency to struggle with doubt. Or was Charles positioning himself in his letter to his brother Samuel. After all, he still valued how Samuel viewed him. When Charles told Samuel that someone was misrepresenting his thoughts to Samuel was he trying to present his beliefs in a way that he would still receive Samuel's approval? It is probable that in his desire to please both of his older brothers, he presented his views in the way that was most agreeable to the brother he was addressing.

Another result of Charles's 'Pentecost' experience was the belief that faith could be experienced in a moment. In the days leading up to his 'Pentecost' Charles was reading the *Life of Mr Halyburton*.[119] His openness to the instantaneous nature of faith is reflected in his comment, "I stayed behind, and read them the *Life of Mr Halyburton*—one instance, but only one, of instantaneous conversion."[120] Later, after his 'Pentecost', he not only accepted that faith could be given in an instant, he was teaching this belief as necessary in some instances. One example of this is his interaction with William Delamotte who was struggling with the instantaneous nature of faith. Charles replied that this "alone hindered his receiving it just now, no more preparation being absolutely necessary thereto than what God is pleased to give."[121]

Another result of Charles's new understanding of faith and assurance related to how he viewed God. As long as Charles was striving to live up to the requirements of holiness in order to be accepted of God, his view of God was predominantly that of a judge. His earliest sermons reflect a moralism which looked at God as one who was waiting for us to earn the grace he would give. In other words, one needed to act a certain way to earn the grace of God. The difficulty was knowing how much was required? How could one know they had done enough? His new view of God as one who accepted and loved him did not set aside the need to love and please God, but now the motivation was love, not fear. He now saw himself accepted in the cross. There was a certainty of having received the atonement. Maybe most importantly, he now believed that God loved and died for him personally. This change from seeing God as a judge to God as one who loves is also reflected in the language of those who sent their conversion narratives to Charles. One of the earliest extent letters is from Mrs. Claggett. Mrs. Claggett said she "had Christ represented as a Lawgiver & Severe judge. I ignorantly imagined I cou'd not receive it then because I was unworthy." One result of her conversion was that now her "heart overflowed with the Love of God. The Spirit also bearing witness that I was a Child of God."[122]

Charles's preaching after May of 1738 helps to clarify how his beliefs were changing. Newport has rightly noted that there were some changes, but they should not be overstated: "There is a noticeable shift in emphasis between the early ('pre-Pentecost') sermons, and the later ones. The differences should not, however, be overestimated."[123]

In July of 1738, Charles began preaching a sermon on the three states of people. This sermon is divided into two parts. He preached part one fifteen times between July 16, 1738 and March 18, 1739. This sermon was based on I John 3:14, "We know that we have passed from death unto life." In this sermon Charles explained the three states and gave examples of people in each state. He began with a lengthy quote from John Norris's *Practical Discourses on Several Divine Subjects.*[124] According to Norris, every person fits into one of three states. Those in the first state are under "the law of sin" and "are said to be dead in trespasses and sins." They are comfortable in their sin. They are fast asleep in their sin. Those in the second state are under "the law of the mind of conscience" and are in an imperfect state. They are aware of their sin and struggle against it. They are "between sleeping and waking." The third group is under "the law of the Spirit of life." They are in a "state of victory." The person who is in the third state "is born of the Spirit and of God, and doth not commit sin because his seed remaineth in him." Finally, Norris described how each of these states related to the 'state of salvation'.

> The first of these states makes no pretensions to salvation; and the second, though it seem to have something of life and righteousness in it, is yet such as is consistent with the final and absolute prevalency and dominion of sin, and consequently such as cannot qualify a man for pardon, or put him into a state of grace and salvation. Whereas in the last, the principle of divine life is so strong, as not only to resist, but to overcome sin; and he that is thus spiritually alive is alive indeed; alive to himself and alive to God; and if he abide in this life, shall live forever.[125]

After highlighting Norris's definition of these three states, Charles described each state in further detail. In the first state, the image of God has been replaced by the image of the world. In this section he also contrasted the image of God with the image of the devil. Charles asserted that the image of God was restored in baptism, but that this image was soon overwritten by the cares of the world. He wrote,

> It is true, at the moment of our baptism, our second birth, that image was restored to us, a principle of divine life infused, and the child of wrath became the child of God. But alas, the soul of most of us soon lost that second life: again was that image wholly impaired and diffused; and the image of the world so strongly graven on it, that God's is no more discernible there.[126]

One thing this group lacked was a change of their "tempers". According to Randy Maddox, John used the word temper to indicate "an enduring or *habitual* disposition of a person."[127] The group in this state still engaged in worldly habits;

they were still fulfilling their lusts and pleasing themselves. In contrast to this the disciples of Christ would develop godly habits, including the ability to deny themselves.

In contrast to the first group, the second group had renounced themselves and begun the journey towards the straight gate. Charles described the seriousness of this group.

> They use all the means of grace, do all good works, and labour after the renewal of their souls in all heavenly tempers, even the whole mind that was in Christ Jesus. In a word, they are in earnest. They own and pursue the one thing needful, even a participation of the divine nature, the life of God in the soul of man.[128]

Although their pursuit of God begins well, in the end temptation comes and they are left with the feeling that "sin is irresistible."[129] This group had been made aware of their sin but have not yet experienced victory over sin. Charles wrote that one of the greatest obstacles which kept the second group from experiencing true happiness was believing they were already in possession of happiness.[130] What they needed, according to Charles, was to be translated "out of darkness into his marvellous light, out of bondage into the glorious liberty of the sons of God."[131] Later when discussing the gift of the Holy Spirit, Charles again indicated that this second group had not yet experienced justifying faith. He wrote, "And this you may see belongs only to them that believe with a living, saving, justifying faith, which you have not as yet."[132]

Charles indicated that the third group had been justified, and the indication of this was their victory over sin. Charles argued that people would continue to serve sin—and be in the second state—until, "being justified by faith, the law of the spirit of life makes [them] free from the law of sin and death."[133]

The second part of this sermon was addressed to those who were in the third state. He advised them to be thankful for the gift "reserved in heaven for you who are kept by the power of God through faith unto salvation!"[134] Their thankfulness should result in praise and sharing with others what God had done for them. He encouraged them not to hide what had happened, but to share, preach, and sing what the Lord had done for them. One of the greatest obstacles to this was a false humility—not sharing their story because it could appear prideful. Immediately after warning them about a false humility, he reminded them they were to be truly humble. True humility for Charles was having a filial fear; placing confidence in God. For Charles this meant recognizing that it was possible to "fall from grace."[135] One way to avoid falling back was "a constant use of all the means of grace. [Hence,] he that thinketh he can stand without them, is on the brink of falling."[136] His final word of advice was to "show your faith by your works."[137] This was a faith that works by love. Charles stressed that these works are a result of justifying faith. He ended this sermon by referring to 2 Peter 1:4-8.

> Being made partakers of the divine nature, express and manifest it by all good works and all holiness: "giving all diligence to add to your faith virtue, and to virtue knowledge, and to knowledge temperance, and to temperance patience, and to

patience brotherly kindness, and to brotherly kindness charity. For if these things be in you, and abound, they shall make you that ye shall neither be barren (idle, it is in the original) nor unfruitful in the knowledge of our Lord Jesus Christ."[138]

Charles explored this relationship between faith and works in his sermon on Titus 3:38. He began by emphasizing how Paul first preached justification by faith alone and then added that the result of this faith was "holiness and a good life."[139] The beginning was justification. This was followed by the evidence of justification—a "universal obedience; . . . by expressing the whole mind that was in Christ Jesus."[140] He again defined faith as a lively faith which worked by love. The marks of this kind of faith were peace, joy, liberty from sin, loving God and loving people, and the witness of the Spirit.[141] He divided these into inward and outward marks and noted the need for both aspects in the Christian walk. He wrote,

> It is evident from hence, that without obedience, all our pretensions to faith are vain. Without obedience, the inward marks of faith are mere phantasm, or the effect of diabolical illusion: as on the contrary, where the inward marks are not, such as peace, love, joy in the Holy Ghost, all outward obedience is merely formal and Pharisaical. Holiness is the test and evidence, no less than the end of faith.[142]

One "test and evidence" of this faith was the care of the poor. This emphasis of 'Oxford Methodism' continued to be important to Charles. He wrote,

> Let it be your constant employment to serve and relieve your Saviour in his poor distressed members.
> He gives you now a blessed opportunity. For inasmuch as you do it to one of these his little ones the least of these his children, you do it unto him. . . . You should see and revere your Saviour in every poor man you ease, and be as ready to relieve him as you would to relieve Christ himself.[143]

As noted above, it seems that Charles's new understanding of faith had affected how he viewed God. God was now seen primarily as the one who was merciful. God was no longer seen primarily as the lawgiver and judge. His changed view of God and the reliance on the work of God in his life changed his motivation for doing good works. Good works were no longer the means to earn salvation. Good works were now seen as being a result of justifying faith. Good works were not done out of fear, but out of love. Charles noted, "For the right and true Christian faith is not only to believe the holy Scripture to be true, but also to have a sure trust and confidence in God's merciful promises to be saved from everlasting damnation by Christ: whereof doth follow a loving heart to obey his commandments."[144] This involved a change of the inward nature, a nature which now freely choose to serve God.

In a sermon on John 4:41, Charles contrasted the freedom to love God with a theology which saw God's role as coercive. The goal of the former was "union with a good God;" the goal of the latter, to be reconciled with an angry God. Charles argued that a view of God as coercive resulted in a faith which was "dry and spiritless," "pernurious and needy," and lacking permanence.[145] His description of God in this sermon emphasized God's reluctance to punish. God was filled with compassion, whose "mercy triumphs over his justice." God welcomed home the lost son with open arms.[146] He argued that instead of serving God out of a command to obey, a person truly in the 'state of salvation' would serve God out of love, by "virtue of the new nature put into [them]."[147]

The Theology of Early Methodism in *Hymns and Sacred Poems* (1739)

In 1739 John and Charles Wesley published their first joint publication, *HSP* (1739). Like many of John's other publications this was a collection of poems from various sources. This collection includes poems written by 6ohn Wesley, Charles Wesley, and John Gambold. It also includes paraphrases of George Herbert's (1593-1633) *The Temple*, translations from the Moravian Hymnbook, *Das Gesang-Buch der Gemeine in Herrnhut* (1735), and a translation of a poem by Antoinette Bourignon (1616–80).[148]

It is nearly impossible to determine the theology of Charles Wesley by examining this collection. There are two major difficulties. First, both John and Charles included their personal poems anonymously. The difficulty of determining authorship includes the difficulty of determining who composed the paraphrases and the translations. If John did, which seems to be a good possibility in most instances, to what extent did these poems express Charles's theology?

Secondly, this publication does not even represent the theology of John and Charles in 1739. As will be shown, some of the poems expressed a theology that John and Charles had rejected by 1739. In spite of these difficulties, it is still helpful to look at this publication because it serves as a reliable witness to the theologies of early Methodism.

Even though it is difficult to determine which poems Charles wrote, it seems probable that he not only helped to shape the content of this publication, but that because of his involvement in its publication, it impacted his thought. One indication of this is his use of many of these hymns in a collection he edited in 1761.[149] Charles included twenty-nine Hymns for *HSP* (1739) in *Hymns for Those to Whom Christ is All in All*. In the preface of this collection he noted his purpose for publishing this collection:

> The following hymns, it will be easily discerned, are peculiarly designed for the use of those, to whom Jesus Christ "is made of God, wisdom and righteousness and sanctification," and who enjoy in their hearts, the earnest of their compleat and eternal "redemption." In these is "the mind which was in Christ Jesus," enabling them to "walk as he also walked."[150]

When his later writings differ from what is found in *HSP* (1739), one might assume either Charles's thought had either changed or that what was published in *HSP* (1739) did not represent what he thought, even at the time of its publication.

Either way, this publication is an important resource from the earliest period of Methodism with which to compare Charles's later thought.

This collection is also important because it helped to shape the theology and devotional life of early Methodism.[151] S T Kimbrough Jr. noted this impact when he stated, "The 1739 volume is extremely important for the understanding of Wesleyan theology and the nature of the emerging Methodist spirituality and devotional life."[152] Paul Chilcote agreed with this, noting, "This collection functioned as a primer in theology for the Methodist people, perhaps more so than any other in the nascent years of the revival."[153] Proof of this can be seen by the large number of allusions to these hymns by early Methodists, including but not limited to Mary Fletcher, Hester Ann Rogers and Jane Cooper.[154]

The preface of *HSP* (1739) gives some insight into the theology the Wesleys had rejected by 1739:

> *Some Verses, it may be observ'd, in the following Collection, were wrote upon the Scheme of the Mystic Divines. And these, 'tis own'd, we had once in great Veneration, as the best Explainers of the Gospel of CHRIST. But we are now convinced that we therein greatly err'd*: not knowing the Scriptures, neither the Power of GOD.[155]

The preface went on to explain why they had rejected these 'Mystic Divines'. They were deemed no longer acceptable because they "*lay Another Foundation.*"[156] Although the 'Mystic Divines' rejected outward works as leading to justification, they affirmed that inward righteousness was required for justification. John and Charles no longer accepted that either inward or outward righteousness was the "*Ground of our Justification.*"[157] They now viewed holiness of heart (inward righteousness) and life (outward righteousness) as a *result*, not a cause of justification. The sole ground or merit for our "*Acceptance with GOD . . . is the Righteousness and the Death of CHRIST, who fulfilled GOD'S Law, and died in our Stead.*"[158] They denied works were a condition of justification. They believed justification resulted from faith alone. John and Charles did specify the following relationship between faith and works in the preface; faith did not include either good works or holiness, but it did necessarily produce them.[159]

A second difficulty with the 'Mystic Divines' was the way they pursued holiness. According to the preface, they pursued holiness in isolation; "*To the Desert, to the Desert, and GOD will build you up.*"[160] For the Wesleys, there were no "*Holy Solitaries.*"[161] "*The Gospel of CHRIST knows of no Religion, but Social; no Holiness but Social Holiness. Faith working by Love, is the length and breadth and depth and height of Christian Perfection.*"[162] Their rejection of the 'Mystic Divines' in the preface complicates using the poems included in this collection to express the theology of John or Charles in 1739 when these poems were published. At the very least any poem that seems to assert the theology rejected in the preface should be treated with caution. In other words, many of these poems, even if they agree with what we have seen of John and Charles's theology and practice at Oxford and in Georgia, may not be the position they would have held in 1739.

It seems probable that in this publication John and Charles created expectations for the Christian life that they had recently abandoned.

Recapitulation and *Theosis*

HSP (1739) reflects John and Charles's early emphasis on being restored in the image of God. Although there are many aspects to this presentation, the overriding paradigm was the ability of people to recover what had been lost in the fall—a complete unity with God. The themes of recapitulation and 'deification' were used to describe this recovery. Randy Maddox argued that these themes are consistent with Eastern theology. He noted that in Eastern theology "he [Christ] must 'recapitulate' the whole of the human state, and thereby redeem it—making it capable of 'deification'"[163] Eastern theology made a distinction between the image and the likeness of God. "'Image of God' denoted the universal human potential for life in God. 'Likeness of God' was the progressive realization of that potentiality."[164] The realization or the process toward the realization of that potential was called 'deification'. Whether or not Charles differentiated between the image and the likeness of God, his writing does focus on the potential for a life in God that would result in a progressive change of the individual into the image of God. II Peter 1:4 was one of the Scriptures the Wesleys used to support this idea, "Whereby are given unto us exceeding great and precious promises: that by these ye might be partakers of the divine nature, having escaped the corruption that is in the world through lust."[165]

The authors included in this publication used image of God language to describe the creation of the world and what was lost in the subsequent fall of Adam. At first the world was perfect, and people, being created in the image of God, were perfect. Two poems in this collection describe the perfect nature of creation. Ernst Lange's description of creation is found in a poem praising the greatness of God. He began his description of God by focusing on the idea that God was unknowable:

> 1 O God, thou bottomless abyss,
>   Thee to perfection who can know?
> O height immense! What words suffice
>   Thy countless attributes to show:[166]

After describing the eternity of God, he turned his attention to God's role in the creation of the earth. He spoke of how God brought order and perfection out of chaos.

> 3 Thy parent hand, thy forming skill
>   Firm fix'd this universal chain;
> Else empty, barren darkness still
>   Had held his unmolested reign:
> Whate'er in earth, or sea, or sky
>   Or shuns or meets the wandring thought,
> Escapes or strikes the searching eye,

> By thee was to perfection brought.[167]

The work of God in creation as ordering or bringing the chaos to perfection is similar to God's role in the re-creation of people, where he restores or perfects the chaotic life. In creation, God overcame the darkness, the emptiness, and the barrenness to bring all of creation to perfection. The goal for both the perfection of creation and the chaotic life was being formed in the image of God.

> In earth, in heav'n, in all thou art:
>   The conscious creature feels thy nod,
> Whose forming hand on ev'ry part
>   Imprest the image of its God.[168]

A second poem describing the creation is a paraphrase of George Herbert's poem "Misery." In the original poem by Herbert, in the midst of recounting the difficulty of praising God, Herbert described a better day, a day now lost:

> Indeed at first Man was a treasure,
> A box of jewels, shop of rarities,
>   A ring, whose posey was, *My pleasure*:
> He was a garden in a Paradise:
>   Glory and grace
>   Did crown his heart and face.[169]

The paraphrase of this poem, found in *HSP* (1739), focused not on the worth or value of that "first Man" as a treasure, instead, it focused on his moral constitution. He was described as perfect and innocent, as shining in the image of his God, and living for God alone in love and praise. For Herbert what was seen in his heart and face was "Glory and grace," but the paraphraser added, "His heart was love, his pulse was praise." He also changed the word grace to light, a word often used to describe the image of God in the poetry of the Wesleys.

> Perfect at first, and blest his state,
>   Man in his Maker's image shone;
> In innocence divinely great
>   He liv'd; he liv'd to God alone:
> His heart was love, his pulse was praise,
> And light and glory deck'd his face.[170]

How the paraphrase changed the original gives a clue of what was important for the paraphraser. While Herbert focused on the worth of people, the paraphraser focused on the doctrine of creation. According to the paraphrase, people were perfect and blest and they shone in the image of their Maker.

This poem also pointed out the tragedy of the present circumstance. The current state was radically different from the treasure that described in the beginning.

> 12 But alter'd now and *faln* he is,
>   Immerst in flesh, and *dead within*;
> Dead to the taste of native bliss,

> And ever sinking into sin:
> Nay by his wretched self undone.
> Such is man's state—and such *my own*!¹⁷¹

Instead of being perfect and enjoying the blessings of God, people are described as fallen. They were focused on the flesh. What this fallenness included was described in the remainder of this poem. People no longer focused on the voice of God; instead, they focused on themselves. This included a focus on the pleasures and carnal joys of this life. In other words, people had turned from living for God to living to satisfy their pleasures. According to this poem, this was because they had become slaves to sense and sin. This same emphasis can be seen in the paraphrase of Herbert's poem "Frailty."

> 1 Lord, how in silence I despise
> The giddy worldling's snare!
> This beauty, riches, honour, toys
> Not worth a moment's care.
> Hence painted dust, and gilded clay!
> You have no charms for me:
> Delusive breath, be far away!
> I waste no thought on thee. ¹⁷²

Recapitulation is the theological concept used throughout this collection to describe the fall and the recovery from the fall—a theme Paul developed in the fifth chapter of Romans. The fall was a result of Adam's sin. What was lost in the fall was recovered through the work of Christ as the second Adam.

> 5 Far as our parent's fall
> The gift is come to all:
> Sinn'd we all, and died in one?
> Just in one we all are made,
> Christ the law fulfill'd alone,
> Dy'd for all, for all obey'd.¹⁷³

Charles presented the role of Christ's incarnation in several different ways, ways that seem to address a diverse set of problems. In this instance, what was needed because of the fall was for the penalty of death to be fulfilled. At other times, the focus was on healing the infected nature that resulted from the fall.

> 4 Grov'ling on earth we still must lie
> Till Christ the curse repeal;
> Till Christ descending from on high
> Infected nature heal.
>
> 5 Come then, our heav'nly Adam, come!
> Thy healing influence give;
> Hallow our food, reverse our doom,
> And bid us eat and live.¹⁷⁴

In one of Charles's most popular hymns, *Hark how all the Welkin Rings*, he presented the role of Jesus as the second Adam who replaced the fallen likeness of Adam with the image of God. This included being reinstated in the love of God.

> 9 Adam's likeness, Lord, efface,
> Stamp thy image in its place,
> Second Adam from above,
> Reinstate us in thy love.[175]

The ultimate goal of being renewed in the image of God was often described in the collection in ways that are similar to an Eastern Orthodox understanding of *theosis* as the culmination of recapitulation. For instance, one could be lost in the immensity of God.

> 3 Eager for thee I ask and pant,
>   So strong the principle divine
> Carries me out with sweet constraint,
>   Till all my hallow'd soul be thine:
> Plung'd in the Godhead's deepest sea,
> And lost in thy immensity.[176]

In addition to seeing people lost in the immensity of God, Charles also described people as being dissolved in God.[177] The focus was not only on the individual, it was extended to all the saints below. The goal for the saints was to be filled with all the deity and to be "All immerst and lost in love!"

> 6 Ah! Give me this to know
>   With all thy saints below.
> Swells my soul to compass thee,
>   Gasps in thee to live and move,
> Fill'd with all the deity,
>   All immerst and lost in love![178]

The poems in this collection did not explain *how* this union occurred. Charles seemed to be comfortable living with mystery. He often proclaimed what he considered to be the truth without explaining the how or why. The union of people with God was one of those areas where he embraced mystery.

Restoration in the Image of God as an Imitation of Christ

This collection also describes being restored in the image of God as imitating Christ. All of Christ's life became an example to be followed, even his time as a carpenter. The themes of humility and sacrifice were the focus of recounting Christ's life as a carpenter.

> 1 Son of the carpenter, receive
>   This humble work of mine;

> Worth to my meanest labour give,
> > By joining it to thine.
>
> 2 Servant of all, to toil for man
> > Thou wouldst not, Lord, refuse:
> Thy majesty did not disdain
> > To be employ'd for us.
>
> 3 Thy bright example I pursue
> > To thee in all things rise,
> And all I think, or speak, or do,
> > Is one great sacrifice. [179]

To imitate Christ meant following in his footsteps: "That path with humble speed I'll seek / Wherein my Saviour's footsteps shine."[180] One of the best expressions of following the example of Christ is Charles's "Hymn for Easter-Day," better known as "Christ the Lord is ris'n to Day." This hymn includes references to both *theosis* and recapitulation. People were "Made like him," and they received a second life through "our heav'nly Adam." What it meant to follow Christ was also described in its broadest scope. It meant being willing to suffer—even to the point of the cross and the grave—and then to experience the exultation of the resurrection.

> 5 Soar we now, where Christ has led?
> Following our exalted head,
> Made like him, like him we rise,
> Ours the cross—the grave—the skies!
>
> 6 What tho' once we perish'd all,
> Partners in our parent's fall?
> Second life we all receive,
> In our heav'nly Adam live.[181]

In *HSP* (1739) the language used to describe being restored was not limited to being restored in the image of God; sometimes another phrase was used. Sometimes Charles spoke of being restored in the likeness of God.[182] The word likeness was used five times in *HSP* (1739). It was used four times in translations from *Das Gesang-Buch der Gemeine in Herrn-Huth*. In three of these there was a prayer to shine in the likeness of God.[183] In the final translation the prayer was for the likeness to descend and change the person who was praying.

> 6 Send down thy likeness from above,
> > And let this my adorning be:
> Cloath me with wisdom, patience, love,
> > With lowliness and purity,
> Than gold and pearls more precious far,
> And brighter than the morning-star.[184]

The only other reference to likeness in *HSP* (1739) was to the likeness of Adam being replaced by the image of God.[185] Another way being restored in the image of God was expressed was to see people who were renewed in the image of God as a "Transcript of the deity."[186]

Being renewed in the image of God was also expressed as having the mind of Christ. In one poem this mind was described as gentle, patient, and victorious. Having the mind of Christ also drove out the charms of the world.

> 5 Renew thy image, Lord, in me,
> Lowly and gentle may I be;
> No charms but these to thee are dear:
> No anger may'st thou ever find,
> No pride in my unruffled mind,
> But faith and heav'n-born peace be there.
>
> 6 A patient, a victorious mind
> That, life and all things cast behind,
> Springs forth obedient to thy call,
> A heart, that no desire can move,
> But still t' adore, believe and love,
> Give me, my Lord, my life, my all.[187]

Being restored in the image of God not only affected the mind, making it more like Christ, it changed the attitudes and behavior of those renewed. As was noted above, Scougal defined the divine life as a life lived in purity and humility. These virtues and the victory over the temptation to abandon them in a life of pleasure and pride were a major focus of what it meant to be restored in the image of God in *HSP* (1739). In a translation of Clemens Alexandrinus's "Description of a Perfect Christian," the two major barriers to a "simple life divine" are described as "pleasure soft and wily pride."[188]

As noted above, Scougal defined purity as being totally devoted to God. This purity involved a denial of self and the denial of worldly desires and pleasures. Several of the poems in this collection focused on avoiding the pleasures of the world so that one could be single in their love for God. In George Herbert's poem "Frailty," pleasures, even though despised, have become a trap. Herbert's prayer was to be set free from these pleasures and united to God.

> 1 Lord, how in silence I despise
>   The giddy worldling's snare!
> This beauty, riches, honour, toys
>   Not worth a moment's care.
> Hence painted dust, and gilded clay!
>   You have no charms for me:
> Delusive breath, be far away!
>   I waste no thought on thee.
>
> 2 But when abroad at once I view
>   Both the world's hosts and thine!

> These simple, sad, afflicted, few,
> These num'rous, gay and fine
> Lost my resolves, my scorn is past,
> I boast my strength no more;
> A willing slave they bind me fast
> With unresisted pow'r.
>
> 3 O brook not this; let not thy foes
> Profane thy hallow'd shrine:
> Thine is my soul, by sacred vows
> Of strictest union thine!
> Hear then my just, tho' late request,
> Once more the captive free;
> Renew thy image in my breast,
> And claim my heart for thee.[189]

This fear that the pleasures of the world would capture the affections can even be seen in a mealtime prayer. This poem expressed a fear that the senses could keep a person from living a godly life.

> 1 Enslav'd to sense, to pleasure prone,
> Fond of created good;
> Father, our helplessness we own,
> And trembling taste our food.
>
> 2 Trembling we taste: for ah! no more
> To thee the creatures lead;
> Chang'd they exert a fatal pow'r,
> And poison while they feed.[190]

Although avoidance of the world was a major emphasis of being pure in heart, an emphasis the Wesleys probably adopted because of the influence of the 'Mystic Divines', there were also more positive expressions of being pure of heart. A poem translated from Johann Scheffler (1624-1677) emphasized the aspect of loving God alone.

> 1 Thee will I love, my strength, my tower,
> Thee will I love, my joy, my crown,
> Thee will I love with all my power,
> In all my works and thee alone!
> Thee will I love till the pure fire
> Fill my whole soul with chaste desire.[191]

Although this verse focused primarily on the positive aspect of loving God, the last line still talked of a "chaste desire." The rest of the poem lamented the author's late turn to God. He admitted what had kept him from loving God was his divided affections. He confessed, "Thy creatures more than thee I lov'd."[192] These passages express a theology consistent with that of the mystical divines. It may be possible that Charles and/or John had by this point rejected, at least in part, this emphasis on avoiding the world.

A second major emphasis for Charles was that the person restored in the image of God would be humble. As noted above, Freylinghausen described being restored in the image of God as putting on the mind of Christ. Putting on the mind of Christ meant becoming gentle and humble, and desiring only those things dear to Christ. It meant anger and pride were replaced with a "heav'n-born peace."[193] In another poem this humility was further defined as having certain attitudes and disciplines, each of which would lead the individual to being totally focused on Christ. Among these virtues were meekness and lowliness of mind.

> 4 Meek and lowly be my mind,
> Pure my heart, my will resign'd!
> Keep me dead to all below,
> Only Christ resolv'd to know,
> Firm and disengag'd and free,
> Seeking all my bliss in thee.[194]

In a poem reflecting on Galatians 3:22, it was concupiscence and pride that divided the heart. In this poem the plea was for the sin-sick soul to be healed.

> 2 Pity and heal my sin-sick soul,
> 'Tis thou alone canst make me whole,
> Fal'n, till in me thine image shine,
> And cursed I am till thou art mine.
>
> 3 Hear, Jesu, hear my helpless cry,
> O save a wretch condemn'd to die!
> The sentence in myself I feel,
> And all my nature teems with hell.
>
> 4 When shall concupiscence and pride
> No more my tortur'd heart divide!
> When shall this agony be o'er,
> And the old Adam rage no more! [195]

Another major ethical emphasis of being restored in the image of God was the role of love. According to Lindström, "Christian love is a factor both in the objective events of atonement and justification and in the subjective transformation of new birth and subsequent sanctification. In the former we see God's love to man, in the latter man's love to God and his neighbour."[196] Both the means to being restored and the goal of being restored in the image of God involved a certain understanding of the subjective and objective aspects of Christian love. While the love people should show to God and neighbor was a constant theme in early Methodism, the way the Wesleys understood or experienced the love of God seems to change mainly because of their interactions with the Moravians. They had moved from seeing God as judge to seeing God as one who cared for them individually. *HSP* (1739) includes poems that show this developing understanding. Some poems seem to reflect their previous understanding, others contrast the change in their theology, and still others present only the new understanding.[197]

Early Methodist theology seems to have adopted William Law's emphasis on a singular commitment to loving God and loving neighbor. In Law this love was measured not by outward actions but by a change of one's habits and spirit into the image of Christ (inward holiness). It was not a new idea that one should love God and neighbor, but according to Law the newness of the commandment to love given by Jesus was that in addition to giving the commandment, Jesus also served as an example of what it meant to love. One aspect of Jesus' love noted by Law was its universal nature; love was not love until it is extended to all.[198]

Randy Maddox has argued that the Wesley's reliance on Law during the earliest days of Methodism resulted in a love that was rational and legal. Maddox referred to the resulting moral theology as "habituated rational control." The goal of "habituated rational control" was for the passions to be subdued by rational discipline. One result of this was a reliance on the work of the individual.[199] This understanding of love can be seen in two poems. In "In Desertion or Temptation" the recognition of God's love was overshadowed by the lack of love experienced in performing the means of grace. The solution to the heart, which was far away from God, was to pray to God for help and redouble personal effort. The poem began with a recognition of God's love, a love which was both universal and changeless. "Ah! My dear Lord, whose changeless love / To me, nor earth nor hell can part." The problem for the author was that a recognition of God's love had not changed their "faithless heart." Their heart was still divided and unmoved by the time spent pursuing God. Even though there was a recognition of God as a God of love, the person remained distant from God. This can be seen in a description of the emotions while approaching the altar and the conclusion that they remain unrenewed;

> 8 Nigh with my lips to thee I draw,
>   Unconscious at thy altar found;
> Far off my heart: nor touch'd with awe,
>   Nor mov'd—tho' angels tremble round.
>
> 9 In all I do, myself I feel,
>   And groan beneath the wonted load,
> Still unrenew'd and carnal still,
>   Naked of Christ, and void of God.[200]

The solution offered by this poem was two-fold. First, there was a prayer to God as a God of love to come and give his help, but this was followed immediately by the need to act more faithfully. This prayer was consistent with the understanding of humility seen in Scougal—a reliance on God in the work of salvation. There was no emphasis in this poem on feeling the love of God; although the poem did end with a prayer for God to give himself to the one praying.

> 12 O Love! Thy sov'reign aid impart,
>   And guard the gifts thyself hast giv'n:

> My portion thou, my treasure art,
> And life, and happiness, and heav'n.
>
> 13 Would ought with thee my wishes share,
> Tho' dear as life the idol be,
> The idol from my breast I'll tear,
> Resolv'd to seek my all from thee.
>
> 14 Whate'er I fondly counted mine,
> To thee, my Lord, I here restore:
> Gladly I all for thee resign:
> Give me thyself, I ask no more![201]

Because the effort of the individual was an important part of controlling their passions, it was necessary to define the limits and goals of that effort. How could someone know that they loved God or neighbor enough? One answer, the main answer given in early Methodism, was that love was to be singular and ascetic. Following in the footsteps of Christ meant pursuing no other good than God and knowing of no other love than the love of God. This was the focus of the translation of Antoinette Bourignon's poem "Renouncing all for Christ."[202] This same attitude was presented in a translation of Gerhard Tersteegen's poem, "Divine Love." The devotion to God was conveyed as a total commitment.

> 7 Ah no! Ne'er will I backward turn:
> Thine wholly, thine alone I am!
> Thrice happy he, who views with scorn
> Earth's toys for thee his constant flame.
> O help, that I may never move
> From the blest footsteps of thy love!
>
> 8 Each moment draw from earth away
> My heart, that lowly waits thy call:
> Speak to my inmost soul, and say
> I am thy love, thy God, thy all!
> To feel thy pow'r, to hear thy voice,
> To taste thy love is all my choice![203]

Although the poem still has an ascetic emphasis, there was a different motivation to live the life of asceticism. Although there was still a call to love God alone, the way to do this was to hear God say to the inmost soul, "I am thy love, thy God, thy all!"

Although the goal of loving God and neighbor remained basically unchanged from 1725 to 1739, the means used to reach this goal seemed to change because of Charles and John's interaction with Pietism, both in their relationships and through their exposure to Pietistic hymns. "Habituated rational control" was replaced by an emphasis on experiencing the love of God. Maddox gave the following explanation of the change, "rational persuasion of the rightness of loving others is not sufficient of itself to move us to do so; we are ultimately inclined and enabled to love others only as we experience being loved ourselves." According to Maddox, the exposure to Pietism and its "deep emotional fervor" may "have contributed to his [John's] growing realization that the love of God must be felt."[204]

It would be wrong to conclude from this that Charles and John learned that God was a God of love from Pietism. Although they saw God mainly as judge before they were exposed to Pietism, they still recognized that God was a God of love and mercy. It seems probable that their exposure to the poetry of George Herbert and the poetry of their father prepared them for the changes they would make in their view of God in 1738. Two poems included in this collection, one from their father and one from George Herbert, show the love of God for people. In the paraphrase of George Herbert's poem "Misery" the fallenness of people was described; they were trapped in their senses. They were influenced by neither love nor fear. God's response to the wandering of people was to spread his wings of love over them.

> 5 Wayward they haste, while nature leads,
>   To' escape thee; but thy gracious Dove
> Still mildly o'er their folly spreads
>   The wings of his expanded love:
> Thou bring'st them back, nor suff'rest those
> Who would be, to remain thy foes. [205]

Samuel Wesley Sr. wrote that the love of God restored the souls of those who had experienced it. He wrote of humbly praising and loving God. It seems probable that the view of God's love presented in this poem would have been shared with Charles and John, especially because they included it in this publication.

> 5 How good thou art! How large thy grace!
>   How easy to forgive!
> The helpless thou delight'st to raise:
>   And by thy love I live.
>
> 6 Then, O my soul, be never more
>   With anxious thoughts distrest,
> God's bounteous love doth thee restore
>   To ease and joy and rest.
>
> 7 My eyes no longer drown'd in tears,
>   My feet from falling free,
> Redeem'd from death, and guilty fears
>   O Lord, I'll live to thee![206]

If John and Charles already saw God as a God of love, how did their exposure to Pietism change their view of God's love to people? Maddox argued that it was that the love of God must be experienced, it must be *felt*. It was only after someone felt the love of God that they could love others and love God.[207] This emphasis on the love of God can be seen in the German translation of Johann Scheffler's "God's Love to Mankind." This hymn began by asking who would not love God, because Jesus was the lover of people. He wrote that Jesus demonstrated his love through both the incarnation and the crucifixion.

> 7 Hell's armies tremble at thy nod,
> And trembling own th' Almighty God
>   Sov'reign of earth, air, hell and sky.
> But who is this that comes from far,
> Whose garments roll'd in blood appear?
>   'Tis God made man for man to die![208]

Zinzendorf also emphasized the role of love in a person being restored in the image of God. In "Prayer to Christ before the Sacrament," Zinzendorf taught that God's love for sinners could be experienced in the sacrament of communion and that our love could be returned to God on "wings with flames of holy love."

> 1 O thou, whom sinners love, whose care
>   Does all our sickness heal,
>
> 3 From thy blest wounds our life we draw;
>   Thy all-atoning blood
> Daily we drink with trembling awe;
>   Thy flesh our daily food.
> Come, Lord, thy sov'reign aid impart,
>   Here make thy likeness shine!
> Stamp thy whole image on our heart,
> And all our souls be thine![209]

All of these poems were written by those who influenced early Methodism. One poem, believed to be written by Charles Wesley,[210] contrasted the way he had approached trying to love God with the way he now waited, desired, and prayed for the ability to love God as a gift from God. It seems that this poem is an autobiographical reflection. Charles wrote it as a reflection on Galatians 3:22; "But the scripture hath concluded all under sin, that the promise by faith of Jesus Christ might be given to them that believe." In the first six verses he described his fallen state. He next described the failure of his former efforts.

> 7 Long have I vainly hop'd and strove
> To force my hardness into love,
> To give thee all thy laws require;
> And labour'd in the purging fire.
>
> 8 A thousand specious arts essay'd,
> Call'd the deep *Mystic* to my aid:
> His boasted skill the brute refin'd,
> But left the subtler fiend behind.[211]

He then declared that these efforts did not bring a change and were no longer his method of learning to love.

> 9 Frail, dark, impure, I still remain,
> Nor hope to break my nature's chain:
> The fond self-emptying scheme is past,
> And lo! Constrain'd I yield at last.[212]

The new way of learning to love was to acknowledge his inability to do it by his own effort. He recognized that it was entirely God's work. In this poem all that Charles could do was accept the gift of God. He even allowed that God may choose not to move to help his cause, if indeed, a God of love could reject one who desired to know him.

> 10 At last I own it cannot be
> That I should fit myself for thee:
> Here then to thee, I all resign,
> Thine is the work, and only thine.
>
> 11 No more to lift my eyes I dare
> Abandon'd to a just despair;
> I have my punishment in view.
> I feel a thousand hells my due.
>
> 12 What shall I say thy grace to move?
> Lord I am sin—but thou art love:
> I give up every plea beside
> "Lord I am damn'd—but thou hast died!"
>
> 13 While groaning at thy feet I fall
> Spurn me away, refuse my call,
> If *love* permit, contract thy brow,
> And, if thou canst, destroy me now![213]

Conclusion

Charles's time at Oxford helped to shape his idea of what it meant to be restored in the image of God. It involved an ascetic lifestyle in which he sought to love God above everything else. This striving was not optional for Charles, it was a necessary part of being in a 'state of salvation'. It included a commitment to private, personal, and public activities that would transform his life into one that was increasingly like that of Christ. Two of the authors Charles read while at Oxford were Henry Scougal and William Law. Both of them expressed ideas about being restored in the image of God that were similar to those expressed by Charles. This included a singular love of God, a love of neighbor, a purity or singleness, and humility. Charles found the practices and expectations associated with being renewed in image of God difficult to live by from time to time during this early period.

Charles's time in America was difficult. It was a time filled with suffering and perceived persecution. It was during this time that Charles made it clear that suffering was a necessary part of being restored in the image of God. It was during this time that he began preaching. His sermons reflected the practice and theology of the 'Oxford Methodists'. When Charles returned to England his intention was to return to Georgia. One reason he wished to return to Georgia was because he felt he needed to suffer in order to be renewed in the image of God.

Charles's exposure to Pietism, both through their hymns and through personal relationships with people like Peter Böhler, changed his understanding of faith. His changing understanding of faith did not change the goal of being restored in the image of God, but it did modify the means used to reach that goal. Although Charles continued to have doubts, he seems to have a newfound assurance because of his 'Pentecost' experience.

The poetry in *HSP* (1739) reflected and shaped the theology of early Methodism. The poems reflected the practices and beliefs of Charles both before and after his 'Pentecost' experience. The poems did add an emphasis that was missing in the other documents from this time. The poetry explained being restored in the image of God by using the doctrines of *theosis* and recapitulation. They also focused on imitating Christ, a theme prevalent in the reading of Charles at Oxford; this included putting on the mind of Christ. This early period has given us hints of what it meant to be restored in the image of God for Charles Wesley. The next chapter will focus on the next period of Charles's life and the collection of hymns and sacred poems he published on his own in 1749. Looking at this period and collection will show if or how his ideas have been modified by the intervening years of ministry, conflict, and revival.

Notes

1. *HSP* (1739).
2. Rattenbury, *The Evangelical Doctrines of Charles Wesley's Hymns*, 88.
3. Richard Heitzenrater used the language of the three rises of Methodism to present the early years of Methodism. Richard P. Heitzenrater, *Wesley and the People Called Methodists* (Nashville: Abingdon Press, 1995), 33. See also John Wesley, "A Short History of the People called Methodists (1781)," in *The Methodist Societies: History, Nature, and Design*, ed. Rupert Davies, vol. 9 of *The Bicentennial Edition of the Works of John Wesley* (Nashville: Abingdon Press, 1789), 425.
4. This would be true of most of the pamphlets published by John and/or Charles. The pamphlets reflected what had happened to that point in the Methodist movement and they also impacted or shaped the definition and practice of Methodism.
5. See pp. 37-38.
6. John Wesley, "A Short History of Methodism" (1765), §5, in *The Methodist Societies: History, Nature, and Design*, in *Works*, 9:368 and Charles Wesley, Letter to Dr. Chandler (April 28, 1785), Frank Baker's transcriptions of Charles Wesley's letters, where the item is No. 535; and *Charles Wesley: A Reader*, 59.
7. "My first year at College I lost in diversions." (Ibid.).
8. For a description of the organization of the 'Oxford Methodists' see Benjamin Ingham, *Diary of an Oxford Methodist, Benjamin Ingham, 1733-1734*, ed., Richard P. Heitzenrater (Durham: Duke University Press, 1985), 6-11.

52 *The Heart of Charles Wesley's Theology*

9. Ibid., 14.

10. Ibid., 12-28.

11. Ibid., 17. See also *The Country-Parson's Advice to His Parishioners In Two Parts* (London: Printed for Benjamin Tooke, 1680). The author of this popular book is unknown.

12. Ibid., 33.

13. Mark A. Noll, *The Rise of Evangelicalism: The Age of Edwards, Whitefield, and the Wesleys,* A History of Evangelicalism, vol. 1, ed. David W. Bebbington and Mark A Noll (Downers Grove, IL: InterVarsity Press, 2003), 73.

14. Henry Scougal, *The Life of God in the Soul of Man: or, The Nature and Excellency of the Christian Religion: with the Methods of attaining the Happiness it proposes; Also an Account of the Beginnings and Advances of a Spiritual Life. With a preface. By Gilbert Burnet now Lord Bishop of Sarum*, fourth ed. (London: printed for Thomas Bever, 1702)

15. Charles Wesley, Letter to John Wesley (January 22, 1729), *Letters I, in Works,* 25:236.

16. Susanna Wesley, Letter to John Wesley (October 25, [1]732), *Letters I, in Works,* 25:345.

17. Richard P. Heitzenrater, "John Wesley and the Oxford Methodists, 1725-35" (Ph.D. diss., Duke University, 1972), 160.

18. Susanna Wesley, Letter to John Wesley (October 25, 1732), *Letters I, in Works,* 25:345. John may even have read the book earlier while he was at Christ Church, Oxford from 1720-1726. According to D. Butler there was direct knowledge that John Wesley read the book during this time, but Butler failed to give any documentation to support this assertion. (D. Butler, *Henry Scougal and the Oxford Methodists: or, The Influence of a Religious Teacher of the Scottish Church* [London: William Blackwood and Sons, 1899], 112).

19. Heitzenrater, "John Wesley and the Oxford Methodists," 159-60. Butler, *Henry Scougal and the Oxford Methodists*, 104. Heitzenrater also noted that they read it in December of 1733 when Samuel Wesley Sr. was visiting the group. Heitzenrater, "John Wesley and the Oxford Methodists," 248-49.

20. George Whitefield, *George Whitefield's Journals* (London: Banner of Truth Trust, 1960), 46-7. Brackets are from this edition of Whitefield's Journal.

21. Butler, *Henry Scougal and the Oxford Methodists*, 104.

22. *Diary of an Oxford Methodist, Benjamin Ingham*, 255-56.

23. Charles Wesley, September 13, 1737, *Manuscript Journal*, 1:88.

24. Charles Wesley, September 24, 1737, *Manuscript Journal*, 1:90.

25. Questions 14 and 15 from the 1746 Annual Conference recommend a course of study that included reading *The Life of God in the Soul of Man* as a part of their daily meditation time:

Q. 14. In what light should your Assistants consider themselves?
A. As learners rather than teachers, as young students at the university for whom, therefore, a method of study is expedient in the highest degree.
Q. 15. What method would you advise them to?
A. We would advise them:
   1. Always to rise at 4.
   2. From 4 to 5 in the morning, and from 5 to 6 in the evening, partly to use meditation and private prayer, partly to read the Scripture (2 or 3 verses, or 1 or 2 chapters), partly some close practical book of divinity, in particular The Life of God in the Soul of Man, Kempis, The Pilgrim's Progress, Mr. Law's Tracts,

Beveridge's Private Thoughts, Heylin's Devotional Tracts, The Life of Mr. Halyburton, and Monsieur De Renty.
(John Wesley, *John Wesley,* ed., Albert Cook Outler [New York: Oxford University Press, 1964], 161-162).

26. Scougal, *The Life of God in the Soul of Man,* 4.
27. Ibid., 15.
28. Ibid., 15.
29. Ibid., 15. Affection is defined as "the action or result of affecting the mind in some way; a mental state brought about by any influence; an emotion, feeling." (*OED,* Draft Revision June 2009, s.v. "affection.") The affections were a common way to describe the will in the writings of John Wesley. (Randy L. Maddox, *Responsible Grace: John Wesley's Practical Theology* [Nashville, Tenn.: Kingswood Books, 1994]), 69. John Wesley shared a similar understanding of the the role of affections in the Christian life as Jonathan Edwards. For a description of this relationship see Gregory Scott Clapper, "'True Religion' And the Affections: A Study of John Wesley's Abridgment of Jonathan Edward's Treatise on Religious Affections," in *Wesleyan Theology Today: A Bicentennial Theological Consultation,* ed. Theodore Runyon (Nashville: Kingswood Books, 1985), 416-423.
30. Ibid., 16. cf. Matthew 22:37-39.
31. Ibid., 16.
32. John Wesley, "A Plain Account of Christian Perfection," ¶5, *Doctrinal and Controversial Treatises II* in *Works,* 13:137-138.
33. Scougal, *The Life of God in the Soul of Man,* 17.
34. Ibid., 25.
35. Ibid., 26.
36. Heitzenrater, "John Wesley and the Oxford Methodists," 170-173.
37. William Law, *A Serious Call to a Devout and Holy Life: Adapted to the State and Condition of All Orders of Christians* (London: Printed for William Innys, 1729).
38. Heitzenrater, "John Wesley and the Oxford Methodists," 314.
39. Charles Wesley, October 17, 1736, *Manuscript Journal,* 1:57-58.
40. Harald Lindström, *Wesley and Sanctification: A Study in the Doctrine of Salvation* (Grand Rapids: Zondervan Corporation, 1980; reprint, Nappanee, IN: The Francis Asbury Press, 1996), 162.
41. William Law, *A Practical Treatise Upon Christian Perfection* (London: Printed for William and John Innys, 1726).
42. Lindström, *Wesley and Sanctification,* 162.
43. Ibid., 163.
44. Ibid., 163.
45. Ibid., 164.
46. Ibid., 166.
47. Charles Wesley, Letter to Samuel Wesley Sr. ([June 11, 1731]), MARC, DDCW 1/4. Also published in Charles Wesley, *The Letters of Charles Wesley: A Critical Edition, with Introdcution and Notes, Volume I (1728-1756),* Kenneth G. C. Newport and Gareth Lloyd, eds. (Oxford: Oxford University Press, 2013), 33-34. Hereafter cited as *Letters of Charles Wesley.* Kenneth Newport and Gareth Lloyd are working on a second volume of this project that will include letters after 1756.
48. Heitzenrater, "John Wesley and the Oxford Methodists," 140.
49. Ibid., 165. This conclusion is drawn from the July 19, 1732 diary entry of John Wesley, "Charles came, talk of the Sacrament, recovered him. V. F."
50. Charles Wesley, Letter to Samuel Wesley Jr. (February 5, 1733), MARC, DDWES

4/14. Also published in *Letters of Charles Wesley*, 35.

51. Samuel Wesley Jr., Letter to Charles Wesley (October 11, 1735), in *The Proceedings of the Wesley Historical Society* 11 (1917-8): 151. Hereafter cited as *PWHS*.

52. Samuel Wesley Jr., Letter to Charles Wesley (September 21, 1736), in Adam Clarke, *Memoirs of the Wesley Family: Collected Principally from Original Documents.*, 2d ed. (New York: Lane & Tippett, for the Methodist Episcopal Church, 1848), 456.

53. Richard P. Heitzenrater, *Wesley and the People Called Methodists*, 76.

54. Charles Wesley, Letter to James Hutton (October 19, 1735), Moravian Archives, London. Also published in *Letters of Charles Wesley*, 44-46.

55. Ibid. Cf. Philippians 2:5.

56. Charles Wesley, Letter to James Hutton (October 29, 1735), Moravian Archives, London. Also published in *Letters of Charles Wesley*, 46-47.

57. Ibid.

58. Ibid.

59. Ibid.

60. Ibid. Cf. Mark 8:34.

61. Charles Wesley, Letter to James Hutton (November 28, 1735), Moravian Archives, London. Cf. Romans 12:2. Also published in *Letters of Charles Wesley*, 48-49.

62. Ibid.

63. Charles Wesley, Letter to James Hutton (March 23, 1738), Moravian Archives, London. I have omitted those parts crossed out in the MS. Also published in *Letters of Charles Wesley*, 68-69.

64. Charles Wesley, Letter to Samuel Wesley Jr. (November 17, 1735), Drew University Methodist Collection, ATLA: Digital resources for the study of religion, *http://www2.atla.com/digitalresources/*. Hereafter cited as Drew University Methodist Collection. Also published in *Letters of Charles Wesley*, 47-48.

65. Frank Baker, "Charles Wesley to "Varanese," *PWHS* 25 (1945-6): 100. In refuting that this was a letter of John, Frank Baker pointed to this disposition as more in line with what we know of Charles. "This letter fits Charles Wesley perfectly, however, whose rather morbid hankering after death was not removed by his conversion, but was a lifelong trait, for which his wife in later years had taken him to task."

66. Charles Wesley, Letter to V[aranese] (February 5, 1736), MARC, DDCW 1/6. Also published in *PWHS* 25 (1945-6): 17-20 as one of John Wesley's letters. See Frank Bakers article which refuted this claim. Frank Baker, "Charles Wesley to "Varanese," *PWHS* 25 (1945-6): 97-101. Also published in *Letters of Charles Wesley*, 50-53.

67. Ibid. Although this is addressed to Varanese, the use of plural pronouns suggests it was to both her and her sister.

68. Charles Wesley, Sermon 16. "Matthew 6: 22–3," in *Sermons of Charles Wesley*, 308-9.

69. Charles Wesley, Letter to John Wesley (October 15-25, 1736), *Letters I*, in *Works*, 25:484. From MS in MARC, DDCW 1/8.

70. Ibid.

71. Charles Wesley, March 24, 1736, *Manuscript Journal*, 1:10. Bracketed material was added in this edited text. For other examples of Charles finding comfort from the Scriptures in his time of trouble see the entries in his journal from March 22-25, 1736, *Manuscript Journal*, 1:7-13.

72. Charles Wesley, Letter to Samuel Welsey Jr. (July 31, 1734), in *Original Letters, by The Rev. John Wesley, and his Friends . . .*, ed. Joseph Priestley (Birmingham: Printed by Thomas Pearson, and sold by J. Johnson, London, 1791), 15.

73. Charles Wesley, Sermon 1, "Philippians 3:13-14," in *Sermon of Charles Wesley*.

74. Ibid., 100.
75. Charles Wesley, Sermon 2, "I Kings 18:21," in *Sermons of Charles Wesley*, 111.
76. Ibid., 112.
77. Ibid., 118.
78. Ibid., 116.
79. Ibid., 116.
80. Charles Wesley, Sermon 3, "Psalm 126:7," in *Sermons of Charles Wesley*, 126.
81. Charles Wesley, Sermon 16, "Matthew 6:22-3," in *Sermons of Charles Wesley*, 308. Charles noted in his journal that he preached this sermon on Sunday, March 14, 1736. Charles Wesley, *Manuscript Journal*, 1:4. This sermon was copied from his brother John.
82. Charles Wesley, Sermon 16, "Matthew 6:22-3," in *Sermons of Charles Wesley*, 309.
83. Ibid., 311-2.
84. Charles Wesley, Sermon 21, "Luke 10:42," in *Sermons of Charles Wesley*, 361.
85. Ibid., 363-4.
86. Ibid., 364.
87. Ibid., 365.
88. Ibid., 366.
89. Ibid., 367.
90. Ibid., 366.
91. Charles Wesley, Sermon 20, "Mark 12:30," in *Sermons of Charles Wesley*, 346.
92. Ibid., 351.
93. Ibid., 352.
94. Charles Wesley, July 31, 1736, *Manuscript Journal*, 1:46.
95. Charles Wesley, October 28, 1736, *Manuscript Journal*, 1:61.
96. Whether or not Appee was accurate in recounting his conversation with Oglethorpe, the fact remains that the behavior of John and Charles was open to the charges, at the very least from Appee.
97. Charles Wesley, August 26, 1736, *Manuscript Journal*, 1:49-50.
98. Charles Wesley, Letter to Samuel Wesley Jr., February 28, 1738, *Manuscript Journal*, 1:99.
99. Charles Wesley, April 3, 1738 and April 12, 1738, *Manuscript Journal*, 1:99.
100. For a description of Charles Wesley's theology of the necessity of suffering, see Joanna Cruickshank, "'The Cross Shall Bring Me to the Crown': The Suffering of Christ and the Suffering of Christians," in "Charles Wesley and the Construction of Suffering in Early English Methodism," 107-151.
101. Charles Wesley, Letter to John Wesley (Jan 2, 1738), *Letters I*, in *Works*, 25:524.
102. Ibid.
103. John Welsey, *The Christian's Pattern* (1735) as quoted in *Letters I*, in *Works*, 25:525.
104. Charles Wesley, September 28, 1739, *Manuscript Journal*, 1:207.
105. Benjamin Ingham, Letter to Charles Wesley (October 22, 1737), DDWES, 2/1.
106. Ibid.
107. Charles Wesley, April 9, 1737, *Manuscript Journal*, 1:82.
108. Charles Wesley, August 31, 1737, *Manuscript Journal*, 1:87.
109. Charles Wesley, February 24, 1738, *Manuscript Journal*, 1:97.
110. Charles Wesley, April 28, 1738, *Manuscript Journal*, 1:100.
111. Charles Wesley, May 11, 1738, *Manuscript Journal*, 1:101.
112. Martin Luther, *Dr. Martin Luther's Commentary Upon the Epistle to the Gala-*

tians: Abridged, Without Any Alterations. Together with Edwin, Bishop of London's License and Commendation of the Work, As Done by the Translators Out of Latin, 28 April, 1575. . . . Together with the Doctor's Own Preface* (London: Printed for J. Brotherton, and J. Oswald, 1734). This is probably the edition he was looking at, but all he recorded was, "Today I first saw Luther on the Galatians." (Charles Wesley, May 17, 1738, *Manuscript Journal,* 1:103).

113. Charles Wesley, May 17, 1738, *Manuscript Journal,* 1:104.

114. Ibid.

115. Ibid. Bracketed material was added in this edited text.

116. Susanna Wesley, Letter to Charles Wesley (October 19, 1738), in *Susanna Wesley: the Complete Writings,* ed. Charles Wallace (New York: Oxford University Press, 1997), 174.

117. John Wesley, Letter to Charles Wesley (June 28,1738), *Letters I,* in *Works,* 25:554.

118. Charles Wesley, Letter to Samuel Wesley Jr. (May, 1739), MARC, DDCW 1/92. Also published in *Letters of Charles Wesley,* 73-75.

119. Thomas Halyburton, *Memoirs of the Life of the Reverend, Learned and Pious Mr. Thomas Halyburton . . . in Four Parts. Whereof Three Were Drawn Up by Himself, the Fourth Collected by His Friends, . . . The Second Edition. With a Large Recommendatory Epistle by I. Watts* (London: sold by R. Cruttenden, 1718).

120. Charles Wesley, April 25, 1738, *Manuscript Journal,* 1:100.

121. Charles Wesley, June 27, 1738, *Manuscript Journal,* 1:126.

122. Mrs. Claggett, Letter to Charles Wesley (July 24, 1738), in Clive Field, *The People Called Methodists: A Documentary History of the Methodist Church in Great Britain and Ireland on Microfiche: Guide to the Microform Collection.* (Leiden [Netherlands]: IDC Publishers, 1998), MP 639, p. 41. cf. Romans 8:16. Note how Mrs. Claggett personalized the text by changing the we to I.

123. *Sermons of Charles Wesley,* 153.

124. John Norris's *Practical Discourses on Several Divine Subjects,* 4 vols. (London: n. p., 1690). I owe this reference to Newport in *Sermons of Charles Wesley,* 133.

125. Charles Wesley, Sermon 4, "I John 3:14," in *Sermons of Charles Wesley,* 134.

126. Ibid., 135.

127. Maddox, *Responsible Grace,* 69.

128. Ibid., 138.

129. Ibid., 139.

130. Ibid., 143.

131. Ibid., 144. cf. I Peter 2:9; Romans 8:21.

132. Ibid., 147.

133. Ibid., 140. According to Newport the words "being justified by faith" have been written above the line in the manuscript.

134. Ibid., 148.

135. Ibid., 148-149.

136. Ibid., 149.

137. Ibid., 149.

138. Ibid., 151.

139. Charles Wesley, Sermon 5, "Titus 3:8," in *Sermons of Charles Wesley,* 154.

140. Ibid., 155. I have omitted what Charles's has crossed out in the MS.

141. Ibid., 160-162.

142. Ibid., 163.

143. Ibid., 165. For a discussion of Charles's sympathetic response to the suffering

of the poor, see Joanna Cruickshank, "'Feelingly and with tears': Sympathy and the Suffering of others," in "Charles Wesley and the Construction of Suffering in Early English Methodism, 199-235.

144. Charles Wesley, Sermon 6, "Romans 3:23-24," in *Sermons of Charles Wesley*, 176.
145. Charles Wesley, Sermon 11, "John 4:41," in *Sermons of Charles Wesley*, 267.
146. Charles Wesley, Sermon 4, "I John 3:14," in *Sermons of Charles Wesley*, 142.
147. Charles Wesley, Sermon 11, "John 4:41," in *Sermons of Charles Wesley*, 263.
148. *HSP* (1739), Introduction, viii-xiii. Quotes from the preliminary matter in this publication include the section (Introduction or Preface) to avoid confusion. The preface in original publication included in this facsimile also begins on page iii. References to the original will include only the page number.
149. Although this was published anonymously, it seems probable that it was published by Charles Wesley.
150. [Charles Wesley.] *Hymns for Those to Whom Christ is All in All* (London: n.p., 1761).
151. Paul Chilcote claims that this hymnal was widely alluded to in the writing of early Methodists. *HSP* (1739), Introduction, xx.
152. Ibid., Preface, iii.
153. Ibid., Introduction, vi.
154. Ibid., Introduction, xx.
155. Ibid., iii.
156. Ibid., iv.
157. Ibid.
158. Ibid., v.
159. Ibid.
160. Ibid.
161. Ibid., viii.
162. Ibid.
163. Randy L. Maddox, "John Wesley and Eastern Orthodoxy: Influences, Convergences and Differences," *The Asbury Theological Journal* 45, no. 2 (1990): 36.
164. Maddox, *Responsible Grace*, 66.
165. KJV
166. Ernst Lange, "God's Greatness," trans. [John Wesley], in *HSP* (1739), 161.
167. Ibid., 162.
168. Ibid., 163.
169. George Herbert, *George Herbert: The Country Parson, The Temple,* ed. John N. Wall Jr. (New York: Paulist Press, 1981), 221.
170. [John Wesley], "Misery. From the Same [George Herbert]," in *HSP* (1739), 67.
171. Ibid.
172. [John Wesley], "Fraility. From George Herbert," in *HSP* (1739), 41.
173. "IIId Hymn to Christ," *HSP* (1739), 171.
174. [Charles Wesley], "Another [Grace Before Meat]," in *HSP* (1739), 35.
175. Charles Wesley, "Hymn for Christmas-Day, in *HSP* (1739), 208.
176. [John or Charles Wesley], "Hymn to the Holy Ghost," in *HSP* (1739), 184.
177. Charles Wesley, "Congratulation to a Friend, Upon Believing in Christ," in *HSP* (1739), 206.
178. "IId Hymn to Christ.," in *HSP* (1739), 169.
179. "To Be Sung at Work," in *HSP* (1739), 193-4.
180. Antoinette Bourignon, "Renouncing all for Christ. From the French," trans.

[John Wesley or John Byrom], in *HSP* (1739), 123.

181. Charles Wesley, "Hymn for Easter-Day," *HSP* (1739), 209-11.

182. The use of image and likeness as either synonyms or as words with similar yet distinct meanings, can be seen in the different interpretations of Genesis 1:26b.

183. Christian Friedrich Richter, "In Affliction, or Pain," trans. John Wesley in *HSP* (1739), 145; Nikolaus Ludwig von Zinzendorf, "Supplication for Grace. From the Same.

184. [German], trans. John Wesley, in *HSP* (1739), 184; Nikolaus Ludwig von Zinzendorf, "Prayer to Christ Before the Sacrament. From the Same [German]," trans. John Wesley, in *HSP* (1739), 190.

Joachim Lange "A Morning Dedication of Ourselves to Christ. From the German," trans. John Wesley in *HSP* (1739), 180.

185. Charles Wesley, "Hymn for Easter-Day," in *HSP* (1739), 208.

186. Charles Wesley, "A Morning Hymn," in *HSP* (1739), 178.

187. Johann Freylinghausen, "Christ Protecting and Sanctifying. From the Same [German]," trans. John Wesley, in *HSP* (1739), 182.

188. Clemens Alexandrinus's "Description of a Perfect Christian,*"* trans. [John Gambold], in *HSP* (1739), 37.

189. [John Wesley], "Fraility. From George Herbert," in *HSP* (1739), 41.

190. [Charles Wesley], "Another [Grace Before Meat]," in *HSP* (1739), 35.

191. Johann Scheffler, "Gratitude for Our Conversion. From the German," trans. John Wesley, in *HSP* (1739), 198.

192. Ibid., 199.

193. Johann Freylinghausen, "Christ Protecting and Sanctifying. From the Same [German]," trans. John Wesley, in *HSP* (1739), 182.

194. "John xvi. 24," *HSP* (1739), 219-220.

195. [Charles Wesley], "Gal[atians] iii. 22," in *HSP* (1739), 92-93. Although one cannot be certain this is one of Charles Wesley's hymns, this view is accepted by John Tyson. (John Tyson, "Charles Wesley's Theology of the Cross: An Examination of the Theology and Method of Charles Wesley as Seen in His Doctrine of the Atonement [Ph. D. diss., Drew University, 1983], Appendix D, III) and listed as probable in the first line index at the website of The Center for Studies in Wesleyan Tradition, Duke Divinity School. Among the arguments made by Tyson, maybe the most convincing is that this was one of Charles's favorite texts to preach from in 1738, when he preached on this text at least 6 times according to his journal.

196. Lindström, *Wesley and Sanctification*, 161.

197. One of the best examples of Charles presenting his previous attempt to please God by his effort with his new understanding of being completely dependent on God and focusing on God's love is his poem on Gal iii. 22. In verses 7-9, Charles recounted the vanity of his previous efforts. In verse 10, he said the way to peace began with resignation. Poems representing each of these three types are discussed in the following pages, specifically with reference to their definition of love.

198. Ibid., 162-166.

199. Randy L. Maddox, "A Change of Affections: The Development, Dynamics, and Dethronement of John Wesley's Heart Religion," in *"Heart Religion" in the Methodist Tradition and Related Movements*, ed. Richard B. Steele (Pietist and Wesleyan studies, no. 12. Lanham, Md: Scarecrow Press, 2001), 5-10.

200. [John or Charles Wesley], "In Desertion or Temptation," in *HSP* (1739), 149.

201. Ibid., 149-50.

202. Antoinette Bourignon, "Renouncing all for Christ. From the French," trans. [John Wesley or John Byrom], in *HSP* (1739), 123-24.

203. Gerhard Tersteegen, "Divine Love. From the German," trans. John Wesley, in *HSP* (1739), 79-80.
204. Maddox, *Change of Affections,* 27-28.
205. [John Wesley], "Misery. From the Same [George Herbert]," in *HSP* (1739), 66.
206. Samuel Wesley Sr., "Psalm CXVI," in *HSP* (1739), 138-139.
207. Maddox, *Change of Affections,* 12.
208. Johann Scheffler, "God's Love to Mankind. From the Same [German]," trans. John Wesley, in *HSP* (1739), 161.
209. Nikolaus Ludwig von Zinzendorf, "Prayer to Christ Before the Sacrament. From the Same [German]," trans. John Wesley, in *HSP* (1739), 189-190.
210. See footnote 193 for evidence that this poem was written by Charles Wesley.
211. Charles Wesley, "Gal[atians] iii. 22," in *HSP* (1739), 93.
212.. Ibid.
213 Ibid., 94.

2

Methodist Revival and Theological Challenge: 1739-1749

In the initial years of the revival several groups worked together, but as the revival progressed the differences in their beliefs began to splinter their unified effort. Charles Wesley was increasingly troubled by two groups: the Moravians and the predestinarians. Charles taught that the means of grace were a necessary part of being restored in the image of God. He confronted the Moravians' denial of the means of grace, because it made them more likely to adopt antinomian practices. Charles rejected the theology of the predestinarians not only because their theology often led to antinomianism, but also because their theology presented a distorted picture of God. The first two sections of this chapter will develop Charles's interaction with and rejection of these two groups and their theology.

The revival was not universally accepted in England. From the very beginning some of the people involved in the revival were persecuted. Charles saw the persecution as something that was necessary for being renewed in the image of God. The third section of this chapter will examine how Charles presented suffering as a necessary part of being renewed in the image of God.

During this time Charles continued to preach about the necessity of self-denial and of having a 'single eye'. One mark of having a 'single eye' for Charles was a commitment to remaining unmarried. He continued to hold this view right up to the day of his marriage in 1749. Charles Wesley's interest in Sarah Gwynne challenged his commitment to remaining single, and his letters reveal the struggle he had in pursuing marriage. Charles struggled with whether getting married compromised his commitment to having a 'single eye', to loving God, and to serving God's church. The fourth section of this chapter will examine this struggle.

The final section will examine the theology of Charles as expressed in *HSP* (1749). Charles's presentation of the events and conflicts with others will provide a context within which to examine how Charles expressed his theology in this collection. The focus will be on Charles's understanding of becoming sinless, the possible impossibility of being restored in the image of God, the means by which people are restored, the character of those who are restored, and the timing of being restored in the image of God.

Charles Wesley and the Moravians

Charles Wesley's interactions with the Moravians played an important role in shaping his theology. His meetings with Böhler and his involvement with the Fetter Lane society reshaped his theology, specifically his ideas about justification by faith. His initial support of their ideas would be challenged primarily because of the importance he attributed to the means of grace and because of his attachment to the Church of England. The behavior of John Shaw challenged the latter. In April of 1739, Shaw insisted "that there is no priesthood, but he himself could baptize and administer the other Sacrament as well as any man."[1] Because of his staunch Anglicanism, Charles thought Shaw's actions would lead to schism.[2] About this time Charles began reading John Potter's *A Discourse of Church Government* and remarked it was "a seasonable antidote against the growing spirit of delusion."[3] On April 25, a weekly conference moved for the removal of Shaw, and a week later George Whitefield noted that Shaw and others who had fallen into the same errors had left the society at Fetter Lane.[4]

The role of lay preachers was being discussed at the Fetter Lane Society about the same time. On May 16th Charles Wesley noted that both he and George Whitefield stood against allowing lay people to preach. Those who pushed for it most, according to Charles, were "Bray and Fish."[5] Charles's position in both of these discussions speaks of his commitment to the structure and theology of the Church of England. Soon Charles would find himself defending the means of grace. Even though he had accepted that justification was by faith, he did not accept that this excluded using the means of grace.[6]

Charles Wesley was concerned that some would mistake Christian liberty as a freedom to abandon the means of grace even before he addressed what he saw as the error of stillness in the Moravians. After meeting with his brothers and sisters in the Temple Church just outside of Bristol he recorded this concern.

> At six o'clock prayers, with a large company of our brethren and sisters, who have learned of Christ to come to the Temple early in the morning. None of them as yet think of it part of their Christian liberty to forsake the means of grace.[7]

Two months later he "Pressed the use of means, as means, from Isaiah 58, which is full of promises to those that walk in the ordinances with a sincere heart."[8] Both of these reflections preceded the high point of the conflict with the Moravians at Fetter Lane. How Charles viewed his interactions with the Moravians at this time is a bit of a mystery, because there is no extent record of Charles writing anything in his journal from November 6, 1739 (the day his brother Samuel died) to March 14, 1740. In his first entry after this break, he began to address the problem of stillness in London.

In March of 1740, Charles was traveling through the Cotswolds on his way to Oxford. While talking to Mr. and Mrs. Morgan, Charles learned about one of their visits to London. They told him Mr. Bray had urged Mrs. Morgan

> to cast off all the means of grace—not to go to church, or Sacrament; not to read the Scriptures; not to pray in private, but *be still*; and the *"New Light,"* as he called it, would come of itself. She would very soon have it, he promised her, *for he felt her spirit.*[9]

He also learned that Richard Viney was drifting into stillness, but noted his "stillness does not yet consist in trampling upon God's ordinances."[10] The Morgans also told Charles that John Bray (who Charles would identify as the pillar of the Fetter Lane Society when he arrived in London in April)[11] had been teaching a notion of stillness "which had no cross in it, no work of faith, no patience of hope, no labour of love."[12] This report raised two major concerns for Charles. The teaching at Fetter Lane was neglecting the Christian ordinances and it was leading people to live a life devoid of what Charles deemed the Christian virtues: a cross, a work of faith, a patience of hope, and a labour of love. It was not enough to have faith. A person with faith would endure struggles that would lead them to maturity. A person with faith would put that faith in action by living a life of love towards others. A part of this faith included a participation in the ordinances.

Charles taught that there were two errors people had fallen into with regard to the ordinances; either forsaking them or resting in them. If a person either rested in the means of grace or denied the means of grace, they would not be making progress in being restored in the image of God. In his sermon at Oxford, Charles was concerned primarily with those who rested in the means of grace. He used the text; "he who 'having a form of godliness, denies the power thereof [2 Timothy 2:5].'"[13] He went on to recount their commitment to the means of grace, but then noted that they still lacked the 'one thing needful', which was a recovery of the image of God. He asked them,

> Art thou 'meet to be partaker of the inheritance of the saints in light'? Hast thou 'fought a good fight and kept the faith'? Hast thou secured 'the one thing needful'? Hast thou recovered the image of God, even 'righteousness and true holiness'? Hast thou 'put off the old man and put on the new'? Art thou 'clothed upon with Christ'? 7. Hast thou oil in thy lamp? Grace in thy heart? Dost thou 'love the Lord thy God with all thy heart and with all thy mind, and with all thy soul, and with all thy strength'? Is 'that mind in thee which was also in Christ Jesus'? Art thou a Christian indeed? That is, a new creature? Are 'old things past away, and all things become new'? 8. Art thou 'partaker of the divine nature'?[14]

It was not only those who rested in the means that concerned Charles, he was also concerned with those he feared had or would forsake the means of grace. His warning to the woman bands in London illustrates how slighting the ordinances was related to being restored in the image of God:

> I told them that their forsaking the ordinances sufficiently accounted for their being forsaken by Christ. Warned them . . . against the double extreme of resting in the means, of slighting them; but, above all, against stopping short of the glorious image of God.[15]

In April, Charles published a pamphlet with a hymn entitled *The Means of Grace*.[16] He began this poem by noting an error he had personally made concerning the means of grace—he had rested in them. When coming to the altar for communion, he confessed that he only had a form of godliness. He wrote, "A form of godliness was mine, / The pow'r I never knew."[17] The problem, according to Charles, was he lacked the proper motive with which one must participate in the means of grace. He had rested in the outward law, but now his motive was love. The former had led to boasting; the latter rested in the work of God.

> 5 But I of *means* have made my boast,
> Of *means* an idol made,
> The spirit in the letter lost,
> The substance in the shade.
>
> 6 I rested in the outward law,
> Nor knew its deep design;
> The length and breadth I never saw,
> And heighth of love divine.
>
> 7 Where am I now, or what my hope?
> What can my weakness do?
> JESU! To thee my soul looks up,
> 'Tis thou must make it new.[18]

Not only did Charles teach that practicing the means of grace out of duty was replaced by practicing the means of grace out of love for God, he also taught that to be restored in the image of God was the work of God, a work which required a response. Attributing the work of restoration to God did not mean God acted alone. Charles indicated God's work required a response when he asked,

> 8 Thine is the work, and thine alone—
> But shall I idly stand?
> Shall I the written rule disown,
> And slight my God's command?[19]

His answer was "no." Instead, because God had commanded him to obey, he would obey, but not out of duty, he would obey out of love for God. This obedience included fasting, praying, searching the Scriptures, attending church, and taking communion. His purpose in all of this was that he would find the Lord and his loving kindness.[20] Charles presented the means of grace as a "written rule." This is illustrated in an anonymous letter written to Charles during this time. The letter supported keeping the means of grace by referring to several Scriptures. The letter began by noting the growing division in the movement with some claiming to follow Molther, others Wesley, and still others who claimed to be following Christ. The author asked how each side defined following Christ. On one side were those who claimed that all Christ required was for them merely "to believe and be still." While not denying that this was a part of what was required, the author asked if there was not more. Should they not let their light shine before men?[21] Were they not to observe the teachings of those who sat in authority?[22] But how could they do that if they never went to hear them? Were they not also required to obey Christ's commandments, which included taking the sacrament?[23] Finally, he noted that those who break the commandments, and teach others to do the same would be "called least in the kingdom of heaven."[24] The author argued that following Christ involved participating in these means of grace. He also attacked the 'still brethren' for their inaction.[25]

Probably the most complete and mature expression of Charles's approach to the stillness controversy can be found in a letter he wrote to the society at Grimsby in 1743. Throughout the letter Charles emphasized two marks of the Christian life. Those who were true believers, according to Charles, were those who obeyed Christ and had departed from iniquity. This faith would be marked by love. He wrote, "Jesus is the Author of Eternal Redemption to all them (& them only) that obey Him. There can be no True Faith, where there is not Love." He also shared that he did not fear them listening to "Mr. Parker & his German Friends" unless by listening to them they were willing to "cast off the Yoke of Christ, & all Scriptures." Charles believed that the 'still brethren' had rejected much of the canon, but especially James and the Old Testament. He said that some of them were even saying "they saw no Occasion for any more than the Epistle to the Romans." In other words, one had to choose to give up either the 'still brethren' or the Scriptures. Charles was confident they would not give up the Scriptures. Charles told them the antidote to stillness was simply to "Read again & again the Epistle of St. James" with its emphasis on faith and works.[26]

Charles also emphasized the importance of the means of grace by asking who should be the model or example for the Christian? Should it be Christ and his apostles or someone like Mr. Parker? Jesus "fasted—& prayed—& did good." His apostles "were in fasting often; prayed without ceasing—confessed Christ before Men, did all manner of good, & suffered all manner of Evil." For Charles the answer was simple, he would much rather follow in the steps of Christ and his apostles.[27]

The real heart of the difference between Charles and the 'still brethren' was how they defined Christian liberty. For the 'still brethren', liberty seems to be a liberty *from* fulfilling the law and all its requirements, which seemed to include even the commandments of Christ. For Charles, Christian liberty was "Liberty *from* all Sin, Liberty *to* fulfil the whole Law."[28] In other words, liberty was more than being forgiven, it was also living out God's purpose by observing the means of grace. The difference can be illustrated by an entry from Charles's journal. On one occasion, when Charles was dining with Bell and Simpson, the bell rang for

Church. They told Charles they thought it was good that they continue in their discussion and miss the service. Charles indicated he would go on without them and leave them to their "antichristian liberty."[29] Both their willingness to miss the service and their theology bothered Charles. According to Charles, "One of them told a poor man in my hearing, 'That comfort you received at the Sacrament, was given you by the devil.' I should less blasphemously have called it, the drawing of the Father, or preventing grace."[30]

Charles's understanding of the Moravian's view of 'Christian liberty' can also be seen in a letter he wrote to a friend in Bristol.

> My brother came most critically. The snare, we trust, will now be broken and many simple souls delivered. Many here insist that a part of their Christian calling is liberty from obeying, not liberty to obey. The unjustified, say they, are to be still; that is, not to search the Scriptures, not to pray, not to communicate, not to do good, not to endeavour, not to desire; for it is impossible to use means without trusting in them. Their practice is agreeable to their principles. Lazy and proud themselves, bitter and sensorious [sic] toward others, they trample upon the ordinances, and despise the commands, of Christ. I see no middle point wherein we can meet.[31]

Charles ended his letter to the society at Grimsby with an admonition to keep the faith and continue to strive for the goal of the Christian life. For Charles this meant growing up "in all things into Christ our Head, till we all come in the Unity of the Faith unto a Perfect Man to the Measure of the Stature of the Fulness of Christ."[32]

This was more than a theological debate for Charles. What a person believed affected the way they lived. As noted above Charles believed that the 'still brethren' taught a Christianity "which had no cross in it, no work of faith, no patience of hope, no labour of love."[33] He also felt it left them in a state of sin that made it difficult for him to live at peace with them. After a visit to Bray he made the following entry in his journal. "Went with Maxfield to Bray's. . . . I laboured for peace, but only the Almighty can root out those cursed tares of pride, contempt, and self-sufficiency with which our Moravianized brethren are overrun."[34]

Another problem Charles had with the Moravians was that their teaching could be divisive. This can be seen in the Moravians' interactions with the Morgans. Charles recognized that Mr. Morgan did not approve of the behavior of his wife, which he attributed to her association with the London brethren. Because of the influence of two sisters in particular, Mrs. Morgan thought about going to Germany. Mr. Morgan felt they were intent on getting her to be set against him. Because of this incident Charles had gained another witness against the dangers of the 'still brethren'. Charles noted that Mr. Morgan "complains that since she came under their teaching she has lost all desire of being a Christian. I can never enough thank God for this unexpected warning against their diabolical stillness."[35]

Charles also criticized the behavior of the 'still brethren' by contrasting it with the Kingswood colliers. When he visited the colliers, it was not only to teach them, but also to learn of them, because according to Charles they had the true marks of a Christian. Charles recorded the following reflection on a visit to the colliers in June of 1740:

> Went to learn Christ among our colliers, and drank into their spirit. We rejoiced for this consolation. O that our London brethren would come to school to Kingswood! These are what they pretend to be. God knows their poverty, but they are rich, and daily entering into rest, without being first brought into confusion. They do not hold it necessary to deny the weak faith in order to get the strong. Their soul truly waiteth still upon God, in the way of his ordinances. Ye many masters, come learn Christ of these outcasts; for know, except ye be converted, and become like these little children, ye cannot enter into the kingdom of heaven.[36]

Charles's reflection on the colliers stressed that belief should be accompanied by signs or fruit. In the case of the colliers he saw an active waiting on God in the ordinances and a childlike humility. When reflecting on a person's faith, Charles often noted whether they were humble and loving. The presence of these qualities argued for a true faith. One example of the importance of humility and faith was Charles's response to the faith of an individual who had fallen "into gross sin" but had once again claimed to have received God's mercy. Even though Charles had his doubts about the person's claims, he did note that "his deep humility and abundant love are good evidences for him."[37]

Charles Wesley was also concerned with the Moravians' denial of the degrees of faith. According to Charles, the Moravians taught there were "no degrees of faith, no forgiveness of faith where any unbelief remains; any doubt, or fear, or sorrow."[38] They had set the results of having faith too high. In May, Charles met with the leaders of the 'still brethren' at Bray's house. In addition to addressing the question of the ordinances, he affirmed that there was such a thing as a weak faith. To this end he asked them if "forgiveness is never given but together with the abiding witness of the Spirit?"[39] Charles noted the practical effect of denying a faith that was weak or a faith that lacked the witness of the Spirit. Mr. Stonehouse, after accepting the Moravian's definition of faith believed he "was never justified" and was "going to leave his parish, and transport himself—to Germany!"[40] Charles resisted this definition of faith and argued instead that a new believer could experience doubt. Charles used Isaiah 50:10[41] to define the nature of faith:

> Here the fear of the Lord, which is the beginning of wisdom, and obedience which is the fruit of faith, are attributed to one that walketh in darkness and hath no light. Nay and the Spirit saith expressly that this dark disconsolate soul may be a believer. "Let him trust in the name of the Lord, and stay upon his God"—even while he walketh in darkness and hath no light. Therefore a believer can doubt.[42]

During this period of his life, Charles's interactions with the Moravians played an important role in shaping his theology; at first it had a positive impact, but soon he began to define his theology in opposition to many of their positions. One thing that Charles would not abandon was his allegiance to the Church of England. Early challenges to the authority of the Church of England included Shaw's attempt to administer the sacraments and the push for lay preachers. Charles stood against both of these moves. The main difference between Charles and the Moravians was the necessity of the means of grace. Charles taught that to deny the means of grace would undermine necessary parts of the Christian life. These included taking up the cross, and laboring in faith, hope, and love. Because he held the means of grace in such a high regard, he also taught about the dangers associated with them: either resting in them or neglecting them. One of the reasons people denied the means of grace was because they neglected much of the Scripture. Some even focused solely on the book of Romans. Charles looked to the whole Scripture. These beliefs had practical consequences. Besides pointing to the life of Christ and his apostles as example of the faith, he also noted the faith of the colliers who understood what it meant to live out the faith simply and humbly. The Moravians were not the only group that helped Charles to refine his idea of what it meant to be restored in the image of God. Another group with which Charles had a mixed relationship were the predestinarians.

Charles Wesley and the Predestinarians

Charles also had an ongoing struggle with the predestinarians. His journal indicates that while he was in London (near Fetter Lane, the work he and his brother shared with the Moravians) his concern was primarily with the problem of stillness, but when he was in Bristol (the work he and his brother shared with George Whitefield), his major concern was with the doctrine of predestination. A letter to John shows that Charles wanted to maintain a peaceful relationship with George Whitefield, but it also highlighted the differences that were jeopardizing that peace. Charles told John,

> G. W. [George Whitefield] came into the desk [the pulpit] while I was showing the believer's privilege, i.e. power over sin. After speaking some time I desired him to preach. He did—predestination, perseverance, and the necessity of sinning. Afterwards I mildly expostulated with him, asking if he would commend me for preaching the opposite doctrines in his orphan-house; protesting against the publishing his answer to you, and labouring for peace to the utmost of my power. Asked whether he held reprobation,[43] which he avowed, as also his intention of preaching it upon the housetop.[44]

This letter highlights three major points of difference—predestination, preservation of the saints, and "the necessity of sinning." While Charles Wesley did not deny the doctrine of predestination, he did reject reprobation, a doctrine Whitefield still proclaimed. Six months later Charles once again expressed his concern with the preaching of George Whitefield in Bristol. Although stressing many of the things important to the Wesleys, George Whitefield was still teaching the doctrine of reprobation. Charles Wesley pleaded with John to confront this problem and soon:

> For mine, and your own, and theirs, and Christ['s] sake—open your eyes, regard not fair speeches, renounce your credulity, and [[George Whitefield]], till he renounces reprobation. 'But that he does already, and preaches holiness, and free grace for all!'—O that [[damnable]] virtue of credulity!—Send me word, I say, by next post, that you have restrained the unwary, or I shall on the first preaching night renounce [[George Whitefield]] on the housetop.[45]

Notice that both Charles Wesley and George Whitefield had taken this to the people and were proclaiming it "on the housetop." In order to support his case that Whitefield was still preaching reprobation, Charles quoted an extract of a letter he had received from Bristol. According to this letter, George Whitefield had become more dangerous because he was preaching 'free grace' and 'holiness' in a way that implied reprobation. His new way of presenting "the poison" of reprobation had damaged the group. The writer from Bristol concluded his complaints about George Whitefield's preaching with his personal commitment.

> For my part, by the grace of God, I never will be reconciled to reprobation, nor join with those who hold it. I wish there might be a real and thorough union betwixt us.[46]

Charles taught that the doctrine of reprobation distorted the image of God by making God a God of hate instead of a God of love. This could have practical implications. How people understood God was of utmost significance, because it was into their image of God that they were striving to be restored. If God was a God of hate, those who were being restored in God's image would be people who exhibited this 'virtue'. But if God was a God of love, than people would be required to act with that same love. Charles believed that to view God as a God of love would transform people's lives. He also thought that preaching about the love of God would defeat the doctrine of reprobation. He asked, "Who can resist the power of love! A loving messenger of a loving God might drive reprobation out of Wales without once naming it."[47]

Charles reflected on the power of God's love after visiting Hannah Cennick and hearing her dying prayer. She cried out, "Victory, Liberty, liberty! This is the glorious liberty of God's children! O who can name the name of Jesus and not depart from iniquity? God loves me. God loves every man. Jesus Christ the Saviour of the whole world." After hearing her testimony Charles preached on a passage he said was one of the strongest for universal redemption.[48] He told the society,

> I could not but observe, and bless God for, this answer to our dying sister's prayer. At the Room I opened the book on "And I, if I be lifted up from the earth, will draw all men unto me" [John 12:32]. Was I to search after the strongest Scriptures for universal redemption, I could not choose so well as Providence chooses for me.[49]

The centrality of this doctrine in Charles's theology can be illustrated by the perception that he was the primary advocate of universal redemption in the Wesleyan Methodist movement. John Cennick wrote to George Whitefield, "with universal redemption bro. Charles pleases the world. . . . Bro. John follows him in everything."[50] One example of his advocacy for universal redemption are the polemical poems he wrote to combat the doctrine of reprobation. In 1741 Charles published the pamphlet *Hymns on God's Everlasting Love*.[51] The major purpose of this pamphlet seems to be to defend the character of God. He argued that holding the doctrine of reprobation presented God as a God of hate, because God had chosen only 'a limited' number of people to be saved—the elect. Charles, on the other hand, believed in a God of "Everlasting Love," who had chosen to demonstrate God's love to the whole world.

The first hymn illustrates how Charles viewed the difference between himself and those who taught reprobation. He began by noting that the Father's love was everlasting and it was because of the Father's love and mercy that the Father sent his son to save the *whole* world.

> [1] Father, whose everlasting love
>   Thy only Son for sinners gave,
> Whose grace to all did freely move,
>   And sent him down a world to save;
>
> [2] Help us thy mercy to extol,
>   Immense, unfathom'd, unconfin'd;
> To praise the Lamb who died for all,
>   The *general Saviour of mankind*.[52]

Charles used four phrases to define the extent of God's mercy and love. God's "grace *to all* did *freely* move," God's mercy was unconfined, the lamb of God "died for all," and the lamb was "The general Saviour of mankind." Each of these phrases point to the limitless and all-inclusive love of God. Charles emphasized this by repeating the word 'all'. 'All' was the hammer Charles used to drive home the point that God's love was not limited, but universal.

> [4] Jesus hath said, we *all* shall hope;
>   Preventing grace for all is free:
> "And I, if I be lifted up,
>   I will draw all men unto me."[53]

Charles illustrated his commitment to the all-inclusive love of God by focusing not only on those inside the movement, but by also turning his attention to those outside of the movement. He invited them to see the love of God: "[6] O *all ye ends of earth* behold / The bleeding, all-atoning Lamb!"[54] Charles concluded this poem with a set of questions for God. The difficulty for Charles was if God was a God of universal love, why did some continue to reject that love? The closest Charles came to answering this question was his statement of hope in the last verse, "And all shall own thou died'st for all."[55] The reason Charles asked why some refused to believe was so he could attack the answer of the predestinarians which he thought damaged the character of God, that God only intended for a few to be saved. In this view people remained lost not because of their own actions, but because it was God's choice that they would die. To Charles this made God a God of hate. Charles attacked the view that only a select few were saved in the following verses;

> [13] 'Tis we, the wretched abjects we,
>   Our sin and death on thee translate:
> We think that fury is in thee,
>   Horribly think, that God is hate.
>
> [14] "Thou hast compell'd the lost to die;
>   Hast *reprobated* from thy face;
> Hast others sav'd, but them *past by*;
>   Or mock'd with only *damning* grace."[56]

A note at the bottom of the page stated that *damning* grace was normally referred to as "*common* grace." Charles concluded this poem by asking God how long he would continue to allow people to deny God's "faithfulness and love?" How long would he allow the "HELLISH DOCTRINE" to stand?[57] This poem both affirmed Charles's view that God's mercy was all-inclusive and attacked those who argued for a more limited view of God's mercy. In this poem Charles rejected the doctrine of reprobation because it seemed to Charles that any God who could limit mercy to a select few was a God of hate.

Charles was also concerned that the predestinarians' definition of justifying faith could lead to antinomianism. If someone believed they would never fall away from the faith, what motive did they have for living according to the commands of God? One example of this concern was the confrontation Charles had with John Cennick at Kingswood in December of 1740. It seems that at this time Charles was facing strong opposition from Cennick. In his journal he noted he had written his "brother a full account of the predestination party, their practices and designs, particularly 'to have a church within themselves, and to give themselves the Sacrament in bread and water.'"[58] In the letter Charles noted that the major point of difference was the preservation of the saints.[59] He told John, "They tell me plainly they will separate from me if I speak one word against final perseverance, or hint at the possibility of a justified person's falling from grace."[60] Charles argued against the doctrine of final preservation by giving examples of people who used this idea as an excuse to live a life that was unholy. His examples seem extreme and may not reflect a normal occurrence, but they still highlight what he perceived was the danger of believing in final preservation. He recorded the following two stories in his journal in the midst of this struggle.

> A woman spoke to me of her husband. He was under strong convictions while he attended the Word, but the first time he heard the *other gospel* [he] came home *elect*, and in proof of it, *beat his wife*. His seriousness was at an end. His work was done, God doth not behold iniquity in Jacob [Num. 23:21], therefore his iniquity and cruelty towards her abounds. He uses her worse than a Turk (his predestinarian brother), and tells her, if he killed her he could not be damned.
> Today I heard of another in the same delusion, Mrs Grevil's man, who lately favored me with a letter exhorting me to bow down at the foot of sovereign grace.

His mistress has now sent him to Bridewell and dragged her maid out of doors by the hair of the head, although naked, elect, and big with child.[61]

One way that Charles Wesley addressed people who had become lax in their faith (because they felt they were elect) was to preach on the "scriptural marks of election."[62] By doing this, Charles addressed what he saw as the problem promoted by those who taught election (that they did not live lives consistent with the demands of the Scripture) without touching on the controversy of election. On one such occasion Charles Wesley remarked, "Dined at Llanishen and preached to the Society and a few others, chiefly predestinarians. Without touching the dispute, I simply declared the scriptural marks of election; whereby some I believe were cut off from their vain confidence."[63]

Charles Wesley also criticized the predestinarians for having a "faith of adherence."[64] He described a "faith of adherence" as a weak faith that normally kept a person from going on to a stronger faith. There are times he used it to describe someone who rested in the ordinances,[65] but normally he used it to describe the faith of predestinarians. He expressed concern that some trusted in this lowest mark of faith: "Spoke closely to those who trusted to their faith of adherence, and insisted on that *lowest mark* of the new birth forgiveness of sins."[66] Charles taught that relying on the weak "faith of adherence" led people to an incomplete view of perfection: "Dined at a Dissenter's, armed cap-a-pie with her faith of adherence, brim full of the five points, and going on to the perfection of Rom. 7."[67] Charles even seemed to teach that having a "faith of adherence" was a hindrance to having a true faith. The faith he taught people to pursue was the "faith of the gospel." Reflecting on a visit with two Baptists Charles wrote, "I almost persuaded [them] to give up their faith of adherence, so called, for the faith of the gospel, which works by love, and includes peace, joy, power, and the testimony of the Spirit."[68]

Charles's insistence on a faith which worked by love was criticized by the predestinarians. They were critical of what Charles deemed the "*two great truths* of the everlasting gospel." After preaching on Titus 2:11 he wrote, "The power and seal of God is never wanting while I declare the two great truths of the everlasting gospel: universal redemption and Christian perfection."[69] But it was these two doctrines that were most divisive in his relationship with the predestinarians. The emphasis on Christian perfection *seemed* to some to be a denial of justification by faith alone. Charles recorded a conversation he had with one who accused him of denying justification by faith. "Spake with one who once walked in simple faith, but the antinomian tempter has prevailed. Now he expressly renounces us, 'who seek to be justified by works.'"[70] Charles expressed the following contrasts between himself and the predestinarians. The predestinarians hoped for the perfection found in Romans 7,[71] Charles hoped for Christian perfection. They hoped to be saved *in* sin; Charles hoped to be saved *from* sin.[72]

Charles's differences with the predestinarians were similar to those he had with the Moravians. He accused them both of promoting a faith that could lead to antinomianism. As much as this irritated him, it seems that the doctrine of reprobation and its attack on the character of God was a greater concern for Charles.

His polemical publication reflected this concern. Charles's action in this area was so passionate that some even thought his brother John followed him in his affirmation of universal redemption. One area that John did not follow Charles was the role of suffering in the life of the believer.

Persecution and the Necessity of Suffering

The growing popularity of the Methodist movement was accompanied by a rise in persecution.[73] In the midst of these attacks Charles argued that persecution was a necessary part of being a Christian. He privileged several passages from the Scripture to argue for this position. This was not a new position, one that was developed out of the current persecution; instead, it was similar to the response Charles had when he felt persecuted in America.[74]

Charles often quoted Scripture to argue that suffering and persecution should be a normal part of the Christian life. For instance, when the Seward family complained that Charles's message was dividing the family, Charles quoted Luke 12:52, "There shall be five in an house, two against three, and three against two."[75] On another occasion when he was discussing the lesson on John 3 with the minister Mr. Pr., he reminded him, "But as then he that was born after the flesh persecuted him that was born after the Spirit, even so it is now. [Galatians 4:29]"[76]

Charles often reminded people that their suffering was a part of God's plan as revealed in Scriptures, but he also reminded them that there would be a day when the suffering would end. On that day, "The wolf also shall dwell with the lamb. [Isaiah 11:6]"[77] The promise of peace and eternal life were two ways Charles encouraged people to endure the suffering of this life.[78] Charles also showed the necessity of persecution from Matthew 5:10. He wrote, "Tonight I proceeded in the Beatitudes. When I came to the last, 'Blessed are they which are persecuted,' our enemies, not knowing the Scriptures, fulfilled them."[79] To comfort those in the midst of the trial he also referred to the ministry of Paul and Barnabas after they were stoned and left for dead outside of Lystra. In this passage, Paul continued his ministry after being left for dead and even returned to Lystra. Paul's message was summarized in Acts 14:22, the passage Charles quoted as he was leaving those who were facing persecution in Wednesbury. Charles used this passage to remind them "that we must through much tribulation enter into the kingdom of heaven."[80] After challenging the people with the need to persevere in the midst of the persecution he noted, "With many tears and blessings they sent me away, commended to the graces of God."[81] At St. Ives the message was basically the same, but while there he showed that it was a part of their calling as Christians to be hated by all men.[82]

Although Charles Wesley's theology of suffering was based on his reading of the Scriptures, it was strengthened by the witness of those in the movement who were coming to the same conclusion. Charles recorded his thoughts about a young woman who was facing the question, "Could you die for the gospel of Jesus Christ?" She concluded her testimony with the following reflection on persecution: "This thought pursues me still, that I am to suffer for my Saviour, and I should grudge the dying in my bed." Her answer inspired Charles. He wrote, "I never felt more powerful, piercing words. They brought their own evidence, and left me no room to doubt God's special love to this soul. They also confirmed my continual expectations of sufferings."[83]

Charles was also encouraged by how persecution seemed to be impacting the larger movement. Commenting on the persecution at St. Just, Charles noted how a society of twelve had grown to about fifty or sixty. His reflections on this suggest that this was not what he had expected or at the very least it was not what had been reported to him about this society. He wrote,

> I spake with each of the Society, and was amazed to find them just the reverse of what they had been represented. Most of them had kept their first love, even while men were riding over their heads, and they passed through fire and water. Their exhorter appeared a solid, humble Christian; raised up to stand in the gap, and keep the trembling sheep together.[84]

According to Charles, the Methodist societies not only were surviving in the face of persecution, they were growing:

> What have they not done to crush this rising sect? but, lo! they prevail nothing! *Non Hydra secto corpore firmior vinci dolentem crevit in Herculem.* For one preacher they cut off, twenty spring up. Neither persuasions nor threatening, flattery nor violence, dungeons or sufferings of various kinds, can conquer them. Many waters cannot quench this little spark which the Lord hath kindled, neither shall the floods of persecution drown it.[85]

For Charles this suffering was not good in itself, instead, it served a higher purpose. In a letter to his future wife, Sarah Gwynne, Charles wrote, "The Lord only make us perfect thro' suffering, & let us suffer unto ye End!"[86] In other words, suffering was part of what was required for one to become perfect—another word Charles used to describe being restored in the image of God.[87] Part of the path to this perfection was a total resignation to the will of God.[88] When Charles Wesley questioned a woman about to die whether she preferred to live or die, she responded, "All is alike to me, let Christ choose. I have no will of my own." Charles commented, "This is that holiness or absolute resignation or Christian perfection!"[89] As has already been shown, he also argued that to suffer because of one's faith was to follow the example of Christ and his apostles.[90]

Charles not only taught that people should be willing to suffer, but he also taught people how to respond to suffering. He taught that one should respond with love. This can be seen in his comments on an altercation at Walsall: "The street was full of fierce Ephesian beasts (the principle man setting them on), who roared and shouted, and threw stones incessantly. Many struck without hurting me. I besought them in calm love to be reconciled to God in Christ."[91] This response of love was the same whether it was a crowd or an individual: "Set my eyes on the man that had been most violent with me on Sunday, and testified my love. He thanked me, and seemed melted."[92]

Even though Charles emphasized the necessity of suffering, he did not teach people to desire or pursue persecution. His struggle with whether or not they should be willing to suffer can be seen in the contrasting views Charles took at two different times during the persecution. At the beginning of the persecutions he was afraid to leave Evesham because to leave would be to "forsake my Captain, or deny my Master, while any one of them opened his mouth against the truth."[93] But four years later he wondered if he and others had mistaken the "fear of shame" for courage. He reflected,

> I cannot help observing from what passed yesterday that we ought to wait upon God for direction when and where to preach, much more than we do. A false courage, which is fear of shame, may otherwise betray us into unnecessary dangers.[94]

As Methodism grew it started to face opposition. For Charles this was accepted as a part of what would be required from a follower of Christ. Christ and his disciples had suffered, therefore his followers should *expect* to suffer. Charles used Scripture to support this position, but his experiences also strengthened his belief in the necessity of suffering. Charles encouraged people to look beyond the suffering to a better time and a better place. He felt that suffering worked to perfect the Christian and would finally be replaced with peace and eternal life. Because suffering was taught as a necessary part of the Christian life, Charles also taught people how to react to persecution and suffering. He taught and showed people that the best response was to return an attack with love. He recorded the calming effect a response of love had both on individuals and crowds. Although Charles seems committed to the necessity of suffering, his writing still reflected a struggle with the motives of some of their actions. Had they exposed themselves to suffering unnecessarily because of a fear of shame? This was not the only area Charles struggled to define in the 1740's. He also seems to rethink the meaning of singleness, a concept he associated with being restored in the image of God. His decision to marry Sarah Gwynne forced him to rethink how singleness would be lived out.

The Role of Marriage: The Single Life and the 'Single Eye'

Early in their lives John and Charles had decided that a part of what it meant for them to be restored in the image of God was a commitment to remain single and celibate.[95] This commitment was reaffirmed by John in his pamphlet, *Thoughts on Marriage and a Single Life*.[96] At the beginning of this pamphlet he extolled the virtues of marriage, but the last section was dedicated to the call to remain single. Like Paul, John Wesley encouraged all who could to remain single. In the late 1740's, Charles began to question the necessity of remaining single. This does not mean he was abandoning the commitment to theological singleness; he was only abandoning the commitment to remaining unmarried and celibate. If Charles's letters are any indication, this was a difficult decision for him, one he struggled with right up to the moment of the service. Part of the struggle was getting everyone involved to agree to the marriage, especially Sarah's family. He also struggled to get important members of the Methodist movement to agree to the marriage, including his brother John. But what is more significant for understanding how Charles defined being restored in the image of God was how he personally questioned whether he was pursuing this out of worldly or out of godly motivations.

That Charles continued to preach and teach the necessity of having a 'single eye' and a pure heart in the time leading up to his engagement to Sarah Gwynne supports the contention that he had not abandoned his commitment to a purity of intention. In March of 1746 he noted that God had confirmed his word when Charles preached on "the necessity of the single eye" out of Matthew 6:22-23. He emphasized the importance of having a 'single eye' in a letter to Sarah when he noted the success he was having in his attempt to be single. He wrote, "Great Confidence I felt of my own Integrity & Single Eye in the most Important Concern of Life. I knew My Aim was right, & my Design, To secure in every State my Last Appearing with Him in Glory."[97] Charles noted this same commitment to a 'single eye' in one who was to soon inherit £100 a year. Charles was unconcerned how this inheritance would affect the man because he was "a Man of a single Eye, & as much above all Worldly Consideration as his Father."[98] That having a 'single eye' was still the desire of his heart was also demonstrated by his request for Sarah to pray for him and to ask specifically for him to have "a Single Eye, & a Pure Heart."[99] Charles confirmed he was struggling with the idea of being married in one of his prayers for Sarah. There were two possible effects his relationship with her could have—perfection or personal benefit. Charles wrote to her, "And this I wish, your Perfection, infinitely more than any Private Benefit."[100] By expressing this wish Charles revealed one of his fears; that he could not trust his own emotions. He feared that he pursued this relationship for personal gain instead of as a part of loving God.

Charles expressed the fear he was abandoning his beliefs for a personal benefit in several different ways. In his journal he noted that doubts arose immediately after he expressed a desire to spend his life with her. He wrote,

> At night my dearest Sally, like my guardian angel attended me. In the loving openness of my heart, without premeditation I asked her "if she could trust herself with me for life," and with a noble simplicity she readily answered me [that] she could. **Monday, April 4.** Frightened at what I had said last night, I condemned my own rashness and almost wished I had never discovered myself.[101]

As the date for the wedding approached, Charles expressed more and more doubt about whether this was the best thing for his and Sarah's spiritual development. Often he expressed victory over his doubts, but not always. Two questions were of upmost importance to him. First, would marrying Sarah negatively affect his ability to serve God and God's Church, and second, would his love for Sarah diminish his love for God. In January of 1749, about three months before the marriage, he wrote Sarah that he had overcome some of these doubts. Even in the midst of these affirmations he still was leaving the outcome to God; suggesting he still didn't trust his own judgment. He wrote,

> I am equally Persuaded such a Companion wd greatly strengthen my Hands in the Lord, & increase my Serviceablenss to his Church.
> My Fear of Loving you too well is moderated, but not quite removed. And perhaps Tis good, yt it shd continue, as a guard & Protection. But of this I seem assur'd, that rather than let me make an Idol of you, the Jealous GOD will take you to his Bosom, or deliver me from ye Evil to come.[102] Which of the Two Events God will finally appoint: Only of this I am assured, He will chuse the Best; or what is most for his own Glory, & for your good, & mine, & the Edification of his Church.[103]

Two weeks later he again noted his desire to marry Sarah, but prayed that God would prevent it if it would be for their harm.[104] The extent of his doubts can be seen in a letter he wrote to Sarah in March of 1749. His desire to marry her here was replaced by a desire to meet her in heaven. The language he used indicates that his doubts about marrying Sarah were extreme even for the eighteenth century. That it was an unusual way to think is suggested by his plea to Sarah not to be troubled by what gave him delight. He wrote,

> Be not troubled, my Best-beloved Friend, at what gives me calm inexpressible Delight. The Hope of our Meeting in Paradice rather than here. Here we shall, we must meet First, if it be Best: & if not, Let Infinite Mercy chuse for us![105]

He included a poem with this letter that shows that one of his concerns was with becoming too comfortable in this life.

> 5. Thou knowst my every Hope & Fear,
>   Thou seest my Heart without Disguise,
> I would not have my Comfort here. -
>   Or seek an Earthly Paradice:
>
> 6. I would not to thy Creature cleave
>   Obtain the Drop, & lose the Sea:
> Thou, Thou art All, & Thine receive
>   Their Happiness compleat in Thee.
>
> 14. Me, & my happy Partner seize,
>   Renewd, & perfected in One,
> Give us to share that Endless Bliss,
>   And now to meet—before thy Throne.[106]

Charles also feared or at least questioned anything that promised good. One reason he could not really hope for the marriage to come to pass was his tendency to withdraw when faced with blessings. He wrote Sarah, "And the Greater the Good Proposed, the Backwarder am I to fasten on it, or snatch at it beforehand, in sanguine Hope of—what may never be.'"[107] Although this may argue that he avoided wishing for any good thing because he was afraid it would never come to be, it may also be a result of his personality, which tended to see or focus on the darker side of life. This darker view of life can also be seen in a letter he wrote to Sarah about two weeks later. In this letter he explained his lack of hope:

> That we shall <u>meet here</u>, I dare not yet be confident, altho' all appearances promise it; but it seems too-great a Blessing for me to expect. Throughout my Life past, you know, I have been <u>Safe from all expectation</u> of Good.
>
> Safe in the Gulph of Temporal Despair.
>
> And I had gone mourning <u>all</u> my Days, had not Providence unexpectedly led me to G; where <u>my Friend</u> extorted from me my Despair; & the Dark Cloud burst at once, & gave me a Prospect of Comfort even on this side the Grave—How strangely Providence <u>appeared</u> since then, I acknowledge with Thankful Astonishment.[108]

About a week before the wedding Charles was still struggling with his doubts. Once again he based his argument on not being presumptuous.

> Nay, I would even pray our Heavenly Father to prevent our Meeting, unless He has Appointed it for our Endless Happiness. You remember Young
>
> > In Human Hearts what Bolder Thout. can rise
> > Than Man's Presumption on Tomorrow's Dawn?[109]

His relationship with Sarah may seem pretty dark, because of these expressions of doubt, but Charles also shared positive thoughts with Sarah, like why he desired to be married to her and what had drawn him to her. Much of what he said focused on her character and the blessings or help he would receive because of their marriage. Reflecting on their first meeting Charles noted how he was drawn to her and his hope that their relationship would draw them nearer to God. He also recognized that Sarah had a "single Eye & a simple Heart." He continued, "I only wish yt in this behalf I were altogether like you."[110] In another letter he praised her for her care of the poor, "I know no one yt wd be a more faithful Steward for the Poor or more naturally care for them."[111]

In the expression of both his fears and his hopes, Charles expressed the same overarching goal, to be restored in the image of God. He may not have used that exact language, but the focus on being single in his desire to love God above all else had been one part of what it meant for him to be restored in the image of God from the beginning. What happen here was not a change of focus, but a change in the means of being restored. Charles proclaimed he could get married and yet remain single in his love to God. His marriage did not weaken his relationship with God, or his ability to minister, or at least that was what Charles was trying to convince himself of immediately after the wedding. Shortly after the wedding he recorded the way God was working in his ministry in the most positive terms.

Monday, April 17. The Lord was never more with me than he was at Builth, while I spake from those words, "These are they that came out of great tribulation" [Revelation 7:14]. All the hearers were in tears, but it was a blessed mourning.[112]

Saturday, April 22. Cheerfully left my partner for the Master's work, and rode on with Harry to Bristol.[113]

Monday, May 1. Never since I preached the gospel have I been more owned and assisted of God than now. He is always with me in the work of the ministry.[114]

He also tried to convince John that his work for God had not suffered because of his marriage: "More zeal, more life, more power, I have not felt for some years: (I wish my mentioning this may not lessen it) so that hitherto marriage has been no hinderance."[115] On the same day he shared with Ebenezer Blackwell how he took the calm state of his mind as a sign of God's favor on his marriage.[116] These entries and letters attest to his continued zeal for God and God's work, even after his marriage. What he feared would damage his ministry and his love for God, at least according to his initial reflections, had had the opposite effect. Although he had doubts about whether or not marriage was God's best for him, in the end he embraced it.

The pursuit of Sarah Gwynne's hand in marriage affected the way Charles applied his theology of being restored in the image of God. He continued to espouse the same theology, that the goal of the Christian life was to be restored in the image of God, but how he applied this to his everyday life began to change. As has just been noted he abandoned his devotion to celibacy and redefined singleness within the marriage relationship. In both instances his love for God was primary. Another major challenge Charles faced in getting married was that now he had to think about providing a living for someone other than himself. He might be willing to forgo many of the conveniences of this life, but Sarah's family wanted proof that Charles would provide a comfortable life for their daughter. Much of the correspondence between Charles and Sarah leading up to the wedding involved garnering her family's support. One way Charles sought to show he could support Sarah was through a valuation of his and his brother's publications. Vincent Perronet (1693-1785) sent a letter to Sarah's mother indicating someone had valued John and Charles's works at £2,500. He told Mrs. Gwynne he did not believe that was even half their value.[117] In addition to this, Charles was collecting subscriptions for a two-volume collection of his own hymns, which would be called *HSP* (1749).[118] The reflections from Charles's journal and letters noted above will be used to examine the theology of *HSP* (1749).

The Theology of Charles Wesley in *Hymns and Sacred Poems* (1749)

Charles published this collection before John had a chance to edit it.[119] Because of this, it is probable that the ideas presented are Charles's ideas. That there would have been differences in this collection if John would have edited it can be demonstrated by the comments he made in his personal copy. These comments highlight some of the differences the brothers may have had in their approach to the Methodist movement at this point in their lives.[120]

HSP (1749) is more structured than any of the collections that precede it.[121] Unlike any of the collections that precede it, most of its poems are grouped together by subject matter. There are very few poems in this collection that are not grouped with other poems of the same type. This collection is basically structured according to the order of salvation,[122] a pattern which will later be used in the *1780 Collection*. The poems interweaved with the poems on the order of salvation are often related to the stage immediately before or after the poems. Many themes in this collection would be familiar to a member of early Methodism. The section most closely related to being restored in the image of God is "Hymns for Those that wait for full Redemption."[123] The twenty-one poems in this section present Charles's understanding of what it meant to be restored in the image of God. Several issues that were a part of Wesleyan theology during this time are addressed in this section. The primary emphasis of these poems is the ability to live a sinless life. These poems also describe the character of one being restored in the image of God, God's role in this restoration, the necessary response people must have to be restored, and the timing of this restoration.

The Goal of Being Restored in the Image of God: Becoming Sinless

Charles Wesley's primary definition of being restored in the image God in *HSP* (1749) involved the goal of becoming sinless. The goal of being restored for Charles was to be like Christ. Because Christ lived a sinless life, Charles reasoned that those who followed him should also live sinless lives. Charles's desire was to be so redeemed from sin that the very possibility of sinning would be removed. He taught that once a believer experienced complete freedom from sin, that believer would be "pure, and all like [Jesus]." He wrote,

> 13 From all our Foes, our Sins redeem,
> The Possible Offence remove,
> And make us pure & all like Him,
> Renew'd & perfected in love.[124]

In another poem he said the will of God was that people would "live from sin forever free" because they were becoming more and more like Christ and because they felt the "fulness of his Spirit."[125] In other words, being free from sin was a result of the work of the Spirit in their lives, which made them more like Jesus who was without sin.

There were other times when Charles referred to specific sins or attitudes people would be freed from as they moved towards a "sinless love."

> 11 Jesus from pride, from wrath, from lust,
> Our inward Jesus be,

> From every evil thought we trust
>   To be redeem'd by thee.
> When thou dost in our flesh appear,
>   We shall the promise prove,
> Sav'd into all perfection *here*,
>   Renew'd in sinless love. [126]

Charles privileged certain Scriptures to teach the need and the ability to live a sinless life. From Galatians 5:17, "The flesh lusteth against the Spirit, but the Spirit against the flesh (and these are contrary the one to the other) that ye may not do the things which ye would," he argued that one who continued in sin was still striving against the Spirit.[127] In contrast to this, the one who would submit to the work of the Spirit would be freed from both the desire and the necessity of sinning.

> 2 But God is to his promise just,
>   And arms us with sufficient grace,
> The Spirit exerts a stronger lust,
>   We *need* not once to sin give place;
> We do not yield to flesh and blood,
> Or do the things which nature would.[128]

Many of the theological concepts used by early Methodism were used by Charles to define what it means to be sinless. Recapitulation was still seen as recovering what was lost in the fall, but Charles adds the emphasis on being sinless to his ideas of recapitulation. He expressed this hope:

> 1 O Jesus, at thy feet we wait,
>   'Till thou shalt bid us rise,
> Restor'd to our unsinning state,
>   To love's sweet paradise.[129]

Charles also associated purity with being sinless in *HSP* (1749). It may still refer to having a single focus, doing everything out of love for God; but now Charles taught it was also recovering the original purity and becoming sinless like the first 'man'.

> 7 We his life on earth shall live,
> We his image shall retrieve,
> Pure as the first sinless man,
> Modell'd by the perfect plan.[130]

Charles wrote one should be delivered from 'inbred sin'. 'Inbred sin' was one result of the fall of Adam. Charles taught this sin could be removed and someone could become "A new sinless creature."[131] Removing the 'inbred offense' involved removing both the ability to stumble and the infection of sin. The extent to which Charles thought this sin could be removed (at least at this time) is indicated by his use of the word extirpate, which means "To root out, eradicate (an immaterial thing, e.g. heresy, vice, etc.)."[132] In other words, to destroy something by getting rid of its roots. The result was a person who was truly righteous.

> 7 Come, Jesus, and cleanse
>   My inbred offence,
> O take the occasion of stumbling from hence,
>   The infection within,
>   The *possible sin*
> Extirpate, by bringing thy righteousness *in*.[133]

Charles also continued to teach that being attached to the creation was wrong. He still focused on the necessity of an ascetic approach to life. In one poem the love of creation was described as a curse or a plague. "Creature-love" was at least one part of the "inbred sin" which was washed away by the blood of the lamb. His prayer to the "gentle Lamb of God" was,

> 1 O thou gentle Lamb of God,
>   Hear thy ransom'd follower pray,
> Wash me in thy cleansing blood,
>   Bear my inbred sin away;
> All the curse, the plague remove,
> All the hell of creature-love.[134]

Charles's desire to live a sinless life was at least partially motivated by the possibility of some very practical benefits. One motivation was freedom from the sorrow associated with sin. According to Charles, the only way someone could be freed from sorrow in this life was for them to be free from sin.

> 2 I never shall rest,
>   Or be perfectly blest,
> While the tempter hath left any hold in my breast:
>   Thou hast loosen'd the chain,
>   Thou hast softned the pain,
> Yet my sorrow, as long as my sin, *must remain*.[135]

Although he may have made arguments like the one above, which have a positive goal, it is more likely that his motivation was polemical. Charles wanted to promote a certain view of the Christian life, but he was also writing against another view. As has been shown above, Charles was concerned with the antinomian tendencies of both the Moravians and the Calvinistic Methodists. Because of this it is probable that he overstated his own beliefs to combat the errors of others. In the polemical promotion of his theology Charles also had a tendency to use the language of those he spoke against to highlight how they differed from his understanding. For instance, Charles used the language of Calvinistic election to promote living a sinless life. It has already been noted that in one of his sermons, Charles encouraged Calvinists to make their election sure by their actions.[136] The same emphasis can be seen in this poem.

1 Ye servants of God, who trust in his Son,
And feel that his blood for all did atone,
Your songs of thanksgiving delightfully raise,
And praise him by living to Jesus his praise.

2 Believe on his name, 'till inwardly clean
Ye live without blame, ye live without sin:
Go on to perfection, thro' Jesus his power,
Make sure your election, and sin is no more.[137]

The Impossibility of Being Sinless and the Work of God

Charles was aware that what he was presenting seemed unreasonable. In one hymn, based on Mark 9:23, he taught that all things were possible to those who believe. Each verse ended with the phrase, "All things are possible to me." The focus of the hymn was being freed from sin, something that seemed impossible, but something Charles said he knew would happen.

> 2 The most Impossible of all
>   Is, that I e'er from sin sh[oul]d cease;
> Yet shall it be, I know, it shall,
>   Jesu, look to Thy Faithfulness,
> ~~Is any~~ If no thing is too hard for Thee,
> All things are possible to me.
>
> 3 I without Sin on Earth shall live,
>   Ev'n I, The Chief of Sinners I.
> Thy Glory, Lord, to Thee I give,
>   O GOD of Truth Thou canst not lie,
> ~~The Thing Thou sayst~~ What Thou hast said shall surely be:
> All things are possible to Thee.[138]

The reason Charles gave for teaching what seemed impossible was his belief that to teach otherwise was to damage the character of God. He presented the high ideal he found in the Scripture, instead of teaching that which was easily reachable. He reasoned that if people could not be restored to a sinless state, then God must be deceiving them with God's promises. Charles's words to the one struggling with doubts about the possibility of living without sin illustrates this point.

> 3 But may we not strive,
>   Yet never arrive
> To be saints, or to live without sin, while alive?
>
> 4 No, no, never fear,
>   If we look for him here,
> But our uttermost Saviour in us shall appear.

> 5 We dare not believe,
>   That God can deceive,
> And never intend what he promis'd to give.
>
> 6 He hath said, from all sin
>   Ye here shall be clean,
> All-holy, all-pure, and all-glorious within.
>
> 7 We rest on his word,
>   We shall here be restor'd
> To his image; the servant shall be as his Lord.[139]

Charles emphasized the ability to live without sin in part because he was concerned about the dangers of antinomianism. Charles's perception of the Moravians and the predestinarians was that they taught that a believer would continue in sin. Charles addressed the idea of continuing in sin through a set of questions. He ended this hymn by affirming his belief in the promises of God. He asked,

> 1 And shall we then abide in sin,
>   Nor hope on earth to be set free?
> Hath Jesus bled to wash us clean,
>   To save from all iniquity,
> And can he not his blood apply,
> And cleanse, and save us—'till we die?
>
> 2 Alas! If their report be true,
>   Who teach that sin must still *remain*,
> If sin we scarcely can subdue,
>   But never *full* redemption gain,
> Where is thy power, Almighty Lord?
> Where is thine everlasting word?
>
> 5 Where are the spirits to Jesus join'd,
>   Freed from the law of death and sin?
> The Saviour's pure and spotless mind?
>   The endless righteousness brought in?
> The heavenly man, the heart renew'd,
> The living portraiture of God?
>
> 8 Lord, we believe, and rest secure,
>   Thine utmost promises to prove,
> To rise restor'd, and throughly pure,
>   In all the image of thy love,
> Fill'd with the glorious life unknown,
> Forever sanctified in one.[140]

Charles used the tension between the impossibility of being restored in the sinless image of Christ and the promises of God that it would happen, to emphasize that the work of restoration was God's work. He emphasized God's work by contrasting two approaches to the impossibility of living without sin. The first group believed in the power of God and the second focused on the weakness of people.

> 2 The power of our Lord doth all things subdue,
> We shall by his word be fashion'd anew;
> Our souls and our bodies shall bow to his reign,
> The weakness of God is far stronger than men.
>
> 3 Men, devils agree to tell us in vain
> Poor sinners like thee must always complain,
> "My leanness, my leanness, my inbeing load,
> The weakness of men is far stronger than God."[141]

For Charles, people should not focus on their limitations, instead they should focus on the work of Christ. People should not cling to the "idol of inbeing sin." Charles probably was using this language to challenge the predestinarians' belief that all were and will continue to be affected by Adam's sin. Charles did not deny the affects of "inbeing sin," but he did teach that Christ was able to cleanse and perfect a person from "inbeing sin,' and Christ was able to do this in a day:

> 7 Let others from themselves remove,
>   And chase salvation far away;
> But thou canst perfect *me* in love,
>   Canst perfect me in love *to-day*
>
> 8 Let others madly hug their chains,
>   Their idol of inbeing sin;
> I cannot plead for sin's remains,
>   When thou hast said, Ye shall be clean.
>
> 9 If thou hast power and will to save,
>   Sav'd to the utmost I shall be,
> The fulness of the Godhead have;
>   For all the Godhead is in thee.[142]

Charles not only credited the work to God in a general way, at times he described the specific actions of God that made the renewal possible. Sometimes Charles would focus on the Trinitarian nature of being restored in the image of God. Christ received the gift from God the Father and the Holy Spirit brought the gift down to those who believed. In this verse Charles tied the gift of the Holy Spirit to the desire to be freed from sin.

> 3 Give me what GOD to Thee did give,
> The grace Thou didst for me receive,
>   When all thy Pangs were o'er;
> Send down thy Spirit from above,
> Spirit of Power, & Health, & Love,
>   And let me sin no more.[143]

At other times Charles would focus on the work of just one member of the Trinity, but the message was the same: it is God's work! Sometimes he would present the work of Christ in a general way, proclaiming people are saved for Jesus' sake with only a passing mention of Christ's death.

> 4 Sav'd from the guilt and power of sin,
>   For Jesu's sake forgiven,
> We trust to have the grace brought in,
>   The new-created heaven.
>
> 5 Forgetting still the things behind,
>   To'ward the high prize we press,
> And look the pretious pearl to find,
>   The perfect holiness.
>
> 6 We shall be wholly sanctified,
>   As many as Christ receive,
> As sure as he for us hath died,
>   He in our hearts shall live.[144]

There are other times when he focused on a specific part of Jesus' life and ministry, when he mentioned certain aspects of Jesus' life in more detail. One reason for his hope was the blood of Christ. The death of Jesus on the cross exhibited God's love. The blood of Christ would thoroughly sanctify the believer. Focusing on the blood of Christ could remove a person's doubts and fears.

> 1 What is the reason of my hope,
>   My hope to live and sin no more?
> After his likeness to wake up,
>   And God in spi'rit, and truth adore,
> To serve him as the hosts above
> In perfect peace, and perfect love?
>
> 2 Faith in the blood of Christ I have;
>   He freely lov'd, and died for me:
> Sinners he came from sin to save,
>   From all, from all iniquity;
> Without the camp he deign'd to die,
> Us by his blood to sanctify.
>
> 3 His blood shall sanctify throughout
>   My spirit, soul, and body *here*:
> Because he died, I cannot doubt,
>   Because he died, I cannot fear;
> His blood shall make me pure within,
> His blood shall cleanse me from all sin.[145]

Later in this hymn he stated that the final goal of this hope was being restored in the image of God here. This included becoming as pure, holy, and perfect as God.

>   5 God hath ordain'd, that I should see
>   In perfect holiness his face,
>   Retrieve his image here, and be
>   Forever sanctified by grace;
>   His truth, and power, and mercy join,
>   The will, and word, and oath divine.
>
>   6 Here then my foot of faith stands sure,
>   And earth, and hell in vain deny;
>   I shall be pure as God is pure,
>   Holy as God is holy I,
>   Perfect, as God is perfect, rise,
>   And take my mansion in the skies.[146]

The Character of Those Being Restored in the Image of God

Charles encouraged people to become more like Jesus by focusing on specific attributes or images of Jesus' character. Some of the character traits Charles promoted were humility, purity of heart, and freedom from fear and sin.

As has already been argued, humility was one of the virtues of early Methodism, a virtue Charles fully embraced in his writings. To promote the need for humility Charles used the image of Jesus as the lovely lamb:

>   1 Lovely Lamb, I come to thee,
>   Thou hast oft invited me;
>   Surely now I would be blest,
>   Give me now the promis'd rest.
>
>   3 Gentle thou, and meek in heart,
>   All humility thou art;
>   Full of wrath, and pride I am,
>   How unlike my lowly Lamb!
>
>   5 Thou art greater than my heart,
>   Thou canst make me as thou art,
>   Sink the proud, and tame the wild,
>   Change me to a little child.
>
>   6 Turn me, Lord, and turn me now,
>   To thy yoke my spirit bow;
>   Grant me now the pearl to find
>   Of a meek and quiet mind.[147]

Charles noted both the attributes associated with humility and the attributes that made attainment of this goal difficult. What stood in the way were wrath, pride, and a wildness. The attributes which would become a part of the life being transformed by the "lowly Lamb" included gentleness, meekness, childlikeness, and a quiet mind. Consistent with the emphasis of the 'Oxford Methodists', this pride resulted from Adam's fall and the selfish lusts associated with that fall. But that nature could and would be overcome because of God's promises.

> 1 While pride and self remain within,
>   While ought of the old Adam lives,
> The fleshly principle of sin
>   Against the Spirit lusts, and strives;
> We groan our evil heart to feel,
> Children in Christ, and carnal still.
>
> 2 But God is to his promise just,
>   And arms us with sufficient grace,
> The Spirit exerts a stronger lust,
>   We *need* not once to sin give place;
> We *do* not yield to flesh and blood,
> Or do the things which nature would.[148]

A second attribute associated with early Methodism was purity. He continued to emphasize the need for purity, but at times he only referred to the need to be pure without giving any description of what it meant to be pure. In this poem he noted that God purifies the heart and prays that the one who is faithful and just, a reference to I John 1:9, would make us pure. Charles ended the poem not with a prayer, but with a declaration, "We shall be pure in heart."

> 7 The Spirit's living law it writes
>   Upon our inward parts,
> Our new-born souls to God unites,
>   And purifies our hearts.
>
> 13 Thy sanctifying word is sure;
>   Lord, we our sins confess,
> Faithful and just, O make us pure
>   From all unrighteousness.
>
> 14 Such power belongeth unto thee,
>   Thy saying we receive;
> We shall be pure in heart, and see
>   Thy smiling face, and live.[149]

For Charles, purity still seems to be tied to a form of asceticism. Charles emphasized ascetic practices by the priority he placed on being freed from sin. God's gift of restoration was more important than any earthly pleasure.

> [4] I ask nor Joy, nor Life, nor Ease,
> No nor thy Heavenly Happiness,
>   But Purity within;
> On others, Lord, thy gifts bestow,
> But let me cease from sin below,
> But let me cease from sin.[150]

Another emphasis of purity was loving God above all else. He wrote all is vanity besides the gift of God's love. True joy could only be found in God's love.

> 3 Whom but thee have we in heaven,
>   Whom have we on earth but thee?
> Only thou to us be given,
>   All besides is vanity;
> Grant us love, we ask no more,
>   Every other gift remove;
> Pleasure, fame, and wealth, and power,
>   Still we all enjoy in love.[151]

One of the benefits of discovering God's gift of love was that it was accompanied with freedom from "sin, and servile fear." In other words, to have the purity of heart which proved "All the Eden of his [Jesus'] Love" would also remove some of the fears associated with living in the world.

> 6 Free from Sin, & Servile Fear,
> Have my Jesus ever near,
> All his Care delight to prove,
> All the Eden of his Love.[152]

Charles preached on these themes in his sermon before the University of Oxford on April 4, 1742.[153] This sermon ended with an admonition to have the character of one who had recovered the image of God. Even though they had success in some of the "grosser abominations" they still lacked "true religion." He wrote,

> 11. And even among those who have kept themselves pure from those grosser abominations, how much anger and pride, how much sloth and idleness, how much softness and effeminacy, how much luxury and self-indulgence, how much covetousness and ambition, how much thirst of praise, how much love of the world, how much fear of man is to be found! Meanwhile, how little of true religion? For where is he that loveth either God or his neighbour, as he hath given us commandment[?]
> . . .
>
> We have not kept ourselves pure. Corrupt are we also and abominable; and few are there that understand any more, few that worship God in spirit and truth.[154]

The Timing of Being Restored in the Image of God

Charles presented the idea of being restored in *HSP* (1749) in a way that suggests he was uncertain of when or how this would happen. At times his poems reveal the struggle he had specifically with the timing of this restoration. The doubts he expressed, though, could also be his way of connecting with where people were in order to lead them to what he was teaching. It seems however, that Charles used different expressions to create an interpretive tension about the timing of the restoration. For instance, in one hymn he progressed from the word "may" (a word that at least expressed some doubts) to the word "shall" (a word which seems to indicate a sense of certainty). He wrote,

> 3 Bounds I will not set to thee,
>   Shorten thine almighty hand:
> Save from all iniquity,
>   Let not sin's foundations stand,
> Every stone o'erturn, o'erthrow;
> I believe it *may* be so.
>
> 4 Wilt thou lop the boughs of sin,
>   Leaving still the stock behind?
> No, thy love shall work within,
>   Quite expel the carnal mind,
> Root and branch destroy my foe;
> I believe it *shall* be so.[155]

Although there is a tension in the way Charles presented being renewed in the image of God, the focus in this section of *HSP* (1749)[156] is primarily on it happening *here*. In one poem he admits that his belief was based on his faith, and if his faith was true, then the restoration would happen here. He was not saying if his faith was strong enough. He was saying if what he believed was correct. He tied his belief in being restored to the goodness and truthfulness of Jesus:

> 5 We shall attain what we pursue,
>   Unless our faith is vain;
> If thou art good, if thou art true,
>   We shall the prize attain;
>
> 6 Partake on earth the heavenly bliss,
>   And pure and holy be,
> And perfect as thy Father is,
>   And one with God in thee.[157]

One of the words he used to emphasize it happening in this life was the word *below*. Many times after he emphasized being restored *below*, he would either pray he would be taken up to heaven or he stated his desire to be taken up.

> 9 Live, till all thy life I know,
> With & in my Lord *below*
> Gladly then from Earth remove,
> Gather'd to the Fold *above*.[158]

Charles stressed that sin could be destroyed or defeated here and now. Many times he did this through a positive proclamation, but other times his approach was more polemical. There were times when he used quotes from those he was opposing. These poems can be especially difficult to interpret if they're not studied in their entirety. Charles indicated his rejection of those who denied the ability of God to remove sin by claiming those people who say these things, "trample on thy [Jesus'] blood." What he opposed in this hymn were those who believed Jesus' death did not allow people to live a sinless life below.

> 1 And hast thou died, O Lamb of God,
>   To take away our inbred sin?
> And shall we trample on thy blood,
>   And say, "It cannot make us clean,
> The truth on earth we cannot know,
> There's no perfection here below?"
>
> 4 "The flesh is weak, and will prevail;
>   We all have our infirmities,
> "Live without sin! Impossible!
>   With God impossible is this:
> At least he *will not* sanctify,
> He will not cleanse us—'till we die."[159]

In *HSP* (1749) there are even hints that Charles thought it could happen in an instant. In one poem he even talked of cutting short the work of Righteousness.

> 2 Surely I have pardon found,
> Grace doth more than sin abound,
> God, I know, is pacified,
> Thou for me, for me hast died:
> But I cannot rest herein,
> All my nature still is sin,
> Comforted I will not be,
> 'Till my soul is all like thee.
>
> 3 See my burthen'd, sin-sick soul,
> Give me faith, and make me whole,
> Finish thy great work of grace,
> Cut it short in righteousness:
> Speak the second time, Be clean,
> Take away my power to sin,[160]
> Now the stumbling-block remove,
> Cast it out by perfect love.[161]

Despite these strong statements about it happening here, Charles acknowledged he could be wrong, and that in the end God would choose when a person would become perfect.

> 8 Perfect when I walk before Thee,
>   Soon, or late, Then translate
> To the Realms of Glory.[162]

In this one section of *HSP* (1749), "Hymns for Those that Wait for Full Redemption," we see what seems to be a new emphasis for Charles, and at the very least an emphasis not present in *HSP* (1739), namely that the goal of being restored in the image of God was to be sinless. Being Sinless included freedom from some of the same sins mentioned in *HSP* (1739), including but not limited to pride, wrath, and lust. Charles's overarching theology still included the themes of recapitulation and singleness, but now focused on the new goal of being sinless. To this end he now wrote about removing inbred sin, which would remove both the ability to stumble and the infection of sin. Charles recognized this seemed impossible, but he continued to present it because to do otherwise would be to damage the character of God. The focus of Charles's work was on God's promises, that God had provided a way for people to overcome the sins of this life and be restored in the character of God, which included humility, purity, and love. Although his primary focus was on this restoration happening in this life, and at times even happening in an instant, he still left room for a different understanding.

Conclusion

The 1740's were a time of challenge and change. The challenges came from groups in the evangelical revival that formerly had a good relationship with Charles. During this time period, he began to speak out against the abuses he observed in the Moravians and the predestinarians. He taught that the Moravian's embrace of stillness was not compatible with his view of the means of grace. He seemed to believe that their embrace of stillness had the potential to be interpreted as a license to sin. Charles had the same objection to the teaching of the predestinarians. Their antinomianism was the result of three doctrines Charles rejected: reprobation, preservation of the saints, and the necessity of sinning. Charles attacked these beliefs because he felt it could lead to antinomianism and because they damaged the view one had of God. He accused them of making God into a God of hate. The ultimate problem with both groups for Charles was that they were settling for something less than being restored in the image of God. For Charles this pursuit include a proper use of the means of grace and a view of God as a God of universal love.

The 1740's were also a time of persecution. Charles used both Scripture and experience to argue that this was a necessary part of the Christian life. He seemed surprised that the effect of persecution was that the movement was made stronger. Charles taught that the way to respond to persecution, whether it was a group or a single individual, was to respond in love. Like many issues in his life, Charles's writing showed that he struggled with how this should be applied. For one thing, he questioned the motivation for putting oneself in a place where persecution was probable. Did they do this because of courage, or did they do it out of a fear of shame?

One of the most important events of the 1740's, for Charles, was his relationship with Sarah Gwynne. Because of this relationship Charles abandoned his commitment to remaining single. In the midst of that decision he worked out a new way of understanding being single in his love for God. He came to believe that contrary to his fears, marriage did not weaken his love for God. Neither did his marriage damage his ability to serve God's church.

As a part of his marriage to Sarah, Charles published a two-volume collection of his poetry and hymns. One part of this collection directly addressed the question of being restored in the image of God. Charles continued to use the language and theological concepts of early Methodism like recapitulation. He still emphasized the need for purity and the love of God and neighbor, but in this section he promoted the possibility of living a sinless life. This life was a result of God's work in the life of the believer and transformed them into the character of God as seen in Jesus. As with so many things in his poetry he presented a tension between this happening in this life (even instantaneously at times) and the commitment to waiting on God's timing (even if it wasn't in this life).

Notes

1. Charles Wesley, April 18, 1739, *Manuscript Journal*, 1:171.
2. For a description of Charles Wesley's Anglicanism see, Leaver, Robin, "Charles Wesley and Anglicanism," in *Charles Wesley: Poet and Theologian*, ed. S T Kimbrough. (Nashville: Kingswood Books, 1992), 157-175.
3. Charles Wesley, April 25, 1739, *Manuscript Journal*, 1:171.
4. Colin Podmore. *The Moravian Church in England, 1728-1760*, Oxford Historical Monographs, ed. R. R. Davis, R. J. W. Evans, et. al. (Oxford: Clarendon Press, 1998), 52-53.
5. Charles Wesley, May 16, 1739, *Manuscript Journal*, 1:173.
6. Harold Knight divided the means of grace into three categories: general, instituted or particular, and prudential. Some of the attitudes and actions included in these categories are: keeping the commandments, self-denial, taking up our cross daily, prayer, fasting, the Lord's supper, searching the Scriptures, classes, bands, and love feasts. (Harold Knight. *The Presence of God in the Christian Life: John Wesley and the Means of Grace*, Pietist and Wesleyan Studies,ed. David Bundy and J. Steven O'Malley (Lanham, MD: The Scarecrow Press, Inc.,1992), 3.
7. Charles Wesley, August 29, 1739, *Manuscript Journal*, 1:191.
8. Charles Wesley, October 27, 1739, *Manuscript Journal*, 1:217.
9. Charles Wesley, March [19], 1740, *Manuscript Journal*, 1:226.
10. Charles Wesley, March [19], 1740, *Manuscript Journal*, 1:227.
11. Charles Wesley, April 22, 1740, *Manuscript Journal*, 1:248.
12. Charles Wesley, March [22], 1740, *Manuscript Journal*, 1:227.
13. Charles Wesley, Sermon 8, "Ephesians 5:14," in *Sermons of Charles Wesley*, 214.
14. Ibid., 217-18. In the opening paragraphs of this sermon Charles noted people lacked even a basic knowledge of their problem. The recovery of the image of God which was lost in the fall was to be the purpose of their lives. A person's "holy business in the present world is to recover from his fall, to regain that image of God wherein he was created. He sees *no necessity* for the 'one thing needful' even that inward universal change, that 'birth from above' (figured out by Baptism) which is the beginning of that total renovation, that sanctification of spirit, soul, and body, 'without which no man shall see the Lord'." (Ibid., 213.)
15. Charles Wesley, April 8, 1740, *Manuscript Journal*, 1:237.
16. [Charles Wesley], *The Means of Grace* (London: Strahan, 1740). There are no extent copies of this pamphlet so the text used is from John Wesley and Charles Wesley,

Hymns and Sacred Poems (London: Strahan, 1740), 35-39.

17. Ibid., 36.
18. Ibid.
19. Ibid., 37.
20. Ibid., 36-37. Similar themes can be found in Charles Wesley, "Isai[ah] lxiv. 5," in [John and Charles Wesley], *A Short View of the Difference between the Moravian Brethren, lately in England, and the Rev. Mr. John and Charles Wesley* (London: Strahan, 1745), 19.
21. Matthew 5:16.
22. Matthew 23:2-3.
23. Luke 22:19.
24. Matthew 5:19.
25. Matthew 11:12, Luke 13:24, Philippians 2:12, and Hebrews 11:6.
26. Charles Wesley, Letter to the Society at Grimsby (April 27, 1743), MARC, DDCW 6/32.
27. Ibid.
28. Ibid. Emphasis mine.
29. Charles Wesley, April 6, 1740, *Manuscript Journal*, 1:235.
30. Ibid.
31. Charles Wesley, April 25, 1740, *Manuscript Journal*, 1:249.
32. Charles Wesley, Letter to the Society at Grimsby (April 27, 1743), MARC, DDCW 6/32.
33. Charles Wesley, March 22, 1740, *Manuscript Journal*, 1:227.
34. Charles Wesley, May 20, 1740, *Manuscript Journal*, 1:261.
35. Charles Wesley, March 19, 1740, *Manuscript Journal*, 1:227.
36. Charles Wesley, June 22, 1740, *Manuscript Journal*, 1:270.
37. Charles Wesley, May 7, 1740, *Manuscript Journal*, 1:253.
38. Charles Wesley, April 5, 1740, *Manuscript Journal*, 1:233.
39. Charles Wesley, May 13, 1740, *Manuscript Journal*, 1:256-57.
40. Charles Wesley, April 5, 1740, *Manuscript Journal*, 1:233.
41. "Who is among you that feareth the LORD, that obeyeth the voice of his servant, that walketh in darkness, and hath no light? Let him trust in the name of the LORD, and stay upon his God." (KJV)
42. Charles Wesley, May 7, 1740, *Manuscript Journal*, 1:253. This passage is omitted in Jackson's edition of the Journal.
43. "Rejection by God; *spec.* the action by which those not forming part of God's elect are predestined to eternal damnation." (*OED*, December 2009 online ed., s.v. "reprobation.")
44. Charles Wesley, Letter to JW ([March 16-17, 1741]), *Letters* II, ed. Frank Baker, vol. 26 of *The Bicentennial Edition of the Works of John Wesley* (Nashville: Abingdon Press, 1982), 54.
45. Charles Wesley, Letter to John Wesley (September 28, 1741), *Letters II*, in *Works*, 26:66. "All the passages enclosed within double square brackets are written in Byrom's shorthand."
46. Ibid., 65.
47. Charles Wesley, July 16, 1741, *Manuscript Journal*, 1:320.
48. Universal redemption was used by John and Charles Wesley to refer to the doctrine of universal atonement in contrast to the predestinarian view of limited redemption or atonement. In other words, Charles was arguing that the benefits of the atonement are available for everyone, that everyone has the possibility of being reconciled to God. John

and Charles were equally clear that this benefit was conditional, and therefore limited in its application. For a discussion of how Charles Wesley's Universal Redemption differs from modern Universalism see, Rattenbury, *The Evangelical Doctrines of Charles Wesley's Hymns*, 129-36.

49. Charles Wesley, May 7, 1741, *Manuscript Journal*, 1:305.

50. [John Cennick], Letter to George Whitefield (January 17, 1741) in *Journal and Diaries* II, ed. W. Reginald Ward and Richard P. Heitzenrater, vol. 19 of *The Bicentennial Edition of the Works of John Wesley* (Nashville: Abingdon Press, 1990), 182-183.

51. [Charles Wesley], *Hymns on God's Everlasting Love; To Which is Added the Cry of a Reprobate and the Horrible Decree* (Bristol: Felix Farley, 1741), The Center for Studies in the Wesleyan Tradition, Duke University, *http://divinity.duke.edu/initiatives/cswt/charles-published-verse*. Hereafter cited as *Hymns on God's Everlasting Love* (1741).

52. Ibid., 3.

53. Ibid.

54. Ibid, 4.

55. Ibid, 5.

56. Ibid., 5.

57. Ibid., 5.

58. Charles Wesley, December 6, 1740, *Manuscript Journal*, 1:293.

59. "Calvinism maintained that the elect could be certain that God would never allow them to fall away from Him." in F. L. Cross and Elizabeth A. Livingstone. *The Oxford Dictionary of the Christian Church*. 3rd ed. rev., s.v. "perseverance."

60. Charles Wesley, Letter to John Wesley (December 3, [1740]), *Letters II*, in *Works*, 26:43-44.

61. Charles Wesley, June 8, 1741, *Manuscript Journal*, 1:312-13.

62. Charles Wesley, July 16, 1741, *Manuscript Journal*, 1:320.

63. Ibid. See also Charles Wesley, March 31, 1745, *Manuscript Journal*, 2:437.

64. The 'Faith of Adherence' is contrasted with 'Assurance' by John Edwards (1637-1716). He argued that assurance was a gift given to those who were more in need of it. Instead he of assurance, he said "we may content our selves with something lower, and remember that Faith of Adherence or Reliance is as safe and secure as that of Assurance, tho' it is not so comfortable." (John Edwards, *a doctrine of faith and justification set in a true light* [London: printed for Jonathan Robinson, John Lawrence, and John Wyat, 1708], 227.) Arthur Bedford makes a similar distinction saying, "Now this *Faith of Adherence* alone is sufficient to bring a Man to Heaven. . . . And therefore, to limit Salvation to a particular Degree of Faith [assurance], is to destroy all those promises, on which Thousands of *Christians* have hitherto depended for their eternal Comfort. (Arthur Bedford, *The Doctrine of Assurance: Or the Case of a Weak and Doubting Conscience*, Second ed. [London: Charles Ackers, 1739], 36.) The Puritan theologian Thomas Goodwin (1660-1680) argued that the only objects of the faith of adherence were the absolute declarations about God and Christ and God's absolute promises of salvation. In other words for Goodwin, the faith of adherence was not based on any merit or actions, but instead rested solely on the promises of God. (Thomas Goodwin, *The Works of Thomas Goodwin, D. D.*, vol. 8, *The Object and Acts of Justifying Faith* [Edinburgh: James Nichol, 1864], 205ff.) John Wesley argued there was only one faith, rejecting the distinction some made between the faith of assurance and the faith of adherence. (John Wesley, January 25, 1740, *Journal and Diaries II*, in *Works*, 19:137.)

65. "This evening Mrs Gilmore received the love of God shed abroad in her heart. A month ago she was a warm opposer. But venturing, out of curiosity, to hear me, the Lord

applied his word, and stripped her all at once of her self-righteousness, faith of adherence, and good works." (Charles Wesley, March 14, 1748, *Manuscript Journal*, 2:526.)

66. Charles Wesley, May 10, 1740, *Manuscript Journal*, 1:255.

67. Charles Wesley, December 27, 1740, *Manuscript Journal*, 1:294. A footnote included the definition of cap-a-pie as "head to toe" (*OED*, December 2009 online ed., s.v. "cap-à-pie.") Charles contrasted a Christianity based on Romans 7 with one based on Romans 8, the later included life in the Spirit and victory over the flesh, compared with the former which had no victory over the flesh.

68. Charles Wesley, October 10, 1747, *Manuscript Journal*, 2:511.

69. Charles Wesley, July 12, 1741, *Manuscript Journal*, 1:319.

70. Charles Wesley, March 11, 1747, *Manuscript Journal*, 2:497.

71. Charles Wesley, June 20, 1740, *Manuscript Journal*, 1:270.

72. Charles Wesley, September 21,1746, *Manuscript Journal*, 2:475-76.

73. Charles discussed several instances of persecution during the 1740's. Sometimes the persecution was a single person or family attacking Charles for the affect the gospel message was having on their lives. One instance of this was the difficulties he was having with the Seward family. (Charles Wesley, March 16, 1740, *Manuscript Journal*, 1:221-24.) At other times the persecution was against the movement in a particular city. A couple of the instances of persecution Charles mentioned were Evesham (Charles Wesley, March 18, 1740, *Manuscript Journal*, 1:224-26.) and Wednesbury (Charles Wesley, October 25, 1743, *Manuscript Journal*, 2:375-77.) One other form of 'persecution' was the attack of the Jacobite forces in 1745 and 1746. (Charles Wesley, May 2, 1746, *Manuscript Journal*, 2:458-59)

74. See pp. 47-48 above.

75. Charles Wesley, March 16, 1740, *Manuscript Journal*, 1:223-24.

76. Ibid.

77. Charles Wesley, March 18, 1740, *Manuscript Journal*, 1:224-25.

78. For instance Charles Wesley wrote to Mrs. Jones, "You are much upon my heart & will be till it ceases to beat. I glorify GOD in yr behalf, that He comforts the Afflicted, & leads you on in the Narrow Way to the Kingdom. Suffer; & you shall reign. The End of all things is at hand. What are all the Troubles of this present Life when set against Eternity. Eternity is at hand." (Charles Wesley, Letter to Mrs. Jones [March 11, (1746)], MARC, DDCW 1/85.) Also published in *Letters of Charles Wesley*, 126.

79. Charles Wesley, March 17, 1740, *Manuscript Journal*, 1:224.

80. Charles Wesley, May 23, 1743, *Manuscript Journal*, 2:344.

81. Ibid.

82. Charles Wesley, July 26, 1743, *Manuscript Journal*, 2:364. See also Charles Wesley, July 27, 1743, *Manuscript Journal*, 2:365 where Charles Wesley quoted John 15:18–20, "If the world hate you, ye know it hated me before it hated you. [...] Remember the word that I said unto you, The servant is not greater than his Lord. If they have persecuted me, they will also persecute you."

83. Charles Wesley, September 1, 1748, *Manuscript Journal*, 2:542-43.

84. Charles Wesley, July 23, 1746, *Manuscript Journal*, 2:467-69.

85. Charles Wesley, July 23, 1746, *Manuscript Journal*, 2:468-69. The latin is translated in the footnote as "'No, the hydra, as its body was hewn, grew mightier against Hercules.' Horace, Odes, IV.iv.61–62." (*Manuscript Journal*, 2:469) See also Charles Wesley, February 8, 1744, *Manuscript Journal*, 2:386-87.

86. Charles Wesley, Letter to Sarah Gwynne (November 10, 1748), MARC, DDCW 5/8. From Frank Baker's transcriptions of Charles Wesley's letters, where the item is No. 102. Also published in *Letters of Charles Wesley*, 170-71.

87. As an heir of the Reformation Charles was always careful to emphasize that Christ's suffering and death were alone responsible or the merit for salvation, but Charles also insisted "on the necessity of extreme suffering as the means to perfection." See, Cruickshank, "Charles Wesley and the Construction of Suffering in Early English Methodism," 140.

88. According to Cruickshank, Charles taught that one part of resigning to the will of God was having a proper response to suffering. Suffering could either lead to purification, or if it was not accepted as a part of God's grace to the individual, it would retain "its primary and permanent meaning of judgement." (Cruickshank, "Charles Wesley and the Construction of Suffering in Early English Methodism," 138)

89. Charles Wesley, May 6, 1741, *Manuscript Journal*, 2:304. Cruickshank has also noted how Charles Wesley used Hebrews 12:10 to argue that "the purpose of suffering is to create in the believer 'the mind, which in our Savior was.'" (Cruickshank, "Charles Wesley and the Construction of Suffering in Early English Methodism," 129)

90. Charles Wesley, Letter to the Society at Grimsby (April 27, 1743), MARC, DDCW 6/32. See pp. 65-66. Also published in *Letters of Charles Wesley*, 102-104.

91. Charles Wesley, May 21, 1743, *Manuscript Journal*, 2:343.

92. Charles Wesley, March 18, 1740, *Manuscript Journal*, 1:224-25.

93. Charles Wesley, March 18, 1740, *Manuscript Journal*, 1:225.

94. Charles Wesley, February 8, 1744, *Manuscript Journal*, 2:386-87.

95. See pp. 35-36 above.

96. John Wesley, *Thoughts on Marriage and a Single Life*, 2d ed. (Bristol: Printed by Felix Farley, 1743).

97. Charles Wesley, Letter to Sarah Gwynne ([March 26-28, 1749]), MARC, DDCW 5/45. Also published in *Letters of Charles Wesley*, 245-47.

98. Charles Wesley, Letter to Sarah Gwynne (January 26, 1749), MARC, DDWES 1/40. From Frank Baker's transcriptions of Charles Wesley's letters, where the item is No. 123a. Also published in *Letters of Charles Wesley*, 216-20.

99. Charles Wesley, Letter to Sarah Gwynne (August 9, 1748), MARC, DDCW 7/47. From Frank Baker's transcriptions of Charles Wesley's letters, where the item is No. 90. Also published in *Letters of Charles Wesley*, 155-56.

100. Charles Wesley, Letter to Sarah Gwynne ([March 10-11, 1749]), MARC, DDCW 5/33.

101. Charles Wesley, April 3-4, 1748, *Manuscript Journal*, 2:527-28.

102. Charles Wesley, Letter to Sarah Gwynne (January 23, 1749), MARC, DDCW 5/22. From Frank Baker's transcriptions of Charles Wesley's letters, where the item is No. 123. Also published in *Letters of Charles Wesley*, 213-16.

103. Charles Wesley, Letter to Sarah Gwynne (January 26, 1749), MARC, DDWES 1/40. Also published in *Letters of Charles Wesley*, 216-20.

104. Charles Wesley, Letter to Sarah Gwynne (February 11, 1749), MARC, DDCW 5/29. Also published in *Letters of Charles Wesley*, 228-29.

105. Charles Wesley, Letter to Sarah Gwynne (March 1, 1749), MARC, DDCW 5/42. Also published in *Letters of Charles Wesley*, 238-39. In this passage, Charles's acceptance and even desire to die can be seen. This desire indicates a strong hope in heaven and the blessings of heaven. Charles's poems on the death of a child help to clarify his attitude towards death. The comfort one has in the face of death is that the loved one is "Safe in the arms of his Beloved," and in the future their will be a reunion with those who have died. (Cruickshank, "Charles Wesley and the Construction of Suffering in Early English Methodism," 195)

106. Charles Wesley, Letter to Sarah Gwynne (March 1, [1749]), MARC, DDCW

5/30. Also published in *Letters of Charles Wesley,* 231-34.

107. Charles Wesley, Letter to Sarah Gwynne (March 2, 1749), MARC, DDCW 5/31. Also published in *Letters of Charles Wesley,* 234-35.

108. Charles Wesley, Letter to Sarah Gwynne (March 12, 1749), MARC, DDCW 5/34. Also published in *Letters of Charles Wesley,* 235-36.

109. Charles Wesley, Letter to Sarah Gwynne (April 3, 1749), MARC, DDCW 5/43. Also published in *Letters of Charles Wesley,* 248. Charles's last two lines are a quote from Edward Young. (Edward Young, *The Complaint: or Night Thoughts on Life, Death, and Immortality,* 5th ed. [London, 1743], 30.)

110. Charles Wesley, Letter to Sarah Gwynne (February 3, 1749), MARC, DDCW 5/24. Also published in *Letters of Charles Wesley,* 222-24.

111. Charles Wesley, Letter to Sarah Gwynne (January 15-17, 1749), MARC, DDCW 5/20. Also published in *Letters of Charles Wesley,* 205-12.

112. Charles Wesley, April 17, 1749, *Manuscript Journal,* 2:572.

113. Charles Wesley, April 22, 1749, *Manuscript Journal,* 2:573.

114. Charles Wesley, May 1, 1749, *Manuscript Journal,* 2:573.

115. Charles Wesley, Letter to John Wesley (April 29, 1749), Frank Baker's transcriptions of Charles Wesley's letters, where the item is No. 148. Also published in *Letters of Charles Wesley,* 253-55.

116. Charles Wesley, Letter to Ebenezer Blackwell (April 29, 1749), Frank Baker's transcriptions of Charles Wesley's letters, where the item is No. 149. Also published in *Letters of Charles Wesley,* 255-56.

117. Vincent Perronet, Letter to Mrs. Gwynne (January 14, 1748) in *Manuscript Journal,* 2:565. Both John and Charles Welsey relied heavily on the advice of Vincent Perronet. He was a Vicar of Shoreham, and two of his sons (Edward and Charles) were Methodist preachers for a time. Charles's respect for him is seen in the title he gave he in 1781: "Archbishop of the Methodists." (*Dictionary of Methodism,* s.v. "Perronet, Vincent," *http://www.wesleyhistoricalsociety.org.uk/dmbi/*).

118. *HSP* (1749).

119. John noted his disapproval of some of what is contained in this publication in *A Plain Account of Christian Perfection*, "In the year 1749, my brother printed two volumes of 'Hymns and Sacred Poems.' As I did not see these before they were published, there were some things in them which I did not approve of." in John Wesley, "A Plain Account of Christian Perfection" (1766) ¶ 18, in *Doctrinal and Controversial Treatises II* in *Works,* 13:164. See also Tyson, "Charles Wesley's Theology of the Cross," 77.

120. See also *HSP* (1749), editorial introduction.

121. By collections I am referring only to those publications which are broader than a single theme. Primarily, I am referring to the other collections entitled "Hymns and Sacred Poems."

122. Other subjects are intertwined, but the Charles put poems associated with the *ordo salutis* in the following order (I have included the number of poems in each section

123. in parenthesizes): "Hymns for One Convinc'd of Unbelief" (10), "Penitential Hymns" (9), "Waiting for Redemption" (4), "Hymns for One Fallen from Grace" (37), "Hymns for Believers" (43), and "Hymns for Those that Wait for Full Redemption" (37). *HSP* (1749), 2:146-195.

124. See Charles Wesley, "Blest be the Lord! By earth & Heaven," MARC, MS Clarke, 94-97; and Charles Wesley, "[Hymns for Those that Wait for Full Redemption.] Hymn IX," in *HSP* (1749), 2:158. At the bottom of the page Charles inserted the following explanation: "* i. e. *The Possibility of offending.*"

125. Charles Wesley, "[Hymns for Those that Wait for Full Redemption.] Hymn

XXIV," in *HSP* (1749), 2:177-178.

126. Charles Wesley, "[Hymns for Those that Wait for Full Redemption.] Hymn XXVIII," in *HSP* (1749), 2:183.

127. Charles Wesley, "[Hymns for Those that Wait for Full Redemption.] Hymn VII," in *HSP* (1749), 2:154-55.

128. Ibid.

129. Charles Wesley, "[Hymns for Those that Wait for Full Redemption.] Hymn XXXII," in *HSP* (1749), 2:189.

130. Charles Wesley, "[Hymns for Those that Wait for Full Redemption.] Hymn XXXIII," in *HSP* (1749), 2:191.

131. See Charles Wesley, "Looking unto Jesus the Finisher," MARC, MS Clarke, 65; and Charles Wesley, "[Hymns for Those that Wait for Full Redemption.] Hymn VIII," in *HSP* (1749), 2:156.

132. *OED*, December 2009 online ed., s.v. "extirpate."

133. Charles Wesley, "[Hymns for Those that Wait for Full Redemption.] Hymn I," in *HSP* (1749), 2:148.

134. Charles Wesley, "[Hymns for Those that Wait for Full Redemption.] Hymn II," in *HSP* (1749), 2:149.

135. Charles Wesley, "[Hymns for Those that Wait for Full Redemption.] Hymn I," in *HSP* (1749), 2:147.

136. For a discussion of election and its relationship to predestination see pp. 119-130 above.

137. Charles Wesley, "[Hymns for Those that Wait for Full Redemption.] Hymn XXVII," in *HSP* (1749), 2:180-81.

138. See Charles Wesley, "All Things are possible to him that Believeth," MARC, MS Clarke, 104-105; and Charles Wesley, "[Hymns for Those that Wait for Full Redemption.] Hymn X," in *HSP* (1749), 2:159. In the published version the final line is "All things are possible to me," changing the focus from God's work in us to our ability to do the work. The change also made the last line the same in every verse.

139. Charles Wesley, "[Hymns for Those that Wait for Full Redemption.] Hymn XXV," in *HSP* (1749), 2:179-80.

140. Charles Wesley, "[Hymns for Those that Wait for Full Redemption.] Hymn XXX," in *HSP* (1749), 2:186-87.

141. Charles Wesley, "[Hymns for Those that Wait for Full Redemption.] Hymn XXXIV," in *HSP* (1749), 2:192.

142. Charles Wesley, "[Hymns for Those that Wait for Full Redemption.] Hymn XIX," in *HSP* (1749), 2: 169.

143. See Charles Wesley, "Groaning for Redemption," MARC, MS Clarke, 68; and Charles Wesley, "[Hymns for Those that Wait for Full Redemption.] Hymn V," in *HSP* (1749), 2:153.

144. Charles Wesley, "[Hymns for Those that Wait for Full Redemption.] Hymn XXXVI," in *HSP* (1749), 2:194.

145. Charles Wesley, "[Hymns for Those that Wait for Full Redemption.] Hymn XVII," in *HSP* (1749), 2:166-67. See also Charles Wesley, "[Hymns for Those that Wait for Full Redemption.] Hymn XXIII," in *HSP* (1749), 2:175-76; Charles Wesley, "[Hymns for Those that Wait for Full Redemption.] Hymn III," in *HSP* (1749), 2:151; and Charles Wesley, "[Hymns for Those that Wait for Full Redemption.] Hymn VI," in *HSP* (1749), 2:154.

146. Ibid.

147. Charles Wesley, "[Hymns for Those that Wait for Full Redemption.] Hymn XII,"

in *HSP* (1749), 2:161.

148. Charles Wesley, "[Hymns for Those that Wait for Full Redemption.] Hymn VII," in *HSP* (1749), 2:154. John Wesley substituted "wrath" for "self" in manuscript in his personal copy of the 2nd edn. (1756).

149. Charles Wesley, "[Hymns for Those that Wait for Full Redemption.] Hymn XX," in *HSP* (1749), 2:170-71.

150. See Charles Wesley, "Groaning for Redemption," MARC, MS Clarke, 68; and Wesley, "[Hymns for Those that Wait for Full Redemption.] Hymn V," in *HSP* (1749), 2:153.

151. Charles Wesley, "[Hymns for Those that Wait for Full Redemption.] Hymn XVIII," in *HSP* (1749), 2:168.

152. Charles Wesley, "Happy Soul that safe from Harms," MARC, MS Clarke, 72-72. The last line reads "All his paradise of love." in Charles Wesley, "[Hymns for Those that Wait for Full Redemption.] Hymn IV," in *HSP* (1749), 2:152.

153. Charles Wesley, Sermon 8, "Ephesians 5:14," in *Sermons of Charles Wesley*.

154. Ibid., 223.

155. Charles Wesley, "[Hymns for Those that Wait for Full Redemption.] Hymn II," in *HSP* (1749), 2:149. Emphasis mine.

156. This statement is true of the verses collected in "Hymns for Those that Wait for Full Redemption."

157. Charles Wesley, "[Hymns for Those that Wait for Full Redemption.] Hymn XXXVII," in *HSP* (1749), 2:195.

158. See Charles Wesley, "Happy Soul that safe from Harms," MARC, MS Clarke, 72-72; and Charles Wesley, "[Hymns for Those that Wait for Full Redemption.] Hymn IV," in *HSP* (1749), 2:152. Emphasis mine.

159. Charles Wesley, "[Hymns for Those that Wait for Full Redemption.] Hymn XXIX," in *HSP* (1749), 2:184-85.

160. "John Wesley substituted 'inbred sin' for 'power to sin' in manuscript in his personal copy of 2nd edn [of *HSP* (1749) published in] (1756). *HSP* (1749), 2:164, The Center for Studies in the Wesleyan Tradition, Duke University.

161. Charles Wesley, "[Hymns for Those that Wait for Full Redemption.] Hymn XIV," in *HSP* (1749), 2:164.

162. See Charles Wesley, "Happy Soul that safe from Harms," MARC, MS Clarke, 68; and Charles Wesley, "[Hymns for Those that Wait for Full Redemption.] Hymn VIII," in *HSP* (1749), 2:156.

3

Methodism in the Midst of Suffering and Conflict:1750-1762

Charles's marriage to Sarah Gwynne began to reshape his role in the Methodist movement. Maybe more important than anything else, it put a strain on his relationship with John. Since their time at Oxford, John and Charles had been working together, but Charles's marriage meant there was someone else who could and would compete for Charles's affection and time. Charles now had to balance his commitment to his wife (and later his family) and his commitment to John. He also had to balance the time spent with his family and in the itinerant ministry. Evidence suggests that Sarah Gwynne Wesley rapidly replaced John's primary place of influence and affection. The strain on John and Charles's relationship was further complicated by John's failed engagement with Grace Murray and his subsequent marriage to Mrs. Mary Vazeille. It was in the midst of these personal difficulties that John and Charles had to deal with the challenges of the rapidly growing Methodist movement. Among the major issues Charles addressed at this time were the role of the lay preachers in the Methodist movement, how to address those claiming perfection in London, and how to deal with the problem of pain (both on a personal and on a national level). This included the death and illness of those closest to him and dealing with the effects of the earthquakes that shook England in the 1750's.

Charles Wesley and the Lay Preachers

Charles Wesley's relationship with the lay preachers was complicated by his complete commitment to the Church of England. This section will show how this commitment affected Charles's responses. At times he was willing to diminish the role of lay preachers in the Methodist movement. He was also concerned about the itinerant lay preachers because some in the Church of England had rejected Methodism's use of lay preachers. Charles also faced a growing desire among the lay preachers to act not only as preachers but as priests—administering the sacrament of communion. Charles continued to teach that their desire to administer the sacraments was motivated by pride and would result in the Methodist movement either leaving or being driven from the Church of England.

Charles Wesley's Commitment to the Church of England

In 1760, after nearly a decade of struggling with lay preachers and their attempt to leave the Church of England, Charles shared his priorities with his wife Sarah:

> My chief Concern upon earth I said, was the Prosperity of the Church of E[ngland,] my next, That of the Meth[odist]s[,] my 3d that of the Preachers. Yt if their Interest shd ever come into competition I wd give up the Preachers, for the Good of the Meth[odist]s & the Meth[odist]s for the Good of the whole Body of ye Ch[urch] of E[ngland]. Yt nothing cd ever force me to leave the Meth[odist]s but their leaving the Church. Yt in that Case they wd in effect leave me, & cast off an old faithful Serv[an]t worn out by serving them.[1]

His desire and calling, a calling of which he often reminded others in the Methodist movement, was "to live and die in the Church of England."[2] This commitment was evident even at his death when he refused John's offer to be buried at Wesley Chapel, preferring to be buried in the parish churchyard of St. Mary's Marylebone.[3]

His commitment to the Church can be best illustrated by the way he dealt with the society at Manchester, a society that was being drawn away from the Church of England, mostly into dissent.[4] According to Charles, Mr. Roger Ball and a new young Baptist preacher had drawn off nearly half of the Methodists in the society at Manchester. Charles gave two reasons for the disorder of the society in Manchester: Methodists in general were worth stealing because they were serious and those in Manchester were in greater danger than normal because of their unsettled situation. According to Charles, they had been saddled by lay preachers who had "neglected, if not abused" them.[5] One way the lay preachers abused the flock was by talking against the Church and her clergy. For instance, Joseph Tucker talked in his "*witty way*" against both the Church and her clergy, and John Hampson (1732-1795) did not go to Church and therefore could not advise others to go. Charles heard that Hampson was even encouraging people not to go to Church.[6] By the time Charles arrived in October of 1756, things were beginning to improve, but there was still work to be done. Brother Johnson had sent the people back to Church, and they were receiving forgiveness in the prayers and sermons of the Church minister. Three other sound preachers in the area were also repairing the damage done by Joseph Tucker and John Hampson. The society, however, was still unsettled enough that Charles planned to spend an additional week with them.[7]

While Charles was in Manchester he suggested some steps which should be taken to avoid future difficulties.[8] They should emphasize the importance of "walking in all the commandments and ordinances."[9] He showed the importance of the commandments and the ordinances by preaching up the ordinances,[10] carrying the society with him to the Church,[11] and encouraging other leaders to practice these same measures.[12] He feared that if they failed to "continue steadfast in the ordinances," they would never prosper and would be "scattered on the Lord's day in the fields" where "all the beasts of the forest" could devour them.[13] According to Charles, Richard Barlow and the rest of the leaders had come to the same conclusion; that the preachers who did not go to the Church and therefore could not advise the Methodists to go to the Church, had resulted in a fickleness among the Methodist about participating in the means of grace.[14] Charles expressed this same concern in a letter to he wrote to Mr. Grimshaw while in Manchester.

> Nothing but grace can keep our children, after our departure, from running into a thousand sects, a thousand errors. Grace, exercised, kept up, and increased in the use of all the means, especially family and public prayer, and Sacrament, will keep them steady. Let us labour, while we continue here, to ground and build them up in the Scriptures, and all the ordinances. Teach them to handle well the sword of the Spirit, and the shield of faith.[15]

According to Charles, some lay preachers had been encouraging people to neglect the means of grace. Because of this, Charles said John had to be more deliberate in the way he admitted new lay preachers. He told John that the mischief carried out by men like Joseph Tucker and John Hampson would continue even after their death if they did not show *"greater, much greater, deliberation and care in admitting preachers."*[16] Charles asked, should any new preacher be received "before we know that he is grounded, not only in the doctrines we teach, but in the discipline also, and particularly in the communion of the Church of England?"[17] If determining their commitment to the Church proved difficult, at the very least they should stop receiving those they knew to be enemies of the Church.[18]

On Sunday, October 24, 1756, Charles read prayers and preached at the Church in Manchester. According to Charles both the morning and the afternoon services were crowded. He preached on two of his favorite passages: Luke 10:42, "The One Thing Needful," and Lamentations 1:12, "Is it nothing to you, all ye that pass by?" and noted, "The Scripture comes with double weight to me in the Church. If any pity me for my bigotry, I pity them for the blind prejudice, which robs them of so many blessings." He repeated this assertion later on the same day asking, "Why does God always accompany the word with a double blessing when preached in the church?" He ended his reflections on this day with what he hoped would be the direction of the Methodist preachers and the Church: "Those of the

Methodist preachers who have faith and patience may, by and by, have all the churches in England opened to them."[19]

Within a couple days Charles was once again fretting about some of the lay preachers. What were they going to do with the lay preachers who did not support the Church? Instead of confronting them, it seems John wanted to take these lay preachers and put them into leadership. Charles said he was incapable of trusting them until their pride and treachery was addressed. The questions he recorded in his journal reflect the tension between him and his brother.

> But what should we do in the meantime? Trust the flock to them, as superintendents? Enlarge their power of doing mischief? Or retrench it? Is it not high time for us *to be* what we profess, ministers and guardians of the Church of England? . . . By doing nothing we give up all into the enemy's hands.[20]

Charles's commitment to the Church is also evident in his attempts to reform the Church. In the midst of the struggles with the lay preachers Charles wrote *An Epistle to the Reverend Mr. John Wesley*.[21] In this poem Charles gave a bleak assessment of the Church of England. He questioned both her theology and the practice of many of her clergy. Like John, Charles wanted the theology of the Church to reflect the theology of the early reformers as stated in the Homilies. Charles also questioned the commitment level of many of her preachers and leaders. He felt they were lazy, greedy, sensual, and proud.[22] Absenteeism was one problem that illustrated their laziness:

> The altars theirs, who will not light the fire,
> Who spurn the labour, but accept the hire,
> Who not for souls, but their own bodies care,
> And leave to underlings the task of pray'r?[23]

Charles and John's assessment of the Church of England and their desire to see her reformed resulted in their use of lay preachers and other irregular means such as preaching outside, praying extemporaneously, and forming societies. Charles seemed torn between either supporting the Church or being involved in practices that were irregular. Gareth Lloyd described this tension as a divided loyalty between his high Church upbringing and his support of the Methodist movement and its irregularities.[24] As the conflict with the lay preachers intensified, Charles began to look for new ways to *both* support and reform the Church. Sometimes it seems Charles would be happy if there were no itinerant lay preachers. Instead he wished that those who wanted to preach would seek ordination in the Church of England. For example, in a letter to Christopher Hopper he showed he understood the difficulties both the Methodist movement and the lay preachers faced, especially after John and Charles were dead. First and foremost, he noted the lay preachers would be unable to support themselves and their families unless they became either a dissenting or a Church minister. He saw no middle way, it would have to be one or the other. Because of this he told Christopher Hopper that he would use all his interest to get the poor Methodist preachers ordained in the Church, and if he didn't, he would never blame them for becoming dissenting ministers. Charles believed that the Church would admit as many as would commit themselves to God's service in the Established Church, but whether this would have been possible is questionable.[25]

Charles's epistle to John was met with a rebuke by a member of the Church of England going by the pseudonym Christophilus.[26] Christophilus accused Charles of pride by setting his private judgment above the judgment of people God had placed in authority. Christophilus also argued that true holiness was always accompanied "with true humility and charity, as well as faith that worketh by love."[27]

These challenges and Charles's responses, illustrate his commitment to the Church of England and his desire to reform her doctrine and practices. Gareth Lloyd argued that Charles was not alone in these desires. Lloyd argued that the majority of Methodists saw the relationship between the Church of England and the Methodist movement in ways that were very similar to Charles Wesley.[28] Even if it is true that many agreed with Charles, it does not negate the struggle Charles encountered. As will be shown in this chapter, there were many times in the 1750's and early 1760's that Charles responded to a movement within Methodism, which he feared would lead to either the Methodist movement leaving or being driven from the Church of England.

The Church of England's Growing Discomfort with the Use of Lay Preachers

Itinerant lay preachers were seen as an important part of the Methodist movement but were rejected by many in the Church of England. Charles Wesley's fear that the extraordinary ministry of lay preaching would become ordinary explains, at least in part, his desire to limit the role and influence of the itinerant lay preachers in the 1750's.[29] The use of lay preachers created four major problems for the Wesleys. This section will document each of these problems. First, the character of some of the itinerant lay preachers had damaged the Methodist movement. Second, the use of itinerant lay preachers was seen by some as leading to a separation from the Church of England. Third, the itinerant lay preachers were not satisfied with just preaching; they soon began pushing for the administration of communion, a rite that was reserved for the priests in the Church of England. Fourth, the itinerant lay preachers began to acquire licenses as dissenting Protestants.

Although Charles initially resisted the use of lay preachers,[30] it seems he had become more comfortable with lay preaching as the 1740's progressed, but in the early 1750's, Charles was once again resisting the use of itinerant lay preachers. It seems likely that one of the reasons Charles began to resist their use was because of the scandal caused by the Wheatly affair.[31] It was at this time that John asked Charles to review and purge the lay preachers.[32] During his review of the lay preachers, Charles questioned the character of many of them. Some were lazy; some were proud; some saw entering the ministry as a way to gain respect. Charles's attitude toward these types of preachers, preachers his brother had appointed, can be found clearly stated in a journal entry omitted in Jackson's edition of the Journal.

> Spoke kindly to Jo. Hewish and got from him his *Book and Licence to preach.* I wish he were the only worthless, senseless, graceless man to whom my brother had given the same encouragement under his hand.[33]

Charles also confronted Michael Fenwick, another lay preacher he thought was lazy. Charles recorded the following reflections on his conversation with Fenwick, "I talked closely with him, utterly averse to working, and told him plainly he should either labour with his hands, or preach no more."[34]

Charles was also concerned that the use of lay preachers was straining the Methodists' relationship with the Church of England. Christophilus accused Charles of pride because he was encouraging people to preach who had not been sent by the Established Church. Charles feared that in the end John and Charles's attempt to reform the Church would end in division from the established Church. Others were criticizing the Methodist movement at this time. According to Donald Kirkham, the primary criticisms of the Methodist movement were that: "the Methodists were contemptuous of the clergy, they altered the Church's doctrine, they depreciated the liturgy, they rejected the Church's discipline, [and] they engineered schism."[35] Even some who saw value in what the Methodist movement had accomplished were now arguing that it was time to recall or suppress the itinerant lay preachers before their ministry led to schism.[36]

One way the lay preachers were driving a wedge between Methodism and the Church of England was their desire to administer communion. John and Charles had to face not only their desire to leave the Church of England in 1755 and 1756, they also had to confront those administering communion in 1760. In the midst of each of these challenges, Charles fought for Methodism to stay connected to the Church of England. It was his insistence on not separating from the Church of England that earned Charles his reputation as a 'Church Methodist'. Charles not only fought against the urge to separate, he also fought to keep the itinerant lay preachers from administering communion.

In June of 1754, Mr. Gardiner was excommunicated by Thomas Sherlock, the bishop of London, for preaching without a license. It seemed to John that the Methodist movement would soon have to decide to silence the lay preachers or be forced out of the Church of England.[37] These circumstances called for a decision, and Charles was disappointed not only with the path John seemed to be taking, but also with his personal influence on his brother John. Part of the problem, at least at this time, was John's wife. Charles wrote:

> Besides—how could I act in concert[,] join with my Brother whom I cannot trust, no more than he can me? Neither were that sufficient unless I could act with his wife also. She stands betwixt & forbids the Bans of Friendship[38]

In the fall of that same year, Charles Wesley complained to John Wesley that Charles Perronet (1723-1776) and Thomas Walsh (1730-1759) had administered the Lord's Supper.[39] Charles feared that this would lead to a separation from the Church of England. This reached its climax at the Leeds Conference in May of 1755, when John presented the treatise, "Ought We to Separate from the Church of England?"[40] In the midst of these developments, Charles wrote to Walter Sellon (1715-1792). Charles thanked Walter Sellon for the letter he had sent to C[harles] P[erronet]. It appears that Charles Wesley and Walter Sellon both agreed that pride was the source of the problems brought by Charles Perronet and his supporters. Charles wrote, "You see thro' him, & his fellows. Pride, cursed Pride has perverted him & them: & unless ye Lord interpose, will destroy the Work of God, & scatter us all as Sheep upon ye Mountains."[41] This pride had not only led Charles Perronet, Thomas Walsh, and three others to administer the sacrament, according to Charles Wesley they were also urging John Wesley to separate from the Church of England. Soon Charles was writing to Walter Sellon to ask him to write a corrective letter to John, and to attend the conference to be held in Leeds in May of 1755.[42] Charles's next letter to Walter Sellon revealed Charles's fear that separation was imminent. Charles noted that John seemed to have taken no notice of Walter Sellon's letter. Other concerns Charles had included; 1) being excluded from John's cabinet council, 2) John taking council with people who were for separation, people Charles called Melchisedechians,[43] 3) John's belief that he could lay on hands without separating, and 4) John's belief that it was lawful to separate, but not yet expedient. Charles's solution to the difficulties he and John were experiencing with the itinerant lay preachers was to prepare the sound itinerant lay preachers for ordination. Perhaps because of Walter Sellon's background, Charles believed there was no one better than him and John Jones (1711-1785) to prepare these young men for holy orders.[44]

Charles's frustration with the itinerant lay preachers was expressed in a letter to Samuel Lloyd: "If my Brother *will* answer for all his wild Preachers, he must. To Him I shall willingly give them up."[45] At about the same time he was working on an Epistle for his brother about remaining in the Church of England. After the conference he was still frustrated. He wrote his wife: "I left the Brethren in Conference; but had quite enough of them first. Yet I don't repent my Trouble. . . . I have done with conferences, forever. All agreed Not to separate. So the Wound is healed—slightly."[46] Just over a year later Charles was once again working with the preachers to strengthen the Methodists movement's ties to the Church of England. John planned another conference for August 23, 1756, which would once again address the question of separation. In order to shore up his brother's resolve, Charles wrote to Samuel Walker (1714-1761) and asked him to attend the conference and speak a word to John, whom both Charles Wesley and Samuel Walker thought was "almost overcome by his Preachers."[47] Part of Charles's strategy was to remind John of a document they and four others had signed on March 10, 1752. In that document they agreed that for the Methodist work to succeed they must be united in their labors and committed to the Church of England. Based on that understanding they agreed:

1. To abide in the closest Union with each other, & ne[ver speak, do, or suffer any thing, wch tends to weaken that Union.]⁴⁸

2. Never to leave the Communion of the Church of E[ngland] without the consent of all whose names are subjoined.⁴⁹

Charles Wesley, William Shent (1715-1787), John Wesley, John Jones, John Downes (1722-1774), and John Nelson (1707-1774) signed this letter. Charles also suggested that they change their approach to the itinerant lay preachers. Charles wanted John to remove unsound and unrecoverable preachers and move to having the rest prepared for orders as fast as possible.⁵⁰ Charles wrote to Samuel Walker again on August 21, 1756. This letter dealt more with his own role in Methodism. Charles's reason for staying was "not so much to do good, as to prevent Evil. I stand in the way of my Brother's violent Counsellours, the object both of their Fear & Hate." Later in the letter he questioned whether he should remain in the Methodist movement or give the preachers formally over to John. He wrote that the best reason to continue in Methodism was "the restless Pains of bad men to thrust me out . . . ."⁵¹

Charles's response to John after the conference was mixed at best. Immediately after the conference he wrote a letter that was supportive of John. Specifically, he noted his pleasure and implied his trust in John. He wrote,

> I have done you much wrong by supposing you capable of any wrong impression(?). I shall never be so uncivil and so idle as to justify my suspicion. . . . Neither shall I dispute with you, which is the greatest friend of the Church. You gave me great pleasure, by insisting, I am of the 2 the most likely to leave it. Most glad am I to believe you; if you stand by it, it is no great matter whether I leave it or no.⁵²

Less than two weeks later, the trust Charles expressed in this letter was replaced by doubts that John was presently or ever would follow through on their agreement. Charles complained to John: "The short remains of my life are devoted to this very thing, to follow your sons . . . with buckets of water, and quench the flame of strife and division which they have, or may kindle."⁵³

This uneasy peace continued until another group of itinerant lay preachers began administering communion in February 1760. Charles informed John of his desire to go to Norwich and address the error of three preachers in the area. His fear was that others would "follow the Example of those Three, & draw as many Disciples after ym as they can, into a Formal Separation."⁵⁴ In addition to administering communion, Charles complained to Sarah that many of the itinerant lay preachers were taking out licenses as dissenting Protestants. According to Charles, taking out licenses indicated the duplicitous nature of their actions. He told Sarah,

> To the Government they therefore say "We are Dissenting ministers": to the Methodists they say "We are not the Dissenters; but true Members of the Ch[urch] of E[ngland]." To a Press-Warrant or Persecuting Justice they say again "We are Dis-

senters[.]" [T]o me at our next Conference they will unsay it again. This is their Sincerity, & my Brother applauds their Skillfulness—& his own.⁵⁵

Charles's frustration with the itinerant lay preachers, who were licensing themselves as Protestant dissenters, is evident in a letter to John Nelson: "John, I love thee from my heart: yet rather than see thee a Dissenting Minister, I wish to see the[e] smiling in thy Coffin."⁵⁶ On the same day Charles wrote a letter to William Grimshaw (1708-1763) and Christopher Hopper (1722-1802) asking for their help in this time of crisis. In his letter to Grimshaw he talked about how taking licenses as Protestant Dissenters helped the Norwich preachers rationalize giving the sacrament.⁵⁷ In a letter to Christopher Hopper, Charles once again suggested the solution to the problem with the itinerant lay preachers was to help them become ordained ministers of the Church of England. Charles said if he failed to use all his interest to help the old faithful preachers become ordained, he would never blame them for turning dissenter. Part of the pressure Charles recognized was the responsibility of the preacher to feed his family. If a preacher found it difficult to feed his family, while John and Charles were alive and supporting them, how would they be able to do it after John and Charles were gone? Charles admitted their only choice would be between becoming a dissenting minister or a Church minister. It was because of this difficulty that Charles committed himself to helping the itinerant lay preachers gain ordination in the Church of England. He answered his own question about helping the itinerant lay preachers gain ordination, "I answer for myself yes:& will begin tomorrow."⁵⁸ Charles also asserted that those who committed themselves to God's service in the established Church would be accepted and that God would take care of his preachers and their needs as long as they did not "ruin themselves & the Work by their Precipitation [or haste]."⁵⁹

In London, the itinerant lay preachers not only desired to be ordained as Protestant Dissenters, they were also claiming to be witnesses of perfection. Charles connected these two concerns in a letter to Sarah. He wrote,

> At Noon I gave the Sacram[en]t to the Pretenders to (I sh[oul]d say the Witnesses of) Perfection, & read some letters about the Separation. I ask a Preacher, how he reconciled it with sincerity, his licensing himself as a Protestant Dissenter while he continued a member of the Ch[urch] of E[nglan]d?⁶⁰

The next section will deal with what Charles calls the pretenders to perfection. Charles alluded to at least three major ways separation from the Church of England was contrary to his understanding of being restored in the image of God. First, Charles believed those who were moving for separation exhibited characteristics incompatible with restoration. Chief among these was pride. Secondly, those who are pushing for separation were minimizing the importance of the ordinances or the means of grace. As has already been shown in Charles's response to the Moravians, the means of grace played an important part in being restored in the image of God. During the controversy in 1756, one of Charles's most frequent sermon themes was the importance of keeping the ordinances. Charles used Isaiah

64:5 to press "the Duties of constant Communicating, of hearing reading practising [sic] the Word, of Fasting, of private, Family, & Public Prayer."[61] Charles Wesley tried to undo the harm caused by the itinerant lay preachers. One of his visits to Manchester was extended because the preachers had scattered the society "as sheep upon the mountains."[62] He told William Grimshaw, "I have once more persuaded them to go to Church, and sacrament, and state to carry them thither the next Lord's day."[63] Charles's insistence on attending the Church of England services was perverted by some to say that Charles believed, "*The Church could save you.*"[64] Charles could easily be misinterpreted on this point. He reminded the people at Manchester:

> I...sent you *in* and *through* all the means to Jesus Christ....Continue in the old ship. Jesus hath a favour for our Church, and is wonderfully visiting and reviving his work in her.... Blessed be God, ye see your calling. Let nothing hinder your going constantly to Church and Sacrament. Read the Scriptures daily in your families, and let there be a church in every house. The word is able to build you up. And if ye watch and pray all ways, ye shall be counted worthy to stand before the Son of Man.[65]

Third, Charles began to speak of restoration in corporate terms. Earlier in his ministry he talked almost exclusively of being sinless. It will be argued in the section on his theology in *Short Hymns on Select Passages of the Holy Scriptures*[66] that he began speaking of the 'spotless' bride of Christ. When Charles used the word 'spotless' it was usually with reference to the bride of Christ, and either implicitly or explicitly had a corporate aspect to it. For Charles, the desire to separate from the Church of England denied the corporate nature of the Church as the 'spotless' bride of Christ.

The Perfectionist Controversy

Another major controversy that threatened Methodism during the 1760's was the radicalization of the doctrine of Christian perfection as proclaimed by those whom Charles called "Pretenders to (I sh[oul]d say the Witnesses of) Perfection."[67] This radicalization strained the already fragile relationship between Methodism and the Church of England. It also had a negative impact on the societies, especially at London. The person who seems to have been the most radical in this movement was George Bell (d.1807), who not only preached Christian perfection as an unqualified and instantaneous work, but also predicted that the world would end on February 28, 1763. These predictions were met with rebukes in the popular press, not only of Bell, but also of Methodism. For instance, 'Philodemas', while denouncing Bell's false prediction, noted that he had "always considered *Methodism,* taken in the most favorable light, as the most destructive and dangerous system to government and society, that ever was established."[68] This opinion was not held by everyone. Some people seemed to accept John Wesley's claim that Bell was not a Methodist.[69] For instance, someone writing under the name 'Impartiality' noted that Bell was "supposed to belong to the Methodists: but he advances things which many Methodists utterly abhor."⁷⁰ He noted that "many of his [Bell's] followers think themselves perfect, and declare they shall never die, 'Because (as they say) our dear Lord, who certainly will come a second time, is at the door, and we shall see him come. . . .'"⁷¹ After the fervor had subsided, Charles noted the extent of the damage when he admitted that Bell's teaching had hurt every sober-minded Christian. He also stated his hope that the "nonsense & blasphemy of our brethren. . . . The floud [sic] of delusion is much subsided here; & I trust in ye Lord he will not suffer the folly & credulity of any man to raise it again."⁷²

According to Thomas Maxfield (d. 1784) (a leader associated with Bell during this controversy), there were three main complaints made against the perfectionists in London: antinomianism, enthusiasm, and fanaticism.⁷³ One of John Wesley's immediate responses to the controversy was published in *Cautions and Directions* in 1762, which addressed each of these charges.⁷⁴ Charles Wesley indicated that antinomianism was one of his concerns when he compared the perfectionists in London to the Ranters and the French Prophets, both who had antinomian tendencies.⁷⁵ A clearer indication that this was one of the problems Charles had with Maxfield and the perfectionists can be seen in the letters he received from Fletcher after the controversy had subsided and Maxfield was attempting to rejoin the movement. Fletcher told Charles that he was "tempted to believe that he [Maxfield] sometimes goes too far towards a philosophy of some Antinomians. But I confess to you that all things considered I believe him innocent of that Article."⁷⁶ About a month and a half later Fletcher stated he believed Maxfield was clear of the charges of being an Antinomian.⁷⁷

A second charge against Maxfield and the perfectionists was enthusiasm. John addressed this in *Cautions and Directions*⁷⁸ and in a letter to Maxfield:

> I dislike something that has the appearance of *enthusiasm*: overvaluing *feelings* and *inward impressions*; mistaking the mere work of *imagination* for the voice of the Spirit; expecting the end without the means; and undervaluing *reason*, *knowledge*, and *wisdom*, in general.⁷⁹

Even though John Wesley rejected enthusiasm in both of these documents, Charles Wesley still wondered if John would not succumb to the tendency of enthusiasm. Charles wrote to his wife, "Who knows but God may by me save my B[rother] from the Gulph of Enthusiasm! . . . If your next comes without a promise of riding out daily—expect me to leave my B[rother] & the flock in the Hands of the Enthusiasts: for you are my First Care."⁸⁰ The third charge, fanaticism, referred mainly to George Bell's prophetic predictions noted above.⁸¹

Charles also had problems with the London perfectionists claiming an instantaneous work of perfection which was unqualified (even speaking of angelic perfection),⁸² exhibiting a pride and spiritual superiority which Charles thought was inconsistent with those who were perfect, and claiming they were perfect in the wrong settings and with the wrong people.

The question of whether perfection was an instantaneous work or a gradual work was taken up at a conference in 1761, a conference Charles was unable to attend because of illness.[83] John Wesley summarized the results of this conference in a letter to Samuel Furly:

> What all our brethren think concerning that circumstance of entire sanctification—that it is instantaneous, although a gradual growth in grace both precede and follow it, you may see in the *Minutes* of the Conference, wherein it was freely debated.[84]

In the wake of this Conference, some claimed there was an immediate work that was both instantaneous and unqualified. In a letter to Lady Huntington, Charles Wesley expressed what he thought was Thomas Maxfield's greatest mistake (a mistake Charles believed he continued even in 1766): "Believe that you are perfect and you are so: believe you have a clean heart and you have it."[85] John Fletcher reflected the same concern about Maxfield in a letter to Charles in 1762. He was concerned that some were taking what was a valid concept and making it invalid by the presumption of enthusiasm:

> *Crede quod habes & habes*,[86] is not so different from the counsel of Christ, Believe that you are obtaining the things you are asking for, the humility of the believer and the presumptuousness of the Enthusiast draw this doctrine to the right side or to the left.[87]

In spite of the fact that Maxfield later denied he believed perfection was immediate and a result of belief, Charles's response to Maxfield and the perfectionists in London was based on his perception that this was Maxfield's position.[88] Whether or not Charles was correct in his perception, his response to this perception illuminates his position that being restored in the image of God was not something which was immediate or unqualified, neither was it something to be claimed by novices. Charles's response to these beliefs will be examined later when looking at the theology of *SHSPS* (1762).[89]

Charles was also concerned the perfectionists were exhibiting a pride and spiritual superiority inconsistent with those who were truly perfect. One way Charles was receiving information about the group in London was through William Briggs (c. 1722-c. 1788). Briggs said that Bell's sermons were "superficial in themselves & delivered with an air of superiority that necessarily occasions disgust. . . . It was all so forced and unnatural"[90] This spiritual superiority was demonstrated not only in Bell's preaching but also in the way they shared what God was doing in their lives. According to Briggs, talking about perfection was acceptable in the common bands. For him the problem was that what was acceptable in the common bands was not to be spoken of in a mixed meeting. He wrote Charles,

> But what can be said of these brethren to meet in a mixt multitude to talk of the highest attainments in the Christian race? The state itself should be treated of with great humility amongst one another; yet here are a number who with a confidence savouring of presumption, spake of this last great operation of the spirit, as if the most common lesson in the School of Christ! Where can they find any scripture to support such a practice?[91]

One way Charles attempted to counter their pride was to preach perfection as a poverty of spirit:[92]

> 'Tis observable what some tell me, yt on Thursday Night after my preaching poverty of spirit, such a Spirit of humility fell upon the bands at their meeting, as had not been known for months or years past. Every mouth was stopped: not one boasting word of Perfection. They lay low in the dust before the Friend of sinners, ashamed & confounded at his presence. . . . Another witness fairly confessed herself undeceived, & gave up her perfection, because (as she said) she had never been poor in spirit. It is surprizing the readiness of the witnesses to receive my sayings. I don't despair of their all coming right at last.[93]

Many of Charles's struggles with the perfectionists had to do with their claims of the immediate nature of perfection. To claim this was to deny the need for growth and purification through suffering. As will be shown in the next section, Charles taught that growth and suffering played vital roles in bringing about the restoration of the image of God in an individual.

Charles Wesley's response to Suffering

Charles Wesley's response to several tragedies in the 1750's gives an indication of the role suffering played in his theology of restoration. Charles's response to earthquakes, the illness and death of his children, and the threat of war all indicate that Charles was willing to re-examine his theology of suffering in the midst of episodes of extreme suffering. Throughout this period, Charles continued to teach that suffering played a positive role in the Christian life. It can even be argued that Charles saw suffering as a means of grace that played a major role in a person being restored in the image of God. This section will illustrate how Charles re-examined his theology of suffering by showing how Charles argued the earthquakes which shook London in February and March of 1750 were a merciful act of God. Charles could see earthquakes as an act of God's mercy because of the positive role he assigned to suffering in his understanding of being restored in the image of God.[94] Charles saw most instances of suffering as a part of the restoration process; the only exception may be the death of a child. Charles struggled with the death of children and the role they played in God's purpose. Even though he looked for God's purpose in the death of a child, it seems he believed the death of a child only brought sorrow.

In February and March of 1750 earthquakes shook London.[95] Charles Wesley took this opportunity to publish a sermon, "The Cause and Cure of Earthquakes," and a two part hymn-pamphlet, *Hymns Occasioned by the Earthquake, March 8, 1750.*[96] In these publications, Charles Wesley tried to balance two concepts that seemed to be in conflict. On the one hand, he wanted to present the earthquakes as the judgment of an angry God; on the other hand, he wanted to present them as the acts of a merciful God. An examination of the sermon and hymns that Charles wrote in the wake of these earthquakes will illustrate that for Charles Wesley judgment, and the suffering that resulted from it, were in some sense an expression of the mercy of God. In other words, the experience of suffering was not seen as a punishment, but as a means of grace through which one could experience the God of love.

In the introduction to Charles Wesley's sermon on "The Cause and Cure of Earthquakes," Kenneth Newport contended that, "Charles here paints a terrifying picture of God's anger, anger that has already begun to spill over into judgment and destruction."[97] Later, he admitted these "are not just punishments, but also warnings, and through them God gives the sinners a chance to repent."[98] Although this assessment of the sermon may reflect part of what Charles wrote, it misses the tone underlying Charles Wesley's argument. For Charles, the primary quality of God seen in the earthquake was not anger; it was mercy. The only hint that God is a merciful God in Newport's introduction was a reference to repentance. Newport's introduction to this sermon contended Charles was trying to convince the crowds that God was an angry God. One passage Newport focused on to support his contention was Charles's statement that "in the London earthquakes one could hear the fast approaching footsteps of an angry God."[99]

Although Charles talked about the anger of God and the judgment of God in this sermon, there was also a pronounced focus on the mercy of God. According to Charles, God proceeded slowly in his judgment: "How slow is the Lord to anger! How unwilling to punish! By what leisurely steps does he come to take vengeance! How many lighter afflictions before the final blow!"[100] Why does God proceed slowly? Charles argued that it was because God found no pleasure in judgment:

> He pauses on the point of executing judgment, and cries, "How shall I give thee up?" (Isa 1.5) . . . He hath no pleasure in the death of him that dieth. He would not bring to pass his *strange act*, unless your obstinate impenitence compel him.[101]

Charles's presentation of God as a merciful God is even clearer in the hymn-pamphlet. In one hymn, the very design of the earthquake was mercy. Charles called on people to "Answer his [God's] mercy's whole design."[102] In another hymn, God was described as being forgiving, merciful, loving, and full of patient grace. This view of God as a loving and merciful God was juxtaposed with a response that indicated a recognition of God's ability to judge. The praise of the people was sung with trembling:

> [1] Great God, who, ready to forgive,
>   In wrath remembrest mercy still,
> By whose preserving love we live,
>   Though doom'd the second death to feel;
> We magnify thy patient grace,
> And tremble, while we sing thy praise.[103]

Charles did not deny that the earthquakes were an expression of God's judgment, but he did insist that the mercy of God could also be seen in the earthquakes.

He expressed this idea best when he said, "Judgment is MERCY's harbinger."[104] Charles Wesley's emphasis was not on the wrath or judgment of God; it was on God's mercy. It was not on what God could do, but what he wanted to do. The earthquake was yet another expression of God's mercy. The emphasis on the mercy of God is similar to the view he expressed during the Calvinistic controversy examined earlier.[105]

Charles's emphasis on mercy may be related to the emphasis he heard at the communion services, services he attended regularly. As he prepared to approach the table of the Lord, Charles would either hear or read the following words;

> We do not presume to come to this thy Table, O merciful Lord, trusting in our own righteousness, but in thy manifold and great mercies. We are not worthy so much as to gather up the crumbs under thy Table. But thou art the same Lord, whose property is always to have mercy. . . .[106]

It was *always* God's property to have mercy. This was the underlying emphasis of both the sermon and the hymns written on this occasion.

Charles Wesley did not develop this idea of a merciful God in the midst of the earthquakes; instead he used what he already believed about God to describe what happened in the earthquakes. For Charles, this meant turning to the scriptures. Charles said, "Now, that God is himself the author, and sin the *moral* cause, of earthquakes, (whatever the natural cause may be) cannot be denied by any who believe the scriptures. . . ."[107] What did Charles mean that God was the author of the earthquakes? There are some instances where Charles presented God as active in the earthquakes in a very personal or specific way.

> 4 The nations to rebuke,
> When God his power displays,
> Earth trembles at his threatning look,
> And moves, and shifts its place:
> Infernal thunders roar,
> And speak his kindled ire,
> And hills dissolve like wax before
> The sin-consuming fire.[108]

God's power was displayed in the earthquake. God's look caused the earth to tremble. God's active involvement can be seen in the following hymn.

> Yet all are order'd, Lord, by thee;
> The elements obey thy nod,
> And nature vindicates her God.
> 3 The pillars of the earth are thine,
> And thou hast set the world thereon;
> They at thy sovereign word incline,[109]
> The center trembles at thy frown,
> The everlasting mountains bow,
> And God is in the earthquake *now*![110]

Charles emphasized God's active participation in the moment of the event. God made everything, and God's look and frown caused the earth to quake. Charles summarized this in the last line: "God is in the earthquake *now!*"

There were two main reasons Charles gave for God being in the earthquake. First, if God was not the author of earthquakes, God could not prevent them. Second, if God was not the author of earthquakes, they could no longer be seen as a warning from God. Even so, Charles seemed to struggle with this belief that God was the active author of the earthquakes, or at the very least Charles struggled with what that meant; specifically the degree to which Christians would be safe during an earthquake. There were some times when Charles Wesley would proclaim with confidence:

> Lo! We stand secure in God,
>   Amidst a ruin'd world.
>
> 8 For his people in distress
>   The God of Jacob stands,
>   Keeps us, 'till our troubles cease,
>   In his almighty hands:
>   He for us his power hath shewn,
>   He doth still our refuge prove;
>   Loves the Lord of hosts his own,
>   And shall for ever love.[111]

There are other times, however, when he prayed for the protection of the remnant. That he prays seems to unsettle the statement. He moved from proclaiming the protection of God to his prayer that God would deliver. The latter seems to indicate some uncertainty about how God would act.

> 5 But O! Thou dreadful righteous Lord,
>   The praying remnant spare,
>   The men that tremble at thy word,
>   And see the coming snare:
>   Our land if yet again thou shake,
>   Or utterly break down,
>   A merciful distinction make,
>   And strangly save thine own.
>
> 6 If earth its mouth *should* open wide,
>   To swallow up its prey,
>   Jesu, thy faithful people hide
>   In that vindictive day:
>   Firm in the universal shock
>   We shall not then remove,
>   Safe in the clifts of Israel's Rock,
>   Our Lord's expiring love.[112]

This struggle is also evident in the stories Charles recalled in his sermon on "The Cause and Cure of Earthquakes." Charles recounted stories of three earthquakes; two from 1692, and one from Lima in 1746. In his account of the earthquake in Lima he listed the inventory of the damage.

> There were seventy-four churches, besides chapels, and fourteen monasteries, with as many more hospitals and infirmaries, which were in an instant reduced to a ruinous heap, and immense riches buried in the earth.[113]

The evidence of this destruction must have challenged Charles's assumption that God protected the elect. His personal experience showed him that the earthquake affected both the righteous and the unrighteous. Charles's hymns reflect that he struggled with this reality. His answer was to admit the elect were not protected in the earthquake, because there was no security on earth. For him, there was only true security in the next life. So the freedom from fear that at first seemed to be based on temporal protection was replaced by a freedom from fear based on eternal protection.

> 5   How happy then are we,
>   Who build, O Lord, on thee!
> What can our foundation shock?
>   Though the shatter'd earth remove,
> Stands our city on a Rock,
>   On a Rock of heavenly love.
>
> 6   An house we call our own,
>   Which cannot be overthrown,
> In the general ruin sure,
>   Storms and earthquakes it defies,
> Built immoveably secure,
>   Built eternal in the skies.
>
> 7   High on Immanuel's land,
>   We see the fabrick stand,
> From a tottering world remove,
>   To our stedfast mansions there:
> Our inheritance above,
>   Cannot pass from heir to heir. [114]

In his sermon, "The Cause and Cure of Earthquakes," he pressed this same point when he argued that death has no sting for the believer.[115] Why this confidence in God? What was there in Charles Wesley's view of God that allowed him to have this confidence? It was his view that God expressed mercy to us, even in judgment. Charles argued that judgment could be used to bring healing and the full restoration of the image of God. Judgment for Charles has some of the same therapeutic qualities Maddox has associated with John Wesley's view of grace; namely that it is not only pardon, but a participation with God that brings healing and restoration.[116]

How were these earthquakes an act of a merciful and not an angry God; in what ways did Charles see the mercy of God in the earthquake? Charles thought the earthquakes were sent to shake people from their sin. For Charles, the moral cause of earthquakes was sin. Charles at one point argued that earthquakes were a result of the fall. He said, "But reason, as well as faith, doth sufficiently assure us it must be the punishment of sin, and the effect of that curse which was brought upon the earth by the original transgression."[117] It was because people were lost in sin that God needed to send the earthquake.

There were two major ways that Charles claimed earthquakes were a harbinger of mercy. First, earthquakes could and should cause people to repent and turn to God, and second, earthquakes were a sign of God's ultimate plan to judge the world. Charles taught that judgments could lead people to repentance. Charles recounted a report from a minister who had experienced the 1692 earthquake in Jamaica to show how earthquakes could lead to repentance. The minister reported that before the earthquake the people were so wicked that he feared continuing among them. But after the earthquake was over, the people responded to the preacher's call to join him in prayer. They spent an hour and a half together in prayer, with the preacher exhorting them to repent.[118] Charles called for this response in his sermon. The nation should respond to the judgment of God by repenting. He said, "What but national repentance can prevent national destruction."[119] Although he did not deal with his doubts, or the doubts of others, when calling for repentance in this sermon, these doubts were dealt with in his hymns. He recognized that some believed earthquakes were not a sign of the judgment of God. He personally rejected this view; teaching they were a sign of God's judgment.

> 3 The crowd, the poor unthinking crowd,
>   Refuse thy hand to see,
> They will not hear thy loudest rod,
>   They will not turn to thee.
> As with judicial blindness struck,
>   They all thy signs despise,
> Harden their hearts, and madly mock
>   The anger of the skies.[120]

More than the skeptics had their doubts. Although Charles taught that God worked in the earthquake, he did question the effectiveness of earthquakes as a means to call people back to God. Most striking was his recognition of the short-term results of such judgments.

> 2 The crowd alarm'd with short surprize,
>   And spar'd, alas! In vain,
> Started, and half unseal'd their eyes,
>   And dropp'd to sleep again.[121]

It seems obvious that Charles's faith was not a blind faith; instead in his hymns he struggled with those things that seemed inconsistent with his belief. In his hymns he not only stated the weakness of others, he also expressed and struggled with the doubts and fears and questions he had with his own theology.

Charles also taught that earthquakes were a sign of God's mercy because they were a sign of God's ultimate plans; they were a sign of the last days when the world would be restored.

> 9   O might we quickly find
>   The place for us design'd;
> See the long-expected day
>   Of our full redemption here!
> Let the shadows flee away,
>   Let the new-made world appear.
>
> 10   High on thy great white throne,
>   O King of saints, come down;
> In the New Jerusalem,
>   Now triumphantly descend,
> Let the final trump proclaim
>   Joys begun which ne'er shall end![122]

In another hymn the wars, plagues, earthquakes, and other disasters "Mark the times of restitution,/ Speak the great restorer near."[123] The earthquakes, for Charles, were a sign of the final, total restoration: they spoke of hope.

In the wake of the earthquakes that shook London in 1750, Charles Wesley found a note of hope. It was not a note that came easy; there were times when he could shout with confidence that God would protect his own in the midst of the earthquakes, but there were other times when the only true security he proclaimed was eternal. His struggle was to bring together two concepts that seemed at odds, that the destruction caused by earthquakes was an expression of the mercy of God. This was not a new belief; instead it was what he already was teaching about the necessity of suffering. He believed that the scriptures spoke of a merciful God. Those same scriptures said that God acted in the earthquake. Charles Wesley strove to hold these two concepts in tension; God was a merciful God whose love could comfort people who were experiencing the uneasiness of God's judgment in the earthquakes.

Charles also spoke about other sources of suffering in the life of a believer. It has already been shown how Charles embraced suffering as a necessary part of the Christian life. This was applied specifically to the persecution early Methodists were facing.[124] Charles's letters and journal expressed a belief that even personal suffering from sickness could be used by God for the good. In a letter to his wife, he wrote,

> *Your* illness would quite overwhelm *me*, were I not assured that it shall work together for your Good & inhance your Happiness throughout all Eternity. How does this Assurance change the Nature of Things!
>
>   Sorrow is Joy, & Pain is Ease,
>   If Thou, my God, art here!

The slightest Suffering (received from Him) is an Inestimable Blessing, Another Jewel added to our Crown. Go on then, my faithful Partner, Doing & Suffering his blessed Will till out of great Tribulation we both enter His Kingdom & his Joy & his Glory Everlasting.[125]

A few days later, he encouraged her to see that her illness was being used for her good: "Ye shall be Partaker of His Holiness, who in tenderest Love chastens you for y[ou]r Good. And you may be bold to say, When He has tried me, I shall come forth as Gold."[126] In other words, Charles taught that the illness was a result of God's mercy and love and was being used to purify and restore his wife Sarah in the image of God. Cruickshank rightly argued that Charles saw suffering as a part of the restoration process.[127] In a hymn on Hebrews 12:10, Charles argued that suffering restored the mind of Christ in the believer:

> 3 The good, which we could never find
>   Untroubled, unchastiz'd by thee,
> We feel, in pain and grief resign'd,
>   The patient, meek humility,
> The mind which in our Saviour was,
> And all the bearers of his cross.
>
> 4 Then let us still his cross sustain,
>   A Father's chastisements receive,
> And waiting thus the prize to gain,
>   We shall the life divine retrieve,
> And put thy sinless image on,
> Pure members of thy perfect Son.[128]

According to Cruickshank, the last verse "makes explicit, it is through this process of humbly submitting to the 'Father's chastisements' that the 'sinless image' of God is re-formed in the individual. This is 'the crown' to which 'the cross' leads."[129]

There is, however, one experience of suffering which Charles did not easily accept as a means of grace. On the death of his second child, Charles wrote, "Lo, her father's hope expires!"[130] But just two stanzas later he confronted his pain with the question,

> 5 But shall sinful man complain
>   Stript by the divine decree?
> Dares our impious grief arraign
>   Heaven's tremendous majesty?
> Rather let us meekly own
> All is right which God hath done.[131]

In the midst of that pain, he still looked for the purpose and the will of God. It was easier for him to see that the child was indeed happier because she was with God in the 'skies'. But he still struggled to see how this was better for him and his wife. While he admitted the child, who had died, was experiencing a blessing, he still questioned how it was best for him and his wife:

> 8 Best for her so soon to die:
> Best for us how can it be?
> Let our bleeding hearts reply,
> Torn from all, O Lord, but thee,
> To thy righteous will subdued,
> Panting for the sovereign good.[132]

This overview has shown the importance of suffering in Charles Wesley's theology. Although he struggled with the exact meaning of specific events, Charles's primary view of suffering was that it was the act of a merciful God used to purify people. The only exception may be the sorrow associated with losing a child. Here his doubts are voiced more strongly, but even here, his stated desire was to experience the "sovereign good." In general, suffering played a major role in purifying and restoring a person in the image of God. How Charles used the necessity of suffering to check those claiming an instantaneous work of grace will be explored in the next section.

The Theology of "Short Hymns on Select Passages of Scripture."

In 1762, in the midst of the perfectionist controversy, Charles Wesley published a collection of poetry with his reflections on the Scripture.[133] This section will examine his purpose for publishing these hymns and describe the ways Charles Wesley used Scripture in this collection. Charles's purpose for publishing this collection and his approach to the Scripture will provide a context to examine both his reaction to the perfectionist controversy and the theology behind that response. Specifically, how Charles used Scripture and poetry to check the errors of pride and impatience will be examined. It will also be noted how Charles continued to speak of the possibility of being restored here. The theological concepts which continue to be emphasized by Charles are *theosis* and recapitulation. He also stressed the universal nature of restoration, a restoration which would be complete and universal, restoring all people and the creation in God's image. As a part of this examination, some of the people who influenced Charles's approach to Scripture will be examined, specifically the three people he mentioned in the preface: Matthew Henry, Robert Gell, and John Albert Bengel.[134]

Charles Wesley's purpose for publishing *Short Hymns on Select Passages of Scripture*.

Charles stated purpose for publishing *SHSPS* (1762) was both to prove and to guard the doctrine of Christian perfection. He wished to guard the doctrine of Christian perfection against both enthusiasts and antinomians, "who by not living up to their profession, . . . 'cause the truth to be evil spoken of.'"[135] Charles noted the difficulty of this task. He felt he must "check the self-confident without discouraging the self-diffident."[136] Because of the diversity of his opponents—one denying Christian perfection and another claiming they had already attained Christian perfection—Charles noted part of his task was to rightly "divide the word of Truth."[137] For Charles this meant holding in tension things others might call contradictory. For instance, Charles said, "I declare with St. Paul, 'A man is justified by faith, and not by works'; and with St. James, 'A man is justified by works, and not by faith only.'"[138] John Fletcher encouraged Charles to be in London when the collection appeared so he could refute any objections. Fletcher also expressed his pleasure in the preface:

> your preface is Just as I would want: it pacifies and reconciles. St. Paul and St. James extricate you from the difficulty most excellently, I could not change any of it but for the worse.[139]

Even John Wesley seemed to appreciate this emphasis of reproving those who had gone too far while continuing to proclaim the doctrine of being perfected in love. On the cover of his pamphlet, *Cautions and Directions,* he included the following lines from his brother Charles:

> Set the False Witnesses aside,
> Yet hold the Truth for ever fast.[140]

Because Charles wrote in this seemingly contradictory style (using both Paul and James and the tension between their theologies), it is easy to misrepresent his teachings if one focuses on only one pole or the other of this tension. It is also important to examine Charles's approach to Scripture and how Charles used the Scripture and poetry to check the "self-confident" and impatient enthusiasts in London.

Charles Wesley's Use of Scripture

It is impossible to know, let alone list all the people and books which influenced Charles Wesley's approach to the Scripture, but it is worth noting the possible influence of three people Charles mentioned in the preface of *Short Hymns on Select Passages of the Holy Scriptures* (1762): Matthew Henry, Robert Gell, and John Albert Bengel. Charles Wesley's reliance on Henry, Bengel, and Gell may have helped to shape both Charles's approach to the Scripture and his reflections on the Scripture. Bengel endorsed Luther's method of study, which consisted of prayer, meditation, and spiritual attack.[141]

Robert Gell was a tutor of Henry More.[142] Charles's reliance on Gell was probably related to his understanding of holiness. Gell had a reputation for teaching "perfectionism." He argued that the scope of pure religion "is to render the *man like and to his God.*" He also asked people to make it their "resolution, to walk in the *name, nature,* or *being* of the Lord our God for ever and ever; to be *holy* as he is *holy, pure* as he is *pure, merciful* as he is *merciful, perfect* as our heavenly Father is *perfect.*"[143] Gell's view of Scripture may have also influenced Charles. Gell argued for both a literal and a mystical understanding of the text: "The *holy Word* is not onely [sic] *literally* to be understood; but also *mystically*; yea, even the most *literal text*, according to the judgment of the best learned men, may, beside the *Letter*, have also a *spiritual meaning.*"[144] Charles and the three commentators he mentioned all approached the Scripture both rationally and spiritually. To understand the Scripture took time and hard work, but also required reliance upon the Holy Spirit. The goal of studying the Scripture was not to develop a speculative theology; instead the goal was to create a practical theology and to apply the text to one's own life. This approach allowed Charles to use the Scripture in ways that test modern sensibilities, especially in the way he went beyond a historical-critical reading of the text.

Charles dealt with a variety of subjects in *SHSPS* (1762), including several poems that dealt with his understanding of the Scripture. Sometimes he focused on "Trusting in the literal word."

> When the house of Jacob's sons
> Their Canaan repossess,
> Shall not all thy chosen ones
> Abide in perfect peace?
> Trusting in the literal word,
> We look for Christ on earth again:
> Come, our everlasting Lord,
> With all thy saints to reign. [145]

Even though Charles referred to trusting in the literal word in this poem, he used this passage to encourage people to look for the return of Christ. This was not a literal use of the passage. The passage is about Jacob's sons dwelling in the land. Charles used this passage to argue that the God who was faithful in the past will be faithful and fulfill God's promises in the future. Just as the Israelites had possessed the land, so one day Christ would return.

There were other times when Charles referred to more than just the literal word in his poems. He argued that only the Holy Spirit could reveal the deeper sense of the text. Two poems illustrate the importance of relying on the Spirit. The first poem argues that even the most learned person could not understand the saving sense of the Scripture without the help of the Spirit, an emphasis of Luther.

> Proud learning boasts its skill in vain
> The sacred oracles t' explain,

> It may the literal surface shew,
> But not the precious mine below;
> The saving sense remains conceal'd,
> 'Till by the Spirit of faith reveal'd,
> The book is still unread, unknown,
> And open'd by the Lamb alone.[146]

In a second poem stressing the work of the Spirit, Charles noted that the literal sense, even if heard or read ten thousand times, was still unable to dispense saving power. Charles once again insisted that to understand the Scripture required the inspiration of the Holy Spirit.

> 1 Thy word in the bare *literal* sense,
>   Tho' heard ten thousand times, and read,
> Can never of itself dispense
>   The saving power which wakes the dead:
> The meaning *spiritual* and true
>   The learn'd expositor may give,
> But cannot give the virtue too,
>   Or bid his own dead spirit live.
>
> 2 But breathing in the sacred leaves
>   If on the soul thy Spirit move,
> The re-begotten soul receives
>   The quickning power of faith and love;
> Transmitted thro' the gospel-word
>   Whene'er the Holy Ghost is given,
> The sinner hears, and feels restor'd
>   The life of holiness and heaven.[147]

For Charles, the goal of hearing the Scriptures through the witness of the Spirit was more than just a way to heaven; it involved being restored to a "life of holiness." How Charles defined this life will be explored in the next section.

SHSPS (1762) as a Check to the Errors of Perfectionism and Antinomianism

One problem Charles had with the perfectionists in London was that they did not exhibit what he considered a "godly character." According to Charles, they were ambitious, impatient, schismatic, deceived, and worst of all in Charles's thought, they were proud. In other words, they lacked two of the main virtues Charles associated with perfection—humility and patience. Charles responded by emphasizing humility and corporate restoration as a check to their pride. He emphasized patience, singleness, and suffering as a check to their claims of instantaneous perfection. Charles also continued to stress the possibility of being restored as a check to antinomianism.

Humility and corporate restoration as a check to pride

Charles saw humility as one of the most important Christian virtues. Humility was a theme he focused on throughout his life.[148] Instead of exhibiting humility, Charles thought the perfectionists were acting out of pride. They displayed their pride through their ambition and self-promotion. Charles's criticism of those who displayed pride in *SHSPS* (1762) was not limited to the perfectionists, he also attacked his brother John and other lay preachers who were not a part of the perfectionist controversy in London. John's self-promotion and ambition were leading to what Charles saw as an inevitable split from the Church of England. Charles insinuated that the reason John was engaged in "the work" was to immortalize his name, and he even compared John to the "great Babylon."

> 1 And dost thou not thyself suspect,
> Vain founder of the rising sect,
>   Or thine own language see?
> "Is not this Babylon the great,
> 'Stablish'd in her sublime estate,
>   Built up to heaven—by me!"
>
> 2 The plan, and finish'd discipline,
> Th' exact *oeconomy* is mine,
>   The whole, internal frame:
> These mon'ments of my toil and thought
> Now to perfection's summit brought
>   Immortalize my name.[149]

According to Charles, pride not only encouraged John to establish an immortal name for himself, it also drove the "preaching witnesses" to "Usurp the priestly character."[150] Although the perfectionists' spiritual problem was pride, the practical problem was that their actions were leading to a separation from the Church of England. They felt comfortable withdrawing from the Church of England, because they claimed their authority was directly from God. Charles used several Old Testament stories to confront them. He used the story of Eldad and Medad in Numbers 11:27 to criticize those who would hold separate meetings and prophesy with only the authorization of God. He characterized them as "irregularly bold."[151] Charles also compared the desire of the lay preachers to be priests to the admonition to Uzziah not to usurp the role of the priests. To be lawful priests, the lay preachers thought they only needed God's approval, not the approval of the Church. If asked what order of priests they were, Charles said they were "a new Melchizedeck!"[152] He also said they bore the same marks as Uzziah, but their leprosy was "The loathsom leprosy of pride."[153] In addition to the problem of pride, Charles argued that their desire to withdraw from the Church of England was a sign of a partial love or love that had grown cold; it was not a perfect love:

> 2 If my own party I approve,
>   And cleave to my own sect,

> Holding the few with partial love,
>   The many I reject;
> My nature's narrowness I feel,
>   Myself I blindly seek,
> And still a slave in Babel dwell,
>   A shackled schismatick.[154]

Pride also led to self-deception, leading them to mistake their weakness for perfection:

> 1 Weakest, when I strongest seem,
>   Fall'n alas I am thro' pride,
> Sinless then myself I dream,
>   Pure, and wholly sanctified,
> Fold my arms, and take my ease,
> Safe in perfect holiness.[155]

John allowed that this may be the case, that some may have mistaken their initial victories as having become perfect, but John did not go as far as Charles in condemning those lay preachers who seemed to be full of pride. John rejected Charles's portrayal of these lay preachers and their followers as "False saints, false-witnesses, for God!"[156]

Charles was also concerned with the way the perfectionists were proclaiming their perfection. According to Charles, the role of the Christian was not self-reflection or a desire to determine whether or not they had received the goodness of perfection; instead they were to be "Unconscious of the grace bestow'd, / Simply resign'd, and lost in God."[157] This raised a practical question—how should one share what one sensed God was doing in their lives?

Charles definitely believed that people should share what God had done in their lives, and, surprisingly, one of the things that kept people from sharing was their pride.

> Pride may frown, and prudence chide,
>   Bid us keep our faith unknown;
> Faith its light no more can hide
>   Than the meridian sun.[158]

He even had experienced this struggle in his own life. When he first began writing hymns, he stopped in the middle of one hymn because he feared that he was writing out of pride. He was able to overcome that fear and go on to write nearly 9000 poems and hymns, many of which reflect his personal experience.[159] Charles believed it was important to testify about what God was doing. The problem, according to Charles, was that the perfectionists were boasting about their *own* progress and perfection, and not focusing on the work God was doing. The tension between these two ways of testifying can be seen in a poem on Mark 5:19. Charles began this poem by stressing that people should share what God had done for them with a genuine meek humility in order that those who heard their witness would be awakened and that they too would "catch the heavenly fire."[160] In verse three, Charles noted the tension between sharing and remaining silent. He asked,

> 3 Didst thou in me thyself reveal,
> That I thy goodness *might conceal*,
>   Or boastingly proclaim?
> No: but thou wilt my wisdom be,
> And give me true simplicity
>   To glorify thy name.[161]

There was, however, one time Charles insisted a person remain silent. A person should not claim they had attained perfection. He even argued that to profess one had become perfect was in effect to deny that perfection. This was at odds with some including Joseph Cownley (1723-1792). He told Cownley, "You believe a man Perfect, because he says I am: that's the very reason for which I believe & am sure he is *not* perfect. How then are you and I exactly of one mind?"[162] Charles contrasted the one who claimed to be perfect with those who were truly perfect. Those who were perfect would appear to deny their own perfection:

> If perfect I myself profess,
> My own profession I disprove:
> The purest saint that lives below
> Doth his own sanctity disclaim,
> The wisest owns, I nothing know,
> The holiest cries, I nothing am![163]

Charles was struggling with the attitude of the perfectionists and the pride that stood behind their actions. One of the characteristics of being restored in the image of God was humility. What Charles witnessed in the lives of the perfectionists, his brother, and other lay preachers during this time was not humility but pride. This pride was evident for Charles both in their claims of perfection and their desire to separate from the Church of England.

Patience, Singleness, and the Necessity of Suffering
as a Check to Claims of Instantaneous Perfection.

Charles not only struggled with the pride of the perfectionists; he rejected their claims to an instantaneous work. Charles resisted these claims, in part, because he believed they were poor witnesses. They ignored their imperfection claiming the work had been completed in a moment. Their claims of perfection were not consistent with their character, which in Charles's estimation still needed to be reformed.

Charles resisted those claiming instantaneous perfection in several ways. He accused those claiming instantaneous perfection of impatience, of rejecting the means of grace, and of desiring to avoid the perfecting work of suffering. Charles responded by emphasizing the need for patience, a commitment to a 'single eye', a willingness to suffer, and a commitment to see oneself as a part of the body of Christ; more specifically, as the bride of Christ.

The impatience of the perfectionists was evident in their claim to have obtained a sinless character in a moment. Both Charles and the perfectionists took seriously the idea that one could be perfected here, but by stressing the instantaneous nature of perfection, the perfectionists denied Charles's emphasis that perfection only came with time and through suffering. Reflecting on Matthew 5:48, "*Ye shall be perfect,*" Charles wrote,

> 3 He saith, *Ye shall be perfect* here!
>   And should ten thousand souls presume
> T' usurp the sinless character,
>   Before the perfect gift is come,
> Yet on thy faithful mercies cast,
> *We* shall obtain the prize at last.[164]

In this poem, Charles criticized those who claimed or desired perfection in a moment or at least before God's time, but he also affirmed that people could be perfect in the final phrase, "*We* shall obtain the prize at last." The problem Charles had with the perfectionists was that instead of waiting for the gift to come, instead of waiting for God's timing, they had attempted to usurp the gift of God and in the process were doing damage to the idea of being perfected. The major difference between Charles's view of perfection and that of the perfectionists was that Charles emphasized the gradual nature of perfection and that restoration normally occurred late in life. He attacked those who enthusiastically claimed an instantaneous perfection, who claimed they were restored in a moment. Those who were claiming instantaneous perfection were novices, according to Charles, those whose "race had scarce begun."[165] Charles called them "delusion's ranting sons" who taught "all the work is done at once!"[166] He compared them to the seed in Matthew 13, which sprung up in an instant. Like that seed, they were shallow and lacked the "toil of patient hope, / they want [lacked] the root of humble love."[167] Charles also wrote that they desired to find a shorter way to perfection:

> 2 That work of faith the novice blind
>   Would fain, on fancy's horse, leap o'er,
> A shorter way to Sion find,[168]

The emphasis on finding a shorter way was almost always criticized by Charles. Charles did, however, use cutting short the work of God in a positive way when it was related to completing the work of grace just before a person died. He wrote,

> Most sensibly, O Lord, I know,
>   My night of death approaches fast;
> My time for work, my course below,
>   Is in another moment past:
> O then cut short thy work of grace,
>   This moment finish it in me,

> And let the next conclude my race,
>   And bring me to my goal and thee.[169]

It was only in the moment of death that Charles spoke of cutting short the work of God in a positive way. He argued that desiring a shorter way was an attempt to avoid the process of mortifying the flesh, of being willing to labor and suffer to the end, and of being willing to take up the cross and die daily:

> 1 May we not 'scape the killing pain,
>   And perfected this moment be?
> This moment, Lord, if thou ordain,
>   We can the final victory
> O'er hell, the world, and death, and sin,
> With everlasting glory win.
>
> 2 But if thou bidst us mortify
>   Our lusts and passions here below,
> Take up our cross, and daily die,
>   And in thy gracious knowledge grow,
> Who shall thine oracles gainsay,
> Or dare prescribe a shorter way?
>
> 3 We, Jesus, will on thee attend,
>   To thee the times and seasons leave,
> Labouring, and suffering to the end,
>   'Till thou the long-sought blessing give,
> And seal us, perfectly restor'd,
> True followers of our *silent* Lord.[170]

Charles also taught that stressing the instantaneous nature of being restored in the image of God tended to deny or minimize the importance of the means of grace. He labeled this as a teaching of "the smooth dawbing prophets:"[171]

> They teach "be simple, and be still,
> "Nor mind the legal guides, that say
> Ye *must* endure, ye *must* obey:
> We bid you start, and win the race,
> (For patience is a needless grace)
> Repose, before the work is done,
> Before the fight, obtain the crown."[172]

Instead of desiring the easier way, Charles taught they should be willing to be taught of God, to suffer, and tocontinue patiently in the faith. He ended this hymn by focusing on both the timing and the nature of the reward:

> In doing good, and bearing ill:
> And *after* we have serv'd our Lord,
> We trust him for the sure reward,
> Expect his image to regain,
> And then in bliss immortal reign.[173]

Although Charles rejected a shorter way to perfection, he did teach that perfection was the result of *a series* of instantaneous works of grace. The difference between him and the perfectionists was the *result* of this instantaneous grace. The perfectionists were focused on a finished work, Charles on a stage or step along the path towards being restored in the image of God. In other words, God did work with instantaneous grace, but that grace was limited in its effect. Reflecting on Jeremiah 33:27, Charles stated that the work of God in the hour of belief was forgiveness and partial sanctification. Partial sanctification was followed by abiding in the cross in order to be made completely clean.

> When I use the proffer'd power,
>   And to the fountain fly,
> Thou wilt in that self-same hour
>   Forgive, and sanctify;
> Partly sanctify me then;
>   And if I at thy cross abide,
> Wash my inmost nature clean,
>   And take me to thy side.[174]

Charles emphasized that grace was given through *a series* of instantaneous works by using the word degrees. When Charles referred to the degrees by which grace worked in the life of the believer, he also emphasized that those degrees of growth are often imperceptible. For instance, he used the example of the seed being cast to the ground and growing up to explain the work of God in the life of the believer:

> Ye bold t' explain, describe, define
> The progress of the life divine,
> Your learned ignorance allow,
> And own it grows ye know not how!
> No mortal eye the manner sees
> The imperceptible degrees,
> By which our Lord conducts his plan,
> And brings us to a perfect man.[175]

Charles also rejected the idea of instantaneous holiness by claiming that those who would receive it, would not receive it in the first moment, but through both faith and patience. Reflecting on Hebrews 6:12, "Be followers of them, who through faith and patience, inherit the promises," Charles noted,

> Nature would the crown receive
> The first moment we believe,
> But we vainly think to seize
> Instantaneous holiness:
> Faith alone cannot suffice,
> Patience too must earn the prize,
> Both insure the promise given,
> Lead thro' perfect love to heaven.[176]

Charles also attacked the individual nature of their restoration by affirming that God was able to accomplish his purpose of having "a spotless bride" on earth. In other words, he was concerned that the emphasis on individual restoration was leading to corporate disunity. This disunity was not consistent with God having "a spotless bride" on earth:

> 4 Whoe'er thro' ignorance, or pride,
>   Are found false-witnesses for God,
> Thou hast on earth a spotless bride;
>   And trusting thine all-cleansing blood,
> We too thine utmost truth shall prove,
> Compleat in holiness and love.[177]

In this poem Charles used language that focused on a corporate understanding of being restored in the image of God, focusing not so much on a sinless individual, but on the 'spotless' bride of Christ. Charles emphasized corporate perfection to check the individual proclamations of perfection, which had resulted in a growing disunity within the Methodist societies.

The Possibility of Being Restored as a Check to Antinomianism

In the midst of the perfectionist controversy Charles Wesley continued to stress that being restored in the image of God was possible. In fact, one of the weaknesses of the perfectionists noted above was their antinomian tendencies. Charles was not rejecting the goal of restoration in the image of God; he was rejecting their antinomianism, their claims of instantaneous perfection, and the pride associated with proclaiming one had already attained perfection. Charles's presentation of the possibility of being restored in the image of God is filled with tension or even paradox. At times he seemed to indicate it was possible to be restored here, and at other times he seemed to deny that it was possible at all.

Many of Charles's poems in *SHSPS* (1762) stressed the possibility of being restored in the image of God here by referring to walking in the image which meant being "pure in heart," gaining "that perfect love unknown," and shining bright in the image of God's son.[178] Charles also stressed the possibility of being restored here by focusing on living in the image. Charles noted that it was possible to live in the image when the Father spoke the soul restored and created a new heart in the believer:

> To the glory of the Lord
>   How can I all things do?
> Father, speak my soul restor'd,
>   Create my heart anew;
> When thine image I retrieve,
> United to my Saviour I
>   Shall in Jesu's Spirit live,
>   And in his Spirit die.[179]

In this poem Charles claimed that being united to Jesus resulted in being renewed in the image of God both here and when one died.

Charles's most ambitious statement about being restored here focused on doing God's perfect will on earth as it was done in heaven [Matthew 6:10]. In these poems he talked of doing God's will "As angels do above."[180] Charles stated this possibility as a fulfillment of God's promise to Abraham's race:

> God of eternal truth and grace,
>   Thy faithful promise seal,
> Thy word, thy oath to Abraham's race
>   In us, e'en us fulfil:
> Let us to perfect love restor'd
>   Thine image here retrieve,
> And in the presence of our Lord
>   The life of angels live.[181]

Charles also used the promise to the house of David in Zechariah 12:8 to argue restoration involved being "sinless, angelic, and divine!"[182] The earthly goal of perfection was to keep the law in love. This type of life would be a witness to the world that would honor God's name.[183]

A third way Charles implied the possibility of being restored was by referring to heaven as present *here*. Charles argued that heaven was realized on earth in several different ways. Reflecting on the laughter of Abraham and Sarah, Charles noted that what was impossible to them, the birth of a child, should give hope and laughter to believers who were asked to believe in something impossible:

> When first we of thy promise heard,
>   Thro' unbelief we smil'd,
> Impossible the birth appear'd
>   Of Christ the holy child:
> But when thou dost thy Son reveal,
>   And shew'st our sins forgiven,
> We laugh for joy unspeakable,
>   For joy of present heaven.[184]

One characteristic of this present heaven was an obedient life.[185] This obedience produced a joy that was a foretaste of heaven:

> And heavenly joys on earth I prove:
> Heaven on earth is Jesu's love![186]

A fourth way Charles emphasized the possibility of being restored in this life was his reference to full salvation. Reflecting on Isaiah 1:2—"Is my hand shortned at all, that it cannot redeem? Or have I no power to deliver?"—Charles noted that God's hand was still unshortened, that all things were still possible if people dared to believe. Among the things possible through belief was God's ability to

> . . . destroy our pardon'd sin,
> Produce out of a soul unclean

> A saint entire and free,
> From every spot and wrinkle pure,
> And make our full salvation sure,
> And hide our life with thee.[187]

A fifth way Charles talked about being renewed here was by referring to Jesus as the "Physician of the sin-sick soul." According to Charles, Jesus healed people when he forgave them:

> Physician of the sin-sick soul,
>   Thou heal'st us when thou dost forgive,
> Thy mercy makes, and keeps us whole,
>   In perfect health it bids us live,
> In perfect holiness renew'd,
> And fill'd with all the life of God.[188]

Even though Charles argued for a full restoration in this life in these poems, he normally argued for this restoration late in life or even in the article of death.[189] One poem which combined many of these themes is a reflection on Genesis 12:3, God's promise to bless the whole earth through Abraham:

> 1 Come thou universal blessing,
>   Abraham's long-expected seed,
>   Perfect peace, and joy unceasing
>   Thro' the ransom'd nations spread,
>   Devilish pride, and brutal passion
>   Far from every heart remove,
>   Bless us with thy full salvation,
>   Bless us with thy heavenly love.
>
> 2 Happy is the man forgiven:
>   This let every sinner feel,
>   Taste in thee his present heaven,
>   Pant for greater blessings still:
>   O that all anew created
>   Might thine image here retrieve,
>   Then to paradise translated
>   In thy glorious presence live.[190]

It is important to note that Charles described being translated to paradise and living in the glorious presence of God immediately after he talked about retrieving the image. This suggests that for Charles these two events were closely related.

Even when Charles affirmed that restoration happened here, he admitted that the late rise of the false witnesses had caused difficulties and even threatened to move Charles from his hope in the restoration. In a verse directed at the perfectionists he wrote,

> 4 False-witnesses may rise,
>   Me from my hope to move,
>   Pretenders to the glorious prize,

> The pure, consummate love:
> Tho' crouds believe a lie,
> Nor reach the perfect day,
> I set the self-deceivers by,
> And still hold on my way.[191]

Although Charles affirmed the possibility of restoration, he also has several poems which seemed to deny the possibility of perfection here. Sometimes Charles's denial of perfection can be explained by the context. For instance, when he spoke of people being "As perfect as the fiends in hell,"[192] it is important to note that he was addressing those who were boasting about their perfection. In other words, Charles seemed willing to deny that obtaining perfection was possible if it bolstered an argument against those who were inappropriately claiming perfection. It seems he was willing to overstate his position in order to counter what he thought were the more dangerous beliefs of the perfectionists, namely their pride.

One way Charles noted that perfection here would always be incomplete was by referring to Paul's statement in Philippians 3:13, "I count not myself to have apprehended." Charles first stated Paul's case, that although he had been laboring in the world for over 20 years, he had not attained the prize. Instead of boasting of his accomplishments, Paul daily died and claimed to live an imperfect life. Unlike the apostle Paul, the perfectionists had already obtained the prize. Charles put the following boast in their mouths:

> 2 "But we now, the prize t' attain,
> An easier method see,
> Save ourselves the toil and pain,
> And ling'ring agony,
> Reach at once the ladder's top,
> While standing on its lowest round,
> Instantaneously spring up,
> With pure perfection crown'd."[193]

It was this easier method, this shorter way, which drew Charles's negative response. Charles was disappointed in this approach because it seemed to contribute to the idea that holiness was an error:

> 3 *Such* the credulous dotard's dream,
> And *such* his shorter road,
> Thus he makes the world blaspheme,
> And shames the church of God,
> Staggers thus the most sincere,
> 'Till from the gospel hope they move
> Holiness as error fear,
> And start at perfect love.[194]

The next verse included a plea to God to reveal the error of their ways and to restore a desire in people to pursue restoration through lawful striving and humility.[195] Charles did not abandon his emphasis on being restored in the image of God. Instead, he addressed those areas he thought people had misunderstood, specifically their lack of humility, patience and their willingness to suffer.

Theological Concepts in *Short Hymns on Select Passages of Scripture*

Behind each of these checks (the check to pride, the check against instantaneous perfection, and the check against antinomianism) was Charles's theology of restoration. These checks are built on a specific theological framework. Charles made this framework clear at times, but most times this framework was assumed. Charles continued to describe what it meant for people to be restored in the image of God using the ideas of *theosis* and recapitulation. A new theme Charles introduced in this collection was the goal of restoration as a universal restoration of all people and the creation.

Theosis

Charles continued to define being restored in the image of God in ways that are similar to the Eastern Orthodox understanding of *theosis*. One way he expressed this was by talking about being reabsorbed into the divine; something that normally happened at the end of life. It was not at the beginning of the race that one would attain the goal of perfect love, it was at the latter end:

> 2 Saviour, my latter end is come,
>   Now to my parting soul appear,
> The root, the man of sin consume,
>   And let me sink to nothing here,
> Resorb'd into perfection's sea,
> And lost, forever lost in thee![196]

Charles reinforced this happening at the end of life by contrasting the sad sinful days of the pilgrimage on earth with the desire to "die, to be / Restor'd, resorb'd, and lost in thee."[197] Charles taught that people should desire a life of pain and die a good death because it was in death the one was finally totally lost in God. It is important to note that this desire to die a good death was a common feature of eighteenth century thought.

Charles developed two concepts at tension with each other which defined the nature of the union with God. On the one hand, Charles stressed the distance between the Creator and creature, the transcendence of God. One way he did this was by noting that the brightness of God makes the brightest day seem as if it were the middle of the night. It was in this context that Charles proposed that the goal of the creature was to be absorbed in God's immensity.[198] On the other hand, Charles stressed the radical union between Creator and creature, the immanence of God. He once again used the metaphor of light, but in this poem it was the union of God and his creation that was stressed. The goal of restoration was to replace the darkness and sin in a person's life with the light of God and becoming "blended with the light divine." The result of this restoration was both shining in the light divine and being healed:

> Jesus, full of truth and grace,
> Shew my heart thy heavenly face,
> Shine the true eternal light,
> Put my darkness all to flight;
> Then my sin shall disappear,
> Heal'd of all my evils here,
> Then I as my Lord shall shine
> Blended with the light divine.[199]

Charles also stressed the fullness or the plenitude into which one would be restored. Someone who was restored would experience the "Fulness of peace, and joy, and love:" This was possible because God's presence filled "the human shrine / With all the plenitude divine."[200]

Recapitulation

Charles also continued to emphasize the doctrine of recapitulation, a theme which is closely related to *theosis*.[201] One way Charles expressed the doctrine of recapitulation was by describing the descent of Jesus, which made possible the ascent of Jesus' disciples. This ascent included regaining the image of God and gaining eternal joy:

> Was ever grief like thine,
> Jesus, thou Man of Woe!
> The visage and the form divine,
> Why was it mangled so?
> That man thro' thee restor'd,
> God's image might regain,
> And by the sorrows of his Lord
> In joy eternal reign.[202]

The primary way recapitulation was expressed was by having what was lost in Adam restored by Christ. This is reflected in the lines: "As many as in Adam died, / In Christ may be restor'd", "Adam, descended from above, / Answer by forming me again, / By perfecting my soul in love", and "Raise me to my first estate."[203] Like John, Charles thought that this restoration to the first estate would in some way have to be better than the first estate. Charles wrote, "Now our universe create / Fair, beyond its first estate."[204] Charles used the doctrine of recapitulation to argue that what we see in Christ, what he has done, is what the believer can expect to happen in their life. Jesus was willing to be arrayed in "feeble flesh" so that his followers could be all like God:

> In our feeble flesh array'd
> We own the filial deity,

> Jesus like his brethren made,
> To make us all like thee.²⁰⁵

In addition to emphasizing the themes of recapitulation and *theosis* in this collection, Charles included some references to a universal restoration. Not only was redemption offered to all. Charles also expressed the hope that one day all people would be restored.

The Universal Nature of Restoration

In 1783 John Wesley published the sermon, "The General Spread of the Gospel."²⁰⁶ In this sermon he described how the whole earth would one day once again be re-established in "universal holiness and happiness."²⁰⁷ Most of the sermon explained this hope in light of the present condition of the world. What is important for understanding what it meant to be restored in the image of God is not so much his judgment of the world or even his explanation of how it will one day become a place of universal holiness and happiness; instead the most important issue is that one day there will be this universal restoration. It is also interesting that this proclamation was made with full knowledge and examination of the present fallenness of the world. Although John had seen glimpses of this restoration through what he described as a 50-year revival, he still realized that the full realization of a world completely restored seemed unreasonable. In the midst of the controversy with the perfectionists, Charles pointed to the same future. Charles argued that there was a day coming when all people would come to know their universal friend. Charles, like John, thought that this included the restoration of people from other faith traditions, specifically mentioning Jews and Muslims. This restoration also included those who were labeled 'heathens' by Charles:

> 3 Millions more their Lord shall know,
> When he doth his mercy shew,
> Mercy's utmost power display
> In the long-expected day:
> Come, thou universal friend,
> Human miseries to end,
> Jews, and Turks, and heathens call,
> All receive, who diedst for all.²⁰⁸

Charles expressed this same hope of a complete and universal restoration in terms which reflected his understanding of recapitulation. There would be a day when all that was lost in Adam's fall would be restored, and that restoration would be universal. He wrote,

> 2 Yet still we look for happier days,
> When Adam's whole backslidden race
>   Shall be to Israel join'd:
> Jesus, call forth thy holy seed,
> And haste throughout the earth to spread

The church of all mankind.[209]

In both of these instances, Charles used a passage from the Hebrew Bible to argue for a universal restoration that would extend beyond the intent of the passage. His use of Luke 11:2, "Thy will be done, as in heaven, so in earth," seems to be more closely related to the original intention of the passage. Note again the universal emphasis in this hymn and the focus on a communal, not an individual restoration:

> Hasten that happiest gospel-day,
>   When all on earth forgiven,
> As fully shall thy will obey,
>   As angels do in heaven;
> While not one disharmonious string
>   Is heard below, above,
> But all in perfect concert sing,
>   And praise the God we love.[210]

Each of these hymns point to a time when there will be universal holiness and happiness. Charles did not present an argument for this universal restoration or describe the process by which this restoration will take place; instead he just asserted it as an inevitable fact based on his reading of Scripture. Charles did, however, indicate this would be the result of a spread of the Gospel, which implies that it will be gradual. This spread would eventually lead to that day of universal holiness and happiness. This is the same argument John will make twenty years later in his sermon, "The General Spread of the Gospel." Both John and Charles argue that in spite of the present reality, there will be a day when God will completely and universally restore people and the creation in God's image.[211]

Conclusion

The 1750's and early 1760's were filled by struggles with the lay preachers over separation from the Church of England, administering the ordinances, and defining the nature of being restored in the image of God. John and Charles's struggle was complicated by Charles's marriage and his commitment to spend time with his family. John and Charles also seemed to have different priorities with regard to remaining connected to the Church of England; Charles was committed to staying in the Church of England no matter what, whereas John believed it was possible to separate from the Church of England but did not believe it was expedient at this time.

In the early 1760's John and Charles had to deal with the doctrine of perfection. George Bell and Thomas Maxfield were bringing a negative response upon Methodism by their emphasis on the instantaneous nature of perfection and by George Bell's prediction that the world would end on February 28, 1763. Charles responded to these problems in London by emphasizing the importance of humility and a focus on corporate restoration as a check to pride. One of the major changes made by the London perfectionists was a new emphasis on proclaiming perfection. Charles responded by emphasizing the need for humility which excluded a public proclamation of one's perfection. Charles also emphasized patience and a 'single eye' as a check to instantaneous perfection. This included a continued emphasis on the means of grace and the role of suffering in being restored in the image of God.

Charles continued to use themes of *theosis* and recapitulation to describe what it meant to be restored in the image of God. Charles also emphasized the universal nature of being restored in the image of God. This universal restoration included people from various faith traditions, and it included the restoration of creation. Like his brother John, Charles believed the restored or new creation would in some way exceed the original creation.

Notes

1. Charles Wesley, Letter to Sarah Gwynne Wesley ([April 13, 1760]), in Frank Baker's transcriptions of Charles Wesley's letters, where the item is No. 337. Charles later told his brother how he described the difference between John and himself to Mr. Davis: "All the difference betwixt my B[rother] & me (I told him) was yt my B[rother]'s First Object was The M[ethodis]ts; & then the Church: mine was First the Church; and then the M[ethodis]ts. That our different Judgment of Persons was owing to our different Tempers, his all hope, & mine all fear." (Charles Wesley, Letter to John Wesley [January 20, 1774], MARC, DDCW 7/63.)

2. Charles Wesley, September 18, 1756, *Manuscript Journal*, 2:623.

3. *Dictionary of Methodism*, s.v., "Wesley, Charles," http://www.wesleyhistoricalsociety.org.uk/dmbi/.

4. In this section Church refers to the Church of England and the society refers to Methodist societies.

5. Charles Wesley, October 21, 1756, *Manuscript Journal*, 2:639.

6. Ibid.

7. Ibid.

8. Charles noted these steps or similar measures throughout this section of his journal. The goal was to keep people from leaving the societies and/or the Church. See Charles Wesley, October 19, 1756 and October 21, 1756, *Manuscript Journal*, 2:637, 638-40.

9. Charles Wesley, October 21, 1756, *Manuscript Journal*, 2:639.

10. Charles noted several times preaching on the means of grace or the ordinances which included "the duties of constant communicating, of hearing, reading, practising the word, of fasting, of private, family, and public prayer." (Charles Wesley, October 10, 1756, *Manuscript Journal*, 2:632.) See also Charles Wesley, October 4, 1756; October 5, 1756; October 11, 1756; October 12, 1756; October 22, 1756; and October 31, 1756, *Manuscript Journal*, 2:629-31, 633-34, 641, 647-48 and Charles Wesley, Letter to John Wesley (October 11, 1756), Frank Baker's transcriptions of Charles Wesley's letters, where the item is No. 269a.

11. Charles Wesley, October 4, 1756; October 5, 1756; October 10, 1756; and October 26, 1756, *Manuscript Journal*, 2:629-631, 632-33, 643-44.

12. Charles Wesley, October 11, 1756, *Manuscript Journal*, 2:633.

13. Charles Wesley, October 22, 1756, *Manuscript Journal,* 2:641.

14. Charles Wesley, October 25, 1756, *Manuscript Journal,* 2:643.

15. Charles Wesley, Letter to Mr. Grimshaw (October 29, 1756) in *Manuscript Journal,* 2:645. See also, Charles Wesley, Letter to my beloved brethern at Leeds ([October 29, 1756]) in *Manuscript Journal,* 2:645-46.

16. Charles Wesley, October 21, 1756, *Manuscript Journal,* 2:640.

17. Ibid.

18. Ibid.

19. Charles Wesley, October 24, 1756, *Manuscript Journal,* 2:642.

20. Charles Wesley, October 26, 1756, *Manuscript Journal,* 2:643-44.

21. Charles Wesley, *An Epistle to the Reverend Mr. John Wesley* (London: [Strahan,] for J. Robinson, 1755), 3, The Center for Studies in the Wesleyan Tradition, Duke University, *http://divinity.duke.edu/initiatives/cswt/charles-published-verse*

22. For more detailed discussion of Charles's attempt to reform the Church of England without leaving her see, Patrick A. Eby, "Reforming the Church: Charles Wesley's Ecclesiology and the Role of Lay Preachers." *Proceedings of the Charles Wesley Society* 11 (2006-2007): 59-68.

23.. Charles Wesley, *An Epistle to the Reverend Mr. John Wesley*, 3.

24. Gareth Lloyd, *Charles Wesley and the Struggle for Methodist Identity* (Oxford: Oxford University Press, 2007), 82, 87.

25. Charles Wesley, Letter to Christopher Hopper (March 27, 1760), MARC, DDWES 4/92(D).

26. Christophilus [*pseud.*], *A Serious Inquiry whether A late Epistle from the Rev. Mr. Charles Wesley to the Rev. Mr. John Wesley be not ...* ([London?]: Printed for the Author, 1755). Christophilus seems to be a member of the Church of England because he accused John and Charles of being "Apostates from the *Church of England*. . . ." (Ibid., 2)

27. Ibid., 7.

28. Gareth Lloyd, *Charles Wesley and the Struggle for Methodist Identity*, 154-158.

29. Lay preaching was one of the ministries which were outside the normal practice of the Church of England. It seems probable the because of the extraordinary nature of the ministry Charles would be troubled by the appearance that it would become a normal part of Methodism.

30. One example of Charles's early rejection of lay preaching was noted in Chapter One. Both he and George Whitefield's declared their disapproval of lay preaching while still at Fetter Lane. (Charles Wesley, May 16, 1739, *Manuscript Journal*, 1:173.)

31. Charles complained about the obstinacy and sexual misconduct of James Wheatley in his Journal. (Charles Wesley, June 14, 1749; July 10, 1749; June 13, 1751; and *Manuscript Journal*, 2:576, 78, and 608-09.)

32. Richard P. Heitzenrater, "Purge the Preachers: The Wesleys and Quality Control," in *Charles Wesley: Life, Literature & Legacy*, ed. Ted A. Campbell and Kenneth G. C. Newport [London: Epworth, 2007], 489.

33. Charles Wesley, June 12, 1751, *Manuscript Journal* 2:608. Emphasis is in the original.

34. Charles Wesley, August 5, 1751, *Manuscript Journal* 2:617.

35. Donald Henry Kirkham, "Pamphlet Opposition to the Rise of Methodism: The Eighteenth-Century English Evangelical Revival Under Attack" (Ph.D. diss., Duke University, 1973), 236.

36. Richard Hardy, *A letter from a clergyman, to one of his parishioners, who was inclined to turn Methodist...* (London: Printed for the Author, 1763), 80-86.

37. Charles reported the following concerns of John Wesley to Lady Huntington: "It

is probable the Point will now be speedily determined concerning the Church. For if we must either *Dissent* or *be silent*. The matter is over with us! "We have no time to trifle!" (Charles Wesley, Letter to Lady Huntington [June 28, 1755], Drew University Methodist Collection). Also published in *Letters of Charles Wesley,* 388.

38. Ibid.
39. Heitzenrater, *Wesley and the People Called Methodists,* 192.
40. Ibid., 193.
41. Charles Wesley, Letter to Walter Sellon (November 29, 1754), Drew University Methodist Collection. Also published in *Letters of Charles Wesley,* 353-54.
42. Ibid.
43. "Of or relating to Melchizedek, the sect of the Melchizedekians, or the order of priesthood which Melchizedek is taken to represent." (*OED,* December 2009 online ed., s.v. "Melchizedekian.") Charles may have used this to indicated the lay preachers were trying to set up a different type of priesthood and were claiming it was superior to the current priests in the Church of England.
44. Charles Wesley, Letter to Walter Sellon (December 14, 1754), Drew University Methodist Collection. Also published in *Letters of Charles Wesley,* 355.
45. Charles Wesley, Letter to Samuel Lloyd (April 29, 1755), The Frank Baker Collection of Manuscripts, Rare Book, Manuscript, and Special Collections Library, Duke University, photographic copy. Hereafter cited as The Frank Baker Collection of Manuscripts, Duke. Also published in *Letters of Charles Wesley,* 368-69.
46. Charles Wesley, Letter to Sarah Gwynne Wesley ([May 9, 1755]), MARC, DDCW 5/88. Part of the text has been struck through with a line. It seems to be in a different hand. Also published in *Letters of Charles Wesley,* 371-72.
47. Charles Wesley, Letter to Samuel Walker (August 7, 1756), The Frank Baker Collection of Manuscripts, Duke, photographic copy. Charles is quoting Samuel Walker at this point in the letter. Also published in *Letters of Charles Wesley,* 414-15.
48. This section has been cut off at the bottom of the page (at least on my copy). The section in brackets has been supplied from a transcription by Frank Baker. (Charles Wesley, Letter to Samuel Walker [August 7, 1756] in Frank Baker's transcriptions of Charles Wesley's letters, where the item is No. 264.) Also published in *Letters of Charles Wesley,* 414-15.
49. Ibid.
50. Ibid.
51. Charles Wesley, Letter to Samuel Walker (August 21, 1756), Wesley manuscripts and selected Wesleyana from the Collections of Bridwell Library, Southern Methodist University, ATLA: Digital resources for the study of religion, *https://www2.atla.com/digitalresources/*. Hereafter cited as Wesleyana from the Collections of Bridwell Library, SMU. Also published in *Letters of Charles Wesley,* 416-17.
52. Charles Wesley, Letter to John Wesley ([October 11, 1756]), from transcriptions of the shorthand by Frank Baker in Frank Baker's transcriptions of Charles Wesley's letters, where the item is No. 269a(4).
53. Charles Wesley, Letter to John Wesley (October 23, 1756), in Charles Wesley, *Charles Wesley as Revealed by His Letters,* ed. Frank Baker, Revised ed. The Charles Wesley Society (London: The Epworth Press, 1995), 97. Also published in *Letters of Charles Wesley,* 421.
54. Charles Wesley, Letter to John Wesley (March 2, 1760), MARC, DDWES 4/63. According to Gareth Lloyd, the three men involved, "John Murlin, Paul Greenwood, and Thomas Mitchell, were well-regarded preachers of long standing, and their actions represented a significant threat to the connection with the Anglican Church." (Gareth Lloyd,

142   *The Heart of Charles Wesley's Theology*

Charles Wesley and the Struggle for Methodist Identity, 164-165)

55. Charles Wesley, Letter to Sarah Gwynne Wesley (March 26, 1760), MARC, DDCW 1/56.

56. Charles Wesley, Letter to John Nelson, March 27, 1760, MARC, DDWES 4/92(B).

57. Charles Wesley, Letter to William Grimshaw, March 27, 1760, MARC, DDWES 4/92(C).

58. Charles Wesley, Letter to Christopher Hopper (March 27, 1760), MARC, DDWES 4/92(D).

59. Ibid.

60. Charles Wesley, Letter to Sarah Gwynne Wesley (April 11, 1760), MARC, DDCW 7/3.

61. Charles Wesley, Letter to John Wesley (October 11, 1756), Frank Baker's transcriptions of Charles Wesley's letters, where the item is No. 269a. See also Charles Wesley, Letter to William Perronet (October 23, 1756), The Frank Baker Collection of Manuscripts, Duke. Also published in *Letters of Charles Wesley,* 421-22. And Charles Wesley, Letter to John Wesley (October 23, 1756) in Frank Baker's transcriptions of Charles Wesley's letters, where the item is No. 272a. Also published in *Letters of Charles Wesley,* 421.

62. Charles Wesley, Letter to William Grimshaw (October 29, 1756), in *Manuscript Journal,* 2:645.

63. Ibid.

64. Charles Wesley, Letter to Society at Leeds (October 28, 1956) in *Manuscript Journal,* 2:646.

65. Ibid.

66. *SHSPS* (1762).

67. Charles Wesley, Letter to Sarah Gwynne Wesley (April 11, 1760), MARC, DDCW 7/3. According to Fraser, "The Witnesses were professing the most radical possibilities of grace expressed in early Methodism by John and Charles Wesley and Thomas Walsh. Undoubtedly they lacked the spiritual humility and sensitivity of these three, but what they lacked in humility and love they made up in hope and faith (or presumption)." (Fraser, "Strains in the Understandings of Christian Perfection in Early British Methodism," 285).

68. Philodemas [*pseud.*], "*To the* Editor *of* Lloyd's Evening Post," *Lloyd's Evening Post*. March 2-4, 1763, 210.

69. In a letter dated January 7, 1963 John explained why Bell had met in the society room at the Foundry and in the Chapel at West Street. He also made it clear that Bell was no longer allowed to meet in these places. (John Wesley, "*To the Editor of the London Chronicle,*" *The London Chronicle*. January 18, 1763, 63.) About a month later he wrote again and made it clear that Bell was no a member of the Methodist society. John also denounced Bell's claims that the world would end and stated "That not one in fifty (perhaps not one in five hundred) of the people called *Methodists*, believe any more than I do, either this or any other of his prophecies." (John Wesley, "*To the Printer of the London Chronicle,*" *The London Chronicle*. February 10, 1763, 143.)

70. Impartiality [*pseud.*], "*To the Printer of the London Chronicle,*" *The London Chronicle*. January 10, 1763, 34.)

71. Ibid.

72. Charles Wesley, Letter to Joseph Cownley [July 1, 1764], Frank Baker's transcriptions of Charles Wesley's letters, where the item is No. 372.

73. In the preface to *A Collection of Psalms and Hymns* Maxfield noted that he had

been "frequently accused of Enthusiasm, Antinomianism, and Fanaticism. . . . Such a groundless charge (he thinks) deserves no answer." (Thomas Maxfield, *A Collection of Psalms and Hymns,* 3rd ed. [London: printed and sold at his chapel, 1778], iii).

74. John Wesley, *Cautions and Directions: Given to the Greatest Professors in the Methodist Societies* (London: n. p., 1762).

75. "My prophecy is fulfilled. 'Witnesses of sanctification' was my word; and my meaning, 'souls stablished in grace.' many such there are now to be seen among us: but none of them heard to witness his own instantaneous perfection.

You might have heard of another of my prophecies Six years ago. 'Yt a new Sect of French Prophets, or Ranters, would arise: & out of the Witnesses of perfection.' Judge you now, if I am not as good a Prophet as the Immortal Mr. Bell." (Charles Wesley, Letter to Joseph Cownley [July 1, 1764] in Frank Baker's transcriptions of Charles Wesley's letters, where the item is No. 372).

76. John Fletcher, Letter to Charles Wesley (August 8, 1765) in John Fletcher, *Unexampled Labours: Letters of the Revd John Fletcher to leaders in the Evangelical Revival,* ed. Peter Forsaith (Peterborough: Epworth, 2008), 217-18. Hereafter cited as *Unexampled Labours.*

77. John Fletcher, Letter to Charles Wesley (September 23, 1765) in *Unexampled Labours,* 221.

78. John Wesley, *Cautions and Directions,* 4-6.

79. John Wesley, Letter to Thomas Maxfield (October 29, 1762) in John Wesley, October 29, 1762, *Journals and Diaries IV (1755-65),* ed. W. Reginald Ward and Richard P. Heitzenrater, vol. 21 of *The Bicentennial Edition of the Works of John Wesley* (Nashville: Abingdon Press, 1992), 215

80. Charles Wesley, Letter to Sarah Gwynne Wesley (June 21, [1763]). Charles also wrote to Joseph Cownley, "I never was ashamed, or repented of one line against the Enthusiasts." (Charles Wesley, Letter to Joseph Cownley [July 1, 1764], Frank Baker's transcriptions of Charles Wesley's letters, where the item is No. 372).

81. See p. 195-96 above.

82. John Wesley noted his displeasure with Maxfield's claim of angelic perfection: "But I dislike your supposing man may be as perfect as an angel; that he can be absolutely perfect; that he can be infallible, or above being tempted; or that the moment he is pure in heart he cannot fall from it." (John Wesley Letter to Thomas Maxfield [November 2, 1762], John Wesley, *The Letters of the Rev. John Wesley,* ed. John Telford, vol. 4 [London: The Epworth Press, 1931], 192). Hereafter cited as Telford, *Letters of John Wesley.*

83. Fraser, "Strains in the Understandings of Christian Perfection in Early British Methodism," 302-03.

84. John Wesley, Letter to Samuel Furly (September 8, 1761), Telford, *Letters of John Wesley,* 4:163.

85. Charles Wesley, Letter to Lady Huntington (September 6, 1766) in Frank Baker's transcriptions of Charles Wesley's letters, where the item is No. 389a. See also Selina Hastings, *In the Midst of Early Methodism: Lady Huntingdon and Her Correspondence,* ed. John R. Tyson and Boyd S. Schlenther, Pietism and Wesleyan Studies, No. 19: Revitalization: Explorations in World Christian Movements (Lanham, Maryland: The Scarecrow Press, Inc., 2006), 107.

86. "Believe what you have and you have it." (*Unexampled Labours,* 163)

87. John Fletcher, Letter to Charles Wesley (August 22, 1762) in *Unexampled Labours,* 163. Fletcher also wrote Charles: "With regard to instantaneous perfection, I have not yet heard him speak of it; what he presses with fervour is the life of faith from minute to minute, to which those who want to proceed in the way of salvation make no objec-

144 *The Heart of Charles Wesley's Theology*

tion." (John Fletcher, Letter to Charles Wesley [August 8, 1765] in Ibid., 218.)

88. Thomas Maxfield, *Christ the Great Gift of God: and the Nature of Faith in Him* (London: n. p., 1769), 33-34; and Thomas Maxfield, *A Collection of Psalms and Hymns*, v. For instance, Maxfield later emphasized that the work of sanctification could be either instantaneous or progressive, that being renewed in the image of God included growing upward into a likeness of Jesus Christ, and that "With regard to the notion that we may stop in some present attainment of holiness, it is as contrary to common sense, as it is to sober scriptural experience." (Thomas Maxfield, *A Collection of Psalms and Hymns*, ix.)

89. See pp. 220-56 below.

90. William Briggs, Letter to Charles Wesley (October 28, 1762) as quoted in, William Briggs, "George Bell and Early Methodist Enthusiasm: A New Manuscript Source from the Manchester Archives," ed. Kenneth G. C. Newport and Gareth Lloyd, *Bulletin John Rylands Library* (1998), 97.

91. Ibid., 96-97.

92. John used this phrase to refer to the first beatitude, "Blessed are the poor in Spirit." (John Wesley, Sermon 21, "Upon Our Lord's Sermon on the Mount," in *Sermons I*, ed. Albert C. Outler, vol. 1 of The Bicentennial Edition of the Works of John Wesley [Nashville: Abingdon Press, 1984], 469-87.) It seems probable that Charles was preaching on a similar theme if not the same text.

93. Charles Wesley, Letter to Sarah Gwynne Wesley ([May 27, 1764]), MARC, DDCW 7/31.

94. Rattenbury, *The Evangelical Doctrines of Charles Wesley's Hymns*, 311. Rattenbury argued that Charles's theology was marked by the positive role suffering has in the life of the believer, a view that was often at odds with his brother John. This section will examine that contention.

95. *Sermons of Charles Wesley*, 225. Newport noted that the most significant earthquake seems to have been on March 8, 1750.

96. Charles Wesley, Sermon 9, "Psalm 46:8: [The Cause and Cure of Earthquakes]," in *Sermons of Charles Wesley*, 225-37; [Charles Wesley], *Hymns*

97. *Occasioned by the Earthquake, March 8, 1750: [Part I]* (London: [Strahan], 1750), The Center for Studies in the Wesleyan Tradition, Duke University, *http://divinity.duke.edu/initiatives/cswt/charles-published-verse*; and [Charles Wesley], *Hymns Occasioned by the Earthquake, March 8, 1750: Part II* (London: [Strahan], 1750), The Center for Studies in the Wesleyan Tradition, Duke University, *http://divinity.duke.edu/initiatives/cswt/charles-published-verse*. Hereafter *EqH* (1750).

Charles Wesley, Sermon 9, "Psalm 46:8: [The Cause and Cure of Earthquakes]," in *Sermons of Charles Wesley*, 226.

98. Ibid., 226.

99. Ibid.

100. Ibid., 235.

101. Ibid.

102. *EqH* (1750), I:4.

103. Ibid, 3.

104. *EqH* (1750), II:21.

105. See pp. 119-130 above.

106. "Holy Communion" in *The Book of Common Prayer* (Cambridge: Printed by John Baskerville, 1662), [24]. *http://justus.anglican.org/resources/bcp/1662/baskerville.htm*.

107. Charles Wesley, Sermon 9, "Psalm 46:8: [The Cause and Cure of Earthquakes]," in *Sermons of Charles Wesley*, 227. Charles quoted Job 9:5, Psalms 104:32, Psalms 97:5,

and Nahum 1:5-6 to argue God is the author of earthquakes.

108. *EqH* (1750), II:8.

109. "'Sovereign word' changed to 'threat'ning look' in 2nd edn. (1750) and following." *EqH* (1750), I:8.

110. Ibid.

111. *EqH* (1750), I:10-11.

112. *EqH* (1750), I:6.

113. Charles Wesley, Sermon 9, "Psalm 46:8: [The Cause and Cure of Earthquakes]," in *Sermons of Charles Wesley*, 231.

114. *EqH* (1750), II:17-18.

115. Charles Wesley, Sermon 9, "Psalm 46:8: [The Cause and Cure of Earthquakes]," in *Sermons of Charles Wesley*, 237.

116. Randy Maddox, *Responsible Grace*, 84-87, 144-45.

117. Charles Wesley, Sermon 9, "Psalm 46:8: [The Cause and Cure of Earthquakes]," in *Sermons of Charles Wesley*, 228.

118. Charles Wesley, Sermon 9, "Psalm 46:8: [The Cause and Cure of Earthquakes]," in *Sermons of Charles Wesley*, 230.

119. Charles Wesley, Sermon 9, "Psalm 46:8: [The Cause and Cure of Earthquakes]," in *Sermons of Charles Wesley*, 234.

120. *EqH* (1750), I:6.

121. *EqH* (1750), II:3.

122. *EqH* (1750), II:18.

123. *EqH* (1750), II:19.

124. See pp. 131-138 above. Cruickshank also argued that Charles saw the suffering associated with persecution primarily in a positive light. (Cruickshank, 174)

125. Charles Wesley, Letter to Sarah Gwynne Wesley ([August 15, 1749]), MARC, DDCW 5/76. Also published in *Letters of Charles Wesley*, 263-64.

126. Charles Wesley, Letter to Sarah Gwynne Wesley (August 17, [1749]), MARC, DDCW5/74. Also published in *Letters of Charles Wesley*, 264-66. Charles opened a letter to the Foundry with the same sentiment: "You will learn Obedience by the things you suffer." (Charles Wesley, Letter to The Foundry [September 21, {1757}], MARC, DDCW 5/101)

127. Cruickshank, 129.

128. *SHSPS* (1762), 2:374.

129. Cruickshank, 129.

130. Charles Wesley, *Hymns for the Use of Families* (Bristol: Pine, 1767), The Center for Studies in the Wesleyan Tradition, Duke University, *http://divinity.duke.edu/initiatives/cswt/charles-published-verse*, 75.

131. Ibid.

132. Ibid. Cruickshank did not see the death of a child as a means of grace because she focused mainly on Charles's pain when dealing with the death of a child. This approach ignored Charles's own search for a purpose for the death of his child. Cruickshank argued Charles did not see the death of a child as a means of grace because the death of a child presented "suffering of grief as a lifelong burden. It is not triumphantly overcome, like the suffering of persecution, but endured." (Cruickshank, 191) She argued that the hymns on suffering that dealt with the death of a child do not have the emphasis of restoration Charles normally associated with suffering, instead there was only a sad recognition of the sorrows in this life and the hope that the suffering will end in the next. (Cruickshank, 193)

133. Charles worked on this collection during an extended illness during most of

1760 and 1761 and registered it for copyrighted at Stationers Hall on August 23, 1762. (Editorial Introduction, *SHSPS* [1762]).

134. Matthew Henry's commentary was treasured for it's practical piety and good sense. Matthew Henry was a dissenter who preached regularly both in his pulpit and in the churches nearby. (David L. Wykes, "Henry, Matthew" in H. C. G. Matthew and Brian Howard Harrison eds., *Oxford Dictionary of National Biography: In Association with the British Academy: From the Earliest Times to the Year 2000* [Oxford: Oxford University Press, 2004]); Matthew Henry (1662–1714), *An Exposition of the Old and New Testament*, 3 vols. (London: Stratford, 1706–10); Robert Gell (1595–1665), *An Essay towards the Amendment of the English Translation of the Bible; or, A proof, by many instances, that the last translation of the Bible into English may be improved. The first part on the Pentateuch, or five books of Moses* (London: R. Norton, 1659); and Johann Albrecht Bengel (1687–1752), *Gnomon Novi Testamenti: in quo ex nativa verborum vi simplicitas, profunditas, concinnitas, salubritas sensuum coelestium indicatur* (Tübingen: H. Philip Schram, 1742).

135. *SHSPS* (1762), Preface: [i-ii].

136. Ibid., Preface: [ii-iii]. "Wanting in self-confidence; distrustful of oneself; not confident in disposition; timid, shy, modest, bashful." (*Oxford English Dictionary*, 2d ed., s.v. "diffident.")

137. Ibid., Preface: [ii].

138. Ibid., Preface: [ii]. Cf. Galatians 2:16 and James 2:24.

139. John Fletcher, Letter to Charles Wesley (May 5, 1762) in *Unexampled Labours*, 143.

140. John Wesley, *Cautions and Directions*. See Charles Wesley, "[Hymn] 94," in *SHSPS* (1762), 2:149-150.

141. See *Theology the Lutheran Way* for a description of Luther's method. (Oswald Bayer, *Theology the Lutheran Way*, trans. Jeffery G. Silcock and Mark C. Mattes [Grand Rapids: William B. Eerdmans, 2007], 33-65).

142. Henry More (1614-1687) was one of the Cambridge Platonists who influenced early Methodism.

143. Gell, *Essay*, Preface, [2].

144. Ibid., [4-5].

145. Charles Wesley, "[Hymn] 1285. 'They shall dwell in the land that I have given unto Jacob, &c.'—[Ezek.] xxxvii. 25," in *SHSPS* (1762), 2:56.

146. Charles Wesley, "1008. 'Read this; I cannot for it is sealed.'—[Isa.] xxix. 11," in *SHSPS* (1762), 1:324.

147. Charles Wesley, "429. 'It is the spirit that quickneth, the flesh profiteth nothing.'—[John] vi. 63," Ibid., 2:249.

148. See pp. 35-37 above.

149. Charles Wesley, "[Hymn] 1298. 'Is not this great Babylon that I have built?'—[Dan.] iv. 30," in *SHSPS* (1762), 2:60-61.

150. Charles Wesley, "[Hymn] 239. 'And seek ye the priesthood also?'—[Num.] xvi. 10," in *SHSPS* (1762), 1:76.

151. Charles Wesley, "[Hymn] 210. 'There ran a young man, and told Moses and said, Eldad and Medad do prophesy in the camp.'—[Num.] xi. 27'" in *SHSPS* (1762), 1.67. In this passage Joshua wanted Moses to forbid Eldad and Medad from prophesying. Moses did not forbid them from sharing, instead he asked Joshua, "Enviest thou for my sake? would God that all the LORD'S people were prophets, and that the LORD would put his spirit upon them!" (Numbers 11:29) Charles clearly has misused this passage to support his position.

152. Charles Wesley, "[Hymn] 660. 'It appertaineth not unto thee, Uzziah, to burn incense, but to the priests, the sons of Aaron, that are consecrated.'—[II. Chron.] xxvi. 18," in *SHSPS* (1762), 1:207.

153. Charles Wesley, "[Hymn] 661. 'Uzziah was a leper unto the day of his death.'—[II. Chron.] xxvi. 21," in *SHSPS* (1762), 1:207.

154. Charles Wesley, "[Hymn] 223. "The love of the many shall wax cold.'—[Matt.] xxiv. 12," in SHSPS (1762), 2:184.

155. Charles Wesley, "[Hymn] 659. 'When he was strong, his heart was lifted up.'—[II. Chron.] xxvi. 16," in *SHSPS* (1762),1:206. John Wesley underlined "Sinless" and "myself" in line 3 and "wholly sanctified" in line 4 of this stanza in his personal copy, commenting in the margin "Perhaps so." (The Center for Studies in the Wesleyan Tradition, Duke University, *http://divinity.duke.edu/initiatives/cswt/charles-published-verse*.)

156. Charles Wesley, "[Hymn 778.] 'God resisteth the proud, and giveth grace to the humble.'—[1 Pet.] v. 5," in *SHSPS* (1762),2:395. This is one of the verses John marked with φευ, which means "Alas!", (The Center for Studies in the Wesleyan Tradition, Duke University, *http://divinity.duke.edu/initiatives/cswt/charles-published-verse*.) In the original this hymn was improperly numbered as 777. The numbering for this and other hymns which were improperly numbered has been corrected in the text produced by The Center for Studies in the Wesleyan Tradition and has been indicated by including the hymn number in square brackets.

157. Charles Wesley, "[Hymn 829.] 'I know thy works.'—[Rev.] ii. 2," in *SHSPS* (1762),2:415.

158. Charles Wesley, "[Hymn] 32. 'A city that is set on an hill, cannot be hid.'—[Matt.] v. 14," in *SHSPS* (1762), 2:133.

159. "At nine began an hymn upon my conversion, but was persuaded to break off for fear of pride. Mr Bray coming encouraged me to proceed in spite of Satan. I prayed Christ to stand by me and finished the hymn." (Charles Wesley, May 23, 1738, *Manuscript Journal*, 1:109). For a description of false humility earlier in his life see p. 70-71 above.

160. Charles Wesley, "[Hymn] 291. 'Go home to thy friends, and tell them how great things the Lord hath done for thee, and hath had compassion on thee.'—[Mark] v. 19," in *SHSPS* (1762), 2:202.

161. Ibid. Emphasis mine.

162. Charles Wesley, Letter to Joseph Cownley (July 1, 1764), Frank Baker's transcriptions of Charles Wesley's letters, where the item is No. 372. Emphasis mine.

163. Charles Wesley, "[Hymn] 721. 'If I say, I am perfect, mine own mouth shall prove me perverse.'—[Job] ix. 20," in *SHSPS* (1762),1:228.

164. Charles Wesley, "[Hymn] 519. 'Let God be true, but every man a liar.'—[Rom.] iii. 4," in *SHSPS* (1762), 2:278-279.

165. Charles Wesley, "[Hymn 301.] ["Who fed thee in the wilderness with manna, that he might humble thee, and that he might prove thee, to do thee good at thy latter end.'—Deut. viii. 16,]" in *SHSPS* (1762),1:95-96.

166. Charles Wesley, "[Hymn 692.] ['Let us go on unto perfection.'—Heb. vi. 1,] in *SHSPS* (1762), 2:354.

167. Charles Wesley, "[Hymn] 155. 'Forthwith they sprung up, because they had no deepness of earth.'—[Matt.] xiii. 5," in *SHSPS* (1762), 2:165.

168. Charles Wesley, "Hymn [631.] 'Remembring your work of faith, and labour of love, and patience of hope.'—1 Thess. i. 3," in *SHSPS* (1762), 2:323.

169. Charles Wesley, "[Hymn] 439. 'The night cometh, when no man can work.'—[John] ix. 4," in *SHSPS* (1762), 2:253.

148   *The Heart of Charles Wesley's Theology*

    170. Charles Wesley, "[Hymn 629.] ['Mortify therefore your members ...'—Col. iii. 5,]" in *SHSPS* (1762), 2:322. See also Charles Wesley "Hymn [631.] 'Remembring your work of faith, and labour of love, and patience of hope.'—1 Thess. i. 3, in *SHSPS* (1762), 2:323-4 and Charles Wesley, "[Hymn 695.] 'And so after he had patiently endured, he obtained the promise.'—[Heb.] vi. 15," in *SHSPS* (1762), 2:356.

    171. Daub is defined: "To put on a false show; to dissemble so as to give a favourable impression." (*OED*, December 2009 online ed., s.v. "Daub.")

    172. Charles Wesley, "[Hymn] [710.] 'For ye have need of patience, that after ye have done the will of God, ye might receive the promise,'—[Heb.] x. 36," in *SHSPS* (1762),2:365-66.

    173. Ibid., 2:366.

    174. Charles Wesley, "[Hymn] 1196. 'Wilt thou not be made clean? When shall it once be?'—[Jer.] xiii. 27," in *SHSPS* (1762), 2:18.

    175. Charles Wesley, "[Hymn] 285. 'So is the kingdom of God, as if a man should cast seed into the ground . . . and the seed should spring and grow up, he knoweth not how.'—[Mark] iv. 26, 27," in *SHSPS* (1762), 2:200-201. See also Charles Wesley, "[Hymn] 294. 'The Lord thy God will put out those nations before thee by little and little: thou mayst not consume them at once.'—[Deut.] vii. 22," in *SHSPS* (1762), 1.93.

    176. Charles Wesley, "[Hymn 694.] 'Be followers of them, who through faith and patience, inherit the promises.'—[Heb.] vi. 12," in *SHSPS* (1762), 2:355-356. "John Wesley underlined 'instantaneous holiness' in his personal copy. He then wrote in the margin 'φεῦ' (a Greek exclamation of disappointment, like 'Alas!')," (The Center for Studies in the Wesleyan Tradition, Duke University, *http://divinity.duke.edu/initiatives/cswt/charles-published-verse.*)

    177. Charles Wesley, "[Hymn] 519. 'Let God be true, but every man a liar.'—[Rom.] iii. 4," in *SHSPS* (1762), 2:279.

    178. Charles Wesley, "[Hymn] 55. 'I am the Almighty God; walk before me, and be thou perfect.'—[Gen.] xvii. 1." in *SHSPS* (1762), 1:19.

    179. Charles Wesley, "[Hymn 558.] 'Do all to the glory of God.'—[1 Cor.] x. 31," in *SHSPS* (1762), 2:294. See also Charles Wesley, "[Hymn] 57. 'Is any thing too hard for the Lord?'—[Gen.] xviii. 14," in *SHSPS* (1762), 1:20 and Charles Wesley, "[Hymn] 84. 'Knock, and it shall be opened unto you.'—[Matt.] vii. 7," in *SHSPS* (1762), 2:147.

    180. Charles Wesley, "[Hymn] 233. 'As truly as I live, all the earth shall be filled with the glory of the Lord.' [Num.] xiv. 21," in *SHSPS* (1762),1.74. One of the complaints against the perfectionists was their claims of angelic perfection.

    181. Charles Wesley, "[Hymn] 1376. 'Thou wilt perform the truth to Jacob, and the mercy to Abraham, which thou hast sworn unto our fathers from the days of old.'—[Mic.] vii. 20," in *SHSPS* (1762), 2:89.

    182. Charles Wesley, "[Hymn] 1436. 'The house of David shall be as God, as the angel of the Lord.'—[Zech.] xii. 8," in SHSPS (1762), 2:110. Charles also spoke of proving angelic happiness below. (Charles Wesley, "[Hymn 867.] 'Whosoever will, let him take the water of life freely.'—[Rev.] xxii. 17," in *SHSPS* (1762), 2:431.)

    183. "The end of all perfection here, / The law fulfill'd is love." (Charles Wesley, "[Hymn] 868. "I have seen an end of all perfection, the exceeding broad commandment.' (Heb.)—[Psalm] cxix. 96," in *SHSPS* (1762),1.275) and "The honour of thy name retrieve, / And shew the world how Christians live, / When perfected in love." (Charles Wesley, [Hymn] 1065. "For mine own sake, even for mine own sake will I do it; for how should my name be polluted?'—[Isa.] xlviii. 11," in *SHSPS* (1762), 1.350.)

    184. Charles Wesley, "[Hymn] 56. 'Abraham laughed.'—[Gen.] xvii. 17," in *SHSPS* (1762),1:19.

185. "Obedient love is present heaven." (Charles Wesley, "[Hymn] 792. 'In keeping of them there is great reward.'—[Psalm] xix. 11," in *SHSPS* (1762),1:255.)

186. Charles Wesley, "[Hymn] 352. 'Moses went up to the top of Pisgah.'—[Deut.] xxxiv. 1," in *SHSPS* (1762),1:114.

187. Charles Wesley, "[Hymn] 1087. 'Is my hand shortned at all, that it cannot redeem? Or have I no power to deliver?'—[Isa.] l. 2," in *SHSPS* (1762),1:360.

188. Charles Wesley, "[Hymn] 147. 'I am the Lord that healeth thee.'—[Exod.] xv. 26," in *SHSPS* (1762),1:47.

189. "The article of death" was used by the Wesleys to refer to the moment of a persons death.

190. Charles Wesley, "[Hymn] 50. 'In thee shall all families of the earth be blessed.'—[Gen.] xii. 3," in *SHSPS* (1762),1:18. See also Charles Wesley, "[Hymn] 202. 'The Lord lift up his countenance upon thee, and give thee peace.'—[Num.] vi. 26," in *SHSPS* (1762), 1.63; Charles Wesley, "[Hymn] 805. 'And now, Lord, what is my hope?'—[Psalm] xxxix. 8," in *SHSPS* (1762), 1.258; and Charles Wesley, "[Hymn] 1110. 'The righteous perisheth, and no man layeth it to heart; and merciful men are taken away; none considering that the righteous is taken away from the evil.'—[Isa.] lvii. 1," in *SHSPS* (1762), 1.369.

191. Charles Wesley, "[Hymn 623.] "Be not moved away from the hope of the gospel.'—[Col.] i. 23," in *SHSPS* (1762), 2:319.

192. Charles Wesley, "[Hymn] 42. 'Every imagination of the thoughts of man's heart was only evil continually.'—[Gen.] vi. 5, in *SHSPS* (1762), 1:16.

193. Charles Wesley, "[Hymn 621.] 'I count not myself to have apprehended.'—[Phil.] iii. 13," in *SHSPS* (1762), 2:317.

194. Ibid.

195. Ibid.

196. Charles Wesley, "[Hymn] 301. ['Who fed thee in the wilderness with manna, that he might humble thee, and that he might prove thee, to do thee good at thy latter end.'—Deut. viii. 16,]" in *SHSPS* (1762), 1:96.

197. Charles Wesley, "[Hymn] 632. ['He died full of days, riches, and honour.'—I. Chron. xxix. 28,]" in *SHSPS* (1762),1:197. Charles expressed the same sentiment in another hymn where he said, "See then, thy soul's hard travail see, / And die, to make us all divine." (Charles Wesley, "[Hymn] 385. 'I thirst.'—John xix. 28," in *SHSPS* (1762), 2:233)

198. Charles Wesley, "[Hymn] 714. 'Behold he put no trust in his servants; and his angels he charged with folly.'—[Job] iv. 18," in *SHSPS* (1762), 1:225.

199. Charles Wesley, "[Hymn] 840. 'Shew the light of thy countenance, and we shall be whole.'—[Psalm] lxxx. 3," in *SHSPS* (1762), 1:267.

200. Charles Wesley, "[Hymn] 544. 'The fulness of the blessing of the gospel of Christ.'—[Rom.] xv. 29," in *SHSPS* (1762), 2:288. Charles also prayed that God would make him all divine. [Charles Wesley, "[Hymn] 347. 'He shall thrust out the enemy from before thee, and shall say destroy!'—[Deut.] xxxiii. 27," in *SHSPS* (1762),1:111.]

201. See pp. 78-85 above.

202. Charles Wesley, "[Hymn] 1093. 'His visage was so marred more than any man, and his form more than the sons of men.'—[Isa.] lii. 14," in *SHSPS* (1762), 1.361.

203. Charles Wesley, "[Hymn] 248. 'This is my blood, which is shed for many.'—[Matt.] xxvi. 28," in *SHSPS* (1762), 2:190; Charles Wesley, "Hymn [622.] 'Who hath made us meet to be partakers of the inheritance.'—Col. i. 12," in *SHSPS* (1762), 2:318; Charles Wesley, "[Hymn 828.] 'He laid his right hand upon me, saying unto me, Fear not; I am the first and the last.'—[Rev.] i. 17," in *SHSPS* (1762), 2:415.

204. Charles Wesley, "[Hymn] 1146. 'Behold, I create new heavens and a new earth: and the former shall not be remembered, nor come into mind. But be you glad and rejoice for ever in that which I create: for behold, I create Jerusalem a rejoicing, and her people a joy.'—[Isa.] lxv. 17, 18," in *SHSPS* (1762), 1.383.

205. Charles Wesley, "[Hymn] 316. 'I will raise them up a prophet from among their brethren, like unto thee.'—[Deut.] xviii. 18," in *SHSPS* (1762),1:100.

206. John Wesley, Sermon 63, "The General Spread of the Gospel," in *Sermons II,* in *Works*, 2:485-99.

207. Ibid., 499.

208. Charles Wesley, "[Hymn] 1075. 'Sing, O heavens; and be joyful, O earth; and break forth into singing, O mountains: for the Lord hath comforted his people, and will have mercy upon his afflicted.'—[Isa.] xlix. 13," in *SHSPS* (1762), 1:355.

209. Charles Wesley, "[Hymn] 1171. 'And it shall come to pass when ye be multiplied and increased in the land, in those days saith the Lord, they shall no more say, The ark of the covenant, &c.'—[Jer.] iii. 16," in *SHSPS* (1762), 2:8.

210. Charles Wesley, "[Hymn] 344. 'Thy will be done, as in heaven, so in earth.'—[Luke] xi. 2," in *SHSPS* (1762), 2:221.

211. Theodore Runyon has argued that for John Wesley restoration of image of God included restoration of creation. One part of his argument is that John Wesley's approach to soteriology had "*creation* and *new creation*" as bookends. According to Runyon this meant the service of those reconciled to God was a part of the transforming power of God which extended "into every aspect of both individual and social experience." (Theodore Runyon, *The New Creation*, 222-23.)

4

Methodism in Charles Welsey's Waning Years: 1763-1789

Charles Wesley continued to be active in the Methodist movement until the end of his life. In his waning years both he and his family moved to London. This move was mainly to help in the training of his musical sons. Charles continued to minister in ways reminiscent of his time at Oxford. He continued to work among the poor and the prisoners. One of Charles's last publications was a collection of hymns for malefactors.[1] In the final years of his life Charles also continued to emphasize some of the same ideas he was exposed to at Oxford. Charles continued to emphasize the necessity of having a 'single eye' and the role that suffering played in the development of a lifestyle of singleness. How Charles defined having a 'single eye' changed during this period because of his desire to raise his sons as musicians. He did not abandon the necessity of singleness, he only redefined what it meant to have a 'single eye'. His emphasis was less and less like the time at Oxford, when having a 'single eye' included remaining single and avoiding diversions.

One of Charles's most prominent roles at the end of his life was his leadership of the 'Church Methodists'. Charles continued to fight against those who wanted to separate from the Church of England. He resisted the split from the Church of England, both because he thought it would weaken the Methodists and because he thought the push for separation was motivated by pride; an attitude which he believed was contrary to being restored in the image of God.

Charles continued to fight against antinomianism, a problem he had addressed since the beginning of the revival when he began to confront both the Moravians and the Calvinistic Methodists. He struggled against antinomians by stressing that sin was defeated in the work of Christ and could be defeated in the life of the believer. He also spoke against the perfectionists and their emphasis on instantaneous perfection, because their teaching seemed to be filled with pride and denied the necessity of growth and suffering; both were traits Charles believed were a necessary part of being restored in the image of God.

Charles, like many Methodists expressed comfort in the face of dying. This was not new for Charles; he taught the Methodist idea of a 'good death' throughout his life.[2] At the same time Charles expressed a fear that he had not done enough, that he had fallen short of recovering the image of God. The comfort he expressed in the face of death came from the belief that God was long-suffering and would save him at the last hour, not from an assurance that he had recovered the image of God. This chapter will examine how Charles expressed these concepts in his letters and in MS Scriptural Hymns.

Charles Wesley's Continued Emphasis on the 'Single Eye' and Suffering

This section will examine the ways in which Charles continued to emphasize the importance of having a 'single eye' and of the necessity of suffering for the restoration of the image of God. Having a 'single eye' continued to be marked by certain behaviors. One of the most common behaviors Charles encouraged others to adopt was rising early. Specifically with his children, Charles emphasized this as part of living a disciplined life. This discipline extended beyond the spiritual and included the ordering of one's whole life. One area where Charles's commitment to having a 'single eye' was questioned during this period was his support of his sons in their pursuit of music. Some in the Methodist movement were against Samuel and Charles Jr. being involved in concerts. It will be shown how Charles reconciled what some saw as a departure from singleness to his idea of having a 'single eye' which led to being restored in the image of God.

Charles continued to refer to the one thing needful and having a 'single eye' in his correspondence.[3] In his correspondence with John Langshaw he expressed this concept by talking about seeking first the kingdom. This emphasis in some ways challenges what Charles previously meant by having a 'single eye'. For Charles, having a 'single eye' meant living an ascetic life, but Charles used the passage on seeking first the kingdom to argue that God would provide all the other things necessary. A tension between Charles's asceticism and the promise of God's provision of all things can be seen when Charles addressed the condition of John Langshaw's brother:

> If "all these things are not added unto us," we should examine ourselves. Do we seek the kingdom *First*? I fear your brother grew slack, before he grew poor. If he takes care of his soul, God will take care of his body, & of his family also.[4]

The emphasis here seems to be on meeting physical needs, not spiritual needs. During this time specifically, when Charles had a family to support, he seemed to accept that one could be single in their devotion to God and have some of the comforts and entertainments of this life. Like his earlier struggles with whether his desire to marry would cause him to lose his devotion to God, during this period he faced the question of whether he could engage in activities that were associated with the upper class with whom he and his family were now interacting in London. This tension between having a 'single eye' and being involved in activities Charles earlier rejected as diversions was most evident in the way he raised his children.

This struggle should not be seen as an abandonment of his devotion to having a 'single eye'; instead it should be seen as Charles once again accommodating or refining the application of his theology to a new situation. During this period Charles continued to encourage people to live a disciplined life. In his correspondence with the same John Langshaw, Charles stressed the importance of discipline, and chief among his admonitions was the desire that John Langshaw rise early. The importance Charles assigned to this can be seen in his conditions for John's son Jack Langshaw to take lessons from Charles Wesley Jr. Charles said he had only one condition for Jack to take lessons from Charles Wesley Jr.: "namely that he shall rise early, & study regularly."[5] Later Charles once again stressed the importance of rising early. He told John Langshaw that Jack had had difficulty rising early while in London because his music disturbed the family with which he was living. He then reminded John Langshaw of the importance he put on rising early, a discipline Charles said was good for the "Soul, body, and Estate.[6]"

> Jack cannot attain an habit of early rising here, because the family he lives with must not be disturbed by his music. You (I trust) will give him full liberty of conscience. No young man in health requires more than Seven hours sleep. Let him go to bed at Ten and rise at 5.—all the year round.—I had rather leave my children such an Habit than an Estate—but alas! these mothers—put in their thwarting oar. Always except Jack's mother & Sam's.[7]

Another example of Charles's continued emphasis on ascetic practices was his emphasis on the role of suffering and persecution in being restored in the image of God. For instance, when faced with the prospect of an invasion Charles noted that God could deliver people *from* evil, but Charles suspected that God would be more likely to deliver them *in* evil.[8] His advice to Elizabeth Briggs was more direct: "There is more work for you to do, and more affliction for you to suffer, before you are permitted to depart in peace."[9] Charles continued to associate the mercy of the Lord with suffering. In comforting Joseph Cownley at the death of his wife, Charles reminded him that this affliction was consistent with the love and mercy of God: "You shall go to her, & then know perfectly the love of your father in this severe affliction, & comprehend how all the paths of the Lord are mercy and truth."[10] At one point Charles even associated the love of the Methodists growing cold with a lack of persecution.[11] In addressing Joseph Benson's belief that the Methodist were a 'fallen people', Charles said, "You seem a little too severe, when you say: 'We are a fallen people.' The love of many is surely waxt cold; not of all. Considering we have no persecution, and so many witnesses of their own perfection, I wonder there is so much life left among us."[12] Note that it was not only a lack of persecution, but also the witnesses to perfection which concerned Charles Wesley.

During the waning years of Charles's life, he continued to emphasize the need to have a 'single eye'. How this was defined seems to change during this period of his life, primarily because of his role as a father. He continued to stress the importance of rising early and of the need of suffering for a person to be restored in the image of God. He even questioned whether the lack of persecution had contributed to a loss of love in the Methodist community. In his role as a father he was challenged once again to redefine what he meant by a 'single eye', because of his desire to see his sons as accomplished musicians. This will be explored in the next section.

The Single Eye and Music

Charles and Sarah Wesley's two sons, Charles and Samuel, were both gifted musicians. Joseph Kelway[13] may even have preferred Charles's playing to his own.[14] The difficulty for Charles was how to raise such a musically gifted child. Charles initially refused to let Charles take a place at the Chapel Royal, because as Gareth Lloyd said, "the boy's father . . . had no intention of raising his son to be a musician."[15] Charles eventually changed his mind, and by 1769 Charles Wesley, Jr. was playing a concert on Prince Street in Bristol. Two years later the family moved to London so that Charles and Samuel could receive a musical education.[16]

A concert on Prince Street in 1769 became a point of contention between Charles Wesley and some of the people in Bristol.[17] The problem with this concert was that it was seen as a diversion from things that were important. Eleanor Laroche wrote as if she was in favor of the changes brought about by Charles's playing on Prince Street, but one is left wondering if she was not being sarcastic throughout the letter. She began with a statement supporting the recent concert on Prince Street: "The alliance which is at length so happily formed between the Horsefair and Prince Street will, without doubt be attended with the most desirable consequences." In other words, in her opinion, Methodism (Horsefair) had now been joined with the world (Prince Street). Laroche argued that Charles Wesley, Jr.'s concert on Prince Street indicated that Charles Wesley had now accepted diversions. To Laroche these diversions included not only concerts, but also other entertainment such as plays, tragedies, and games. Her stated goal was to encourage Charles to quit preaching against such diversions now that his son was involved in playing a concert on Prince Street.[18] The second letter was written by an anonymous Quaker. The stated intention of this author is clear; the recent performance of Charles was not consistent with Charles's position as expressed in his writing, preaching, and public declarations about the necessity of living a holy life. This author also believed the concert did not glorify God. Her most biting criticism was to remind Charles of the example of Eli and his sons.[19] Charles responded, "I do remember Eli; & excuse a Quaker for seeing no difference between incouraging my Son in music, or incouraging him in Rapine & Adultery."[20] The third letter was written to the society at Bristol. Unlike the previous two letters we only have

Charles's response in this letter. As such it primarily focuses on Charles's defense of his actions. He began by acknowledging the problem he intended to address in this letter: "I understand, my brethren, that some serious persons, both in the Society and out of it, were troubled at my Son's lately playing at a Concert."[21] What is implied in these letters was that this change of behavior was inconsistent with having a 'single eye', that Charles was stepping outside the practice currently accepted by Methodists in Bristol. Allowing or even encouraging his son to play a concert was seen as a new behavior which departed from the practices of the society at Bristol. Both the Quaker and the society of Bristol associated this new behavior with an acceptance of worldliness.

One of the ways people pointed out that this was a departure from Charles's earlier position was to point to two of his hymns published in 1749. The first hymn, written to promote the watch-night services, is entitled, "Innocent Diversions."[22] The first verse deals with pursuing Christian pleasures in the night because the day is too short. Charles then argued against other more harmful pleasures saying that those who engage in them became "slaves of excess." In pursuing these pleasures people seek to please their senses and throw off all the restraints of sobriety. Charles applied this specifically to drunkards and those who misused their time by going to the theater, the masque, and the ball. Charles then returned to the watch-night service and asked whether that was not a better use of a person's time.[23]

A second hymn people used to argue that Charles's position had changed was "The True Use of Musick."[24] Charles began the hymn by arguing against the misuse of music. He argued that music could be misused to lead people into sin. Although this was an important part of the hymn, his overriding purpose was a plea for the recovery of music's virtue; to "rescue the holy pleasure." The rest of the hymn argued for a true use of music, which was praising Christ the King. Laroche mentioned this hymn in her letter as an example of a hymn that she called an "enthusiastick Rhapsody." Charles took this to mean that she thought he was an enemy of music. Charles responded with a question, "Can any impartial reader of the latter ["The True Use of Music"] think us enemies to music? No; it is not the use but the abuse of it we condemn." Laroche's criticism was primarily focused on verse 4:

> 4 The civiller croud,
> In theatres proud,
> Acknowledge his power,
> And Satan in nightly assemblies adore:
> To the masque and the ball
> They fly at his call;
> Or in pleasures excel,
> And chaunt in a grove* to the harpers of hell.[25]

The final phrase, "the harpers of hell" drew the most attention. Laroche argued there was really no difference between "the hellish harpers of Vauxhall and the performers at the assembly room, than between the enthusiastick ravings of a Methodist preacher in the Field and the same jargon vented in a Room in the Horse-fair." In other words, all of these were forms of entertainment. Charles's response to Laroche about this criticism was to note that some, but not all, musicians might deserve the title "the harpers of hell."[26] Charles expanded on his defense of this language in his letter to the society of Bristol. Charles argued that there may be heavenly as well as hellish harpers. What he was resisting in the phrase hellish harpers was those who used their music to encourage drunkenness or even worse vices. He believed there were not many musicians of this type: "Therefore the term is too general and liable to be misunderstood. For which reason I have altered it long ago as you will find, if the hymn is ever reprinted."[27]

Charles not only corrected what he argued was a misunderstanding of this hymn, he also noted positive ways in which he had been a supporter of music. "I was always a lover of music. So was my brother: and you ought to thank God for this very thing. He has been pleased to make good use of vocal music among us. Our hymns have helped to spread the gospel: God himself has owned, and applied them to many of your hearts."[28] Another argument Charles used to show his support and appreciation of music was to talk about the music of Handel. In one letter he quoted several lines from "The Messiah" and said these lines and many more "carries a mind above anything in this world—and I know for himself [Handel] his subject exalted him."[29]

Charles explained why he raised Charles and Samuel as musicians in a letter to the society at Bristol. Charles said it was his intention to raise his sons for clergymen, and that that would be his first choice, but from the earliest days it was clear that nature marked them for musicians. Charles then argued it was the duty of a parent to attend to the natural bent of their children. Instead of forcing his children into a certain profession he was acting in accordance to the wise saying of Mr. Dodd, "give your son a trade and the Bible, and leave him to the grace of God."[30] He even overstated his son Charles's desire to be a musician when he told the people of Bristol, "There is no way to hinder his being a Musician but to cut off his fingers."[31] Charles also noted that it was not for pleasure, but to earn their bread that Charles and Samuel were pursuing becoming musicians. When Charles went to play or perform in a concert it was not as a diversion, but as a part of his business; it was his trade. Charles also noted that both Mr. Whitefield and his brother John had no objections to his son being a musician.[32] Maybe Charles's most important claim was that he had with a good conscience and a 'single eye' brought up his sons as musicians. Charles answered what he saw as their concern, that he in some way was abandoning the pursuit of having a 'single eye'.

In spite of the defense he presented of his actions, it seems that Charles had redefined what it meant to have a 'single eye', just as he had redefined it when he chose to marry Sarah Gwynne. Both of these behaviors would have been rejected by John and Charles in their earlier years. These behaviors would not have been in line with how they defined having a 'single eye' when they were 'Oxford Methodists'.[33]

Charles Wesley's Instructions to his Children

One of the richest sources of information about how Charles presented being restored in the image of God during the later stages of his life are the letters to his children. In these letters he provided guidance for them in their Christian faith. That his general idea of the Christian faith had remained unchanged since the first visible glimmers of that faith can be seen in the following passage to Sally.

> That you gained by the despised Methodist, if nothing more, the knowledge of what True Religion consists in; namely, in Happiness & Holiness; in Peace & Love; in the Favor & Image of God restored; in Paradise regained; in a Birth from above, a Kingdom within you; a Participation of the Divine Nature. The principal means or Instrument of this is Faith; which Faith is the Gift of God, given to every one that asketh.
>
> The two grand Hindrances of Prayer & consequently of faith are Self-Love and Pride: therefore our Lord so strongly enjoins us [to] Self-denial & Humility. 'If any man will come after me, let him deny himself & take up his cross daily & follow me.' And—'How CAN ye believe who *receive honour* one of another, and seek not the honor which cometh from God *only*?' Here you see Pride is an insurmountable Obstacle to believing. Yet the desire of praise is inseparable from our fallen nature. All we can do, till faith comes, is Not to seek it; not to indulge our own will; not to neglect the means of attaining faith & forgiveness, especially private prayer & the scripture.[34]

This passage touches on several themes which have been a consistent part of Charles's definition of being restored in the image of God. The overall emphasis reflects the theology of Scougal.[35] Like Scougal, Charles informed his daughter that he was defining 'true religion'. This 'true religion' was "a Participation of the Divine Nature." The principal means of this 'true religion' was faith. The branches were love of God and neighbor, purity, and humility. Charles specifically mentioned love, but he did not differentiate between love of God and love of neighbor in this short passage. His primary concern throughout the passage seems to be to encourage a godly humility. One of the major obstacles to prayer and to faith was pride. He touched briefly on the need for purity or having a 'single eye' in this letter with his reference to taking up the cross daily. In another letter Charles stressed the necessity of having a 'single eye'. He encouraged Sally to be fully devoted to God:

> In the sacrament you renew yr baptismal Covenant: and devote yourselves <u>intirely</u> to God. It is much easier to be <u>wholly</u> his then partially. He refuses a divided heart. 'A double minded man is unstable in all his ways.' Yet most Christians (so called) halt between God & the world. They are so much as <u>almost</u> Christians.[36]

Charles not only reflected Scougal's definition of true religion, he also included several other things associated with being restored in the image of God. He included the idea that the restoration occurred in two steps when he mentioned receiving first the favor (justification) and then the image (sanctification). He referred to recapitulation when he noted a paradise regained. He also stressed the importance of using the means of grace, specifically prayer and reading the Scripture. Later in this letter he referred to rising early, one of the habits associated with purity (or having a 'single eye') in Methodism. Charles also mentioned two authors who had formed his idea of Christian discipline since Oxford: Thomas á Kempis and William Law.[37] These examples show that Charles continued to focus on the same definition of true religion as he had while at Oxford. What may have changed was how he applied these definitions.

Charles Wesley's Continued Support of The Church of England

John's decision to ordain ministers for America had, according to Charles, already assured that the Methodist preachers would become dissenters. Because of Charles's commitment to the church of England this development angered him. According to Charles, John's ordinations had guaranteed that 70,000 Church of England people would become dissenters.[38] Charles's fear was that after John had ordained people in America, his preachers in England "would never rest till you [John] ordained them."[39] His frustration with John 'turning Presbyterian' can be seen in one of his most cynical comments: "J[ohn] W[esley] the Schismatic Grandson to J[ohn] W[estley] the Regicide! How woud this disturb (if they were capable of being disturbed) my Father & Brother in Paradise!"[40] Charles's frustration with John can also be seen in the motivation he assigned to John's actions. Instead of being open and honest, Charles accused John of being deceitful.

> But why did he not, at first, fairly and plainly avow his Design to make all the Meth(odist)s Dissenters, & to leave them under the Episcopal Care & Government of Dr. C[oke]? because he intended to do it by degrees, secretly & imperceptibly, i.e. To <u>betray</u> them into a Separation! Alas! alas! Where is Simplicity & Godly Sincerity.[41]

Charles pledged he would use all the means in his power "to save the poor Methodist from the Sin of Schism."[42]

One result of this was that Charles began to renounce some of the critical statements he had once made and printed against the Church of England. One of the reasons he did this was because his brother John was using his statements against him. John told Charles, "For these forty years I have been in doubt concerning that question, 'What obedience is due to "heathenish priests, and mitred infidels"?'"[43] Charles responded that he now renounced what he called "That juvenile line of mine." The line, "Heathenish Priest, and mitred infidels" was a line he used based on one account of a mitred infidel, and even that example was not his own, but based on the testimony of Mr. Law.[44] Charles now renounced some of his critical comments referring to the Church of England, because he feared they were being used to justify separation from the Church of England. Charles resisted a split from the Church of England because of his continued support of

Potter's ecclesiology as stated in his book on church government.⁴⁵ More importantly, he thought the split would weaken Methodism. He associated the success of Methodism with their loyalty and support of the Church of England. He wrote, "The Meth(odis)ts are a Part, & but a Part, of that Remnant: & they have prospered, because they love our Jerusalem. If they ever lose their love for her, they will come to nothing."⁴⁶

Although Charles wrote to John about his "Hatred of Methodism," he noted that in addition to his attachment to the Church of England he still had an appreciation of some of the parts of Methodism. He shared with John how he had recently proclaimed these commitments:

> I spoke largely of my Attachment to the Church & you; of my Hatred of Methodism; not the Gospel we preach, not the Rules of our Society, every one of wch has its use; but of the Independant [sic] Scheme—the Selfish Spirit of Separation & Rebellion.—I shewed them nothing coud save them from splitting into 20 Sects, but their keeping together as at the first & continuing steadfast in the Church of E[ngland].⁴⁷

Here Charles made it clear that he still valued some of the practices of Methodism (he mentioned specifically the Gospel they preached and the rules of the societies), but despite his appreciation of these practices, Charles proclaimed his "Hatred of Methodism." This "Hatred of Methodism" was one result of the push to separate from the Church of England, according to Charles, a move driven by selfishness and pride. Later in the same letter Charles reiterated the source of the problem: "there is a Spirit of Independency, a Spirit of pride & Self-seeking, which has more or less infected the body of preachers."⁴⁸ Both of these quotations support the idea that Charles still saw pride as one of the major problems behind the desire for separation. In MS Hymns for Preachers Extraordinary, Charles warned that pride was the only thing that could lead to separation, not only from God, but from each other:

> 4 Pride, only pride can cause divorce,
>   Can separate 'twixt o[u]r souls and Thee;
> Pride, only pride is discord's source,
>   The bans of peace and charity:
> But us it never, Lord, shall part,
> For Thou art greater than our heart.
>
> 5 Wherefore to thine almighty hand
>   The keeping of our hearts we give,
> Firm in one mind and spirit stand,
>   To Thee, and to each other cleave,
> Fix'd on the Rock w[hi]ch cannot move,
> And meekly safe in humble Love.⁴⁹

Charles's disappointment with those who sought to separate from the Church of England should not be taken as a complete rejection of Methodism, but only of those who sought to separate. In 1779 he told his brother,

I assured them [the society at Bristol], I love the gracious preachers; [that is] almost all of them— the best of any persons upon earth;— that I looked upon them as the greatest blessing to this nation, and the greatest friends to the Church of England, &c., and that I had it in my heart to live and die with them.[50]

Charles continued to work against those who desired to separate from the Church of England. During this stage of his life one of the biggest challenges he faced was with his brother's ordinations. John's decision to ordain brought some of the most cynical comments from Charles's lips. Charles was convinced that those who desire to separate were guilty of the sin of schism and were motivated by pride. These behaviors were not consistent with Charles's definition of being restored in the image of God as love of neighbor and humility. His commitment to being restored in the image of God played a role in his resistance to those who wanted to separate from the Church of England. Charles's commitment to being restored in the image of God also impelled his continued rejection of antinomianism.

Charles Wesley's Continued Rejection of Antinomianism

The conflict between Calvinistic and Wesleyan Methodism began early in the revival and continued throughout Charles's lifetime. It was especially prominent in the early 1770's.[51] Once again the problem with Calvinistic Methodism was its antinomianism. The person most prominent in this debate was John Fletcher. Fletcher was held up as a model by Charles Wesley. Fletcher was an example in the way he carried out the ministry, specifically in the way he examined the members of the society, the way he stressed family religion, and in the way that he gave instruction from house to house.[52] This expression of support for Fletcher was in response to the question of whether or not there should be less preaching. Charles does not answer that question; instead he said there should be more doing and listed the traits listed above which he attributed to Fletcher.[53]

Charles also supported Fletcher because of his writing. Charles stated his approval of Fletcher's *Checks to Antinomianism*.[54] Charles told John Fletcher, "My Bror & I read your Third Check together: and approve the whole."[55] In another letter, Charles praised Fletcher's writing, saying that his fourth check would turn even the elect into doubters of election. In this letter he also noted that it was John's ministry "both to write & preach ag[ain]s[t] Antinomianism, alias Calvinism."[56]

Charles's continued disdain for Calvinism, and specifically the way Calvinism led to antinomianism, can be seen in a letter to his daughter Sally.[57] In the letter he favorably compared a Roman Catholic to a Calvinist. His purpose in this comparison was to warn Sally not to follow the path he saw Lady Huntingdon following. According to Charles Wesley, the Lady was becoming too antinomian. He told Sally, "A sensible Roman-catholic is above a match for any Calvinist. Her Ladyship approaches too near the Antinomian Extreme."[58]

Each of these passages show that Charles continued to reject any antinomian approach. As noted above, one of the main reasons was the importance Charles assigned to the means of grace. In the same letter that Charles praised Fletcher's 'more doing', he noted the work being done by the master at Kingswood: "There is life both there and here. Several have been lately quickened; one in baptism, others in the Lord's Supper, & in the word."[59]

Charles Wesley on Dying Well

As Charles approached the end of his life, he continued to stress the necessity of recovering the image of God. In a letter to Samuel Lloyd, in which he noted the shortness of their time left on earth, he encouraged Lloyd to "lose no time to secure the one thing needful."[60] Later he encouraged Lloyd to go forward to the death all must face "in his Image, & be no more seen in this miserable Vale."[61] Charles also spoke of waking "up after his Likeness, & seeing Him as He is"[62] and of being satisfied when he woke "up after his likeness (& not before)."[63] These three letters indicate Charles's focus on recovering the image and likeness of Christ, even in the face of death.

There were two major attitudes Charles expressed as he neared the end of life. First, he expressed his comfort with dying. He told his son Charles, "Tell Sally— I have not the least Objection to her closing my eyes and Laying me with my five children."[64] He expressed a similar sentiment in comforting John Langshaw and his wife on the loss of a loved one: "I hope, your Partner has found Him who comforteth the afflicted. She has always David's Comfort 'I shall go to Him.' [II Samuel 12:23] I have five children waiting for me in one grave. The days of our mourning will soon be ended."[65]

The second major attitude was his fear that he had fallen short of recovering the image of God. He shared this fear with Samuel Lloyd:

> The Good I wish you, & myself, is A recovery of the Favour & Image of God. But how unlike Him am I at ye close of life! How precious our are few remaining moments! Shall we lose our last stake? Then our we lost forever! But He bids us reckon yt his long-suffering is our salvation. Let us believe this practically, & yield to be saved as at the eleventh hour.[66]

Although Charles expressed his fear that he had fallen short and as a result might lose his last stake, he continued to hope in a God who was long-suffering. His hope was that he would recover the image of God in the final hour or at the moment of death.

The Theology of Charles Wesley in MS Scriptural Hymns

The collection of hymns used for this period of Charles's life is different than those used in the previous sections. Unlike the earlier collections, this one was never published by Charles. There is one indication that Charles may have been considering publishing this collection—Charles attached his proposal for publishing *HSP* (1749) to the inside cover of this manuscript. It is probable that this was a collection of poems Charles had written over time because the flyleaf has a date of May 11, 1783, the first page of the New Testament has the date May 18, 1783, and at the end of the collection Charles has noted, "Finished May 26, 1783."[67] It seems unlikely that Charles could have composed 254 hymns that fill 267 pages in such a short time. This manuscript is relatively free of corrections, another indication that they are probably copied from another source. Even if they are copied from another source, they are an example of the way Charles would have presented his theology in the waning years of his life.

It will be argued that Charles continued to emphasize the necessity of having a 'single eye' in this collection. Charles also included poems which seemed directed at those who had embraced antinomianism and perfectionism. In this collection Charles continued to present restoration in the image of God in terms consistent with recapitulation and *theosis*.

Charles Wesley's Continued Emphasis on having a 'Single Eye'

As has been noted above, Charles Wesley came under fire for the way he was raising his sons. Some accused Charles of abandoning his commitment to having a 'single eye'. Charles's embrace of musical training for his sons was a diversion others in Methodism still rejected. In spite of this apparent embrace of diversions, Charles continued to stress the necessity of having a 'single eye'. This emphasis was still marked by an emphasis on asceticism, an emphasis which was a part of Methodism from its beginnings at Oxford. The ascetic emphasis can be seen in those things he was willing to resign or give up in his pursuit of God. In order to gain the life of God, Charles wrote that one needed to be willing to resign every creature to find their all in God.[68] This included renouncing all of one's 'idols'; all those things which caused a person to miss "the riches of [God's] pardoning grace."[69] Charles noted that both empty pleasures and lust were behaviors that could lead a person away from a desire for God alone.[70] Charles also mentioned the dangers of riches, empty enjoyments, and the "rational good." Engaging in these behaviors meant settling for the shadows of this life. These commitments are present in a poem reflecting on Jeremiah 4:14, "Wash thine heart, that thou mayst be saved: how long shall thy vain thoughts lodge within thee?"

> [1.] Man, foolish and impotent man,
>   Attach'd to the things that appear,
> He pants for a shadow in vain,

A shadow of happiness here!
His wants with his riches increase
   His labour and burthen of mind,
And mock'd by the objects he sees,
   He seeks what he never can find.

2. If curst with his wish, he obtains
   His height of ambition below,
With empty injoyments he gains
   Vexation, and sorrow, and woe:
His spirit in bitterness groans,
   Or'ewhelm'd by a mountain of care;
His folly, defeated, he owns,
   And sinks in a gulph of despair.

3. If rational good he desire,
   He misses his laudable end;
Nor wisdom its aim can acquire,
   Or virtue insure us a friend:
No blessing on this side the skies
   Can merit our love or esteem,
When Virtue is pride in disguise,
   And friendship itself is a dream.[71]

One way Charles emphasized the need to be single in one's desire was to speak of purity. Reflecting on Job 14:4, "Who can bring a clean *thing* out of an unclean? not one," Charles contrasted becoming pure with "filthy thoughts" and "unrighteousness."[72] In a later poem on the same passage Charles asked for a pure love to expel "This fleshly filthiness." One reason people failed to be made pure was a reliance on their own work, instead of relying on God's work.

2. This filthiness of pride
   Mocks all our efforts vain,
The plague we from each other hide
   Will in our hearts remain:
Corruption's fountain spreads
   Throughout our lives unclean,
Defiles our thoughts, and words, and deeds,
   Till all we are is sin.[73]

Charles stressed that God's work purified a person. He also taught that God's presence was a part of the process. Charles pointed to the work of Jesus on the cross as a part of the purifying process. The "sprinkling of the blood" purified the heart from lust, self, and pride.[74] Although this was applied by God, Charles wrote that a person was able to rise and wash away their sins by the word. He also emphasized the necessity of praying for the blood to have its full effect. Once again Charles emphasized both God's part and the necessary response of those seeking to be made clean. What finally drove out all the selfish and vain desires was the very presence of God:

> 4. Selfish and vain desires in me
>   Shall never more reside,
> When Thou with all thy purity
>   Dost in my heart reside;
> Thy uttermost salvation then
>   I in thy presence prove,
> The crown of righteousness obtain,
>   The heights and depths of love.[75]

Throughout this collection Charles emphasized the presence of God and at times even talked about being lost in God, concepts which are closely related to the doctrine of *theosis*.[76] This same concept is applied to the work and presence of the Holy Ghost in a reflection on Acts 15:8-9:

> [1.] If God the holy Ghost impart,
>   The living faith bestow,
> His Spirit purifies the heart
>   And makes us white as snow;
> The heart that in his Son believes,
>   Is purg'd from every stain,
> And he who still to Jesus cleaves
>   Needs never sin again.
>
> 2. O woud my gracious God confer
>   The Spirit of faith on me,
> A foul, desponding sinner chear
>   By peace and purity!
> Father, in me reveal thy love
>   If reconcil'd Thou art,
> And all the filth of sin remove,
>   And keep my sprinkled heart.
>
> 3. The heart which in thy Son confides
>   No longer is unclean,
> Where Purity himself abides
>   It must be pure from sin:
> O may he dwell by faith in mine
>   And thus himself explain
> The real Holiness divine,
>   The perfect Love in man![77]

Charles continued not only to warn about the dangers of behaviors contrary to the life of purity noted above, he continued to proclaim the one thing necessary was to know and desire Jesus above all other things. This included the desire to be joined with God noted above, to seek not the gifts of God, but the very presence of God.[78] Charles's desire to pursue the presence of God can be seen in this poem; he desired the Comforter more than the consolation he could receive:

> [1.] My longing heart's desire
>   Is to its Maker known,

> Thou seest it now aspire,
>   Jesus, to Thee alone:
> The one thing necessary,
>   For Thee alone I pine:
> On earth I only tarry
>   To know, that Thou art mine.
>
> 2. More than the consolation
>   The Comforter I want:
> O God of my salvation,
>   In me thyself implant:
> With infinite expansion
>   My spirit pants for Thee
> And swells to be thy mansion
>   Thro' all eternity.[79]

It seems clear that Charles's definition of singleness as purity continue throughout his whole life. Those things he first embraced at Oxford continued to define his theology at the end of his life. He continued to have an ascetic emphasis, although what this required was modified both by his marriage and in the way he raised his children. He continued to emphasize purity as desiring God above all other things. He also continued to use images of recapitulation and *theosis* to describe what it meant to be restored in the image of God. The means by which one became pure were almost exclusively tied to the presence of God in this collection. This does not deny a necessary response from people, but prayer and the use of the other means of grace were an avenue through which one could experience the presence of God and in the end, be lost in God.

Restoration in the Image of God as a Check to Antinomianism and Perfectionism

Charles continued to address the dangers of antinomianism and perfectionism in MS Scriptural Hymns. It will be shown that Charles spoke a message of hope against the antinomians (it was possible to be restored in the image of God) and a word of warning to the perfectionists (it was a sign of pride to proclaim that one had become perfect).

Charles continued to stress the importance of the marks or fruits of belief. To the one who claimed that the image had been stamped upon their heart Charles wrote, "He hears unmoved, and waits to see / The fruit, and then discern the tree."[80] These words addressed both extremes. To those who claimed they were restored in the image of God because of their belief, Charles argued that their faith would be known by their fruits. To the perfectionist who claimed a present knowledge of being marked with the image of God he argued for a process of restoration with the most important fruit being patience. Charles began by implying the need for patience: "The faithful soul doth not make haste / To judge, or think, to speak, or do."[81] In the last verse he made clear that the one uncontested fruit, which proved faith, was patience:

> 6. Cautious in all his works and deeds,
>   He dares on God alone rely,
> With calm, deliberate step proceeds
>   The spirits, and himself, to try,
> Patience the uncontested sign
> Which slowly proves his faith divine.[82]

In a reflection on I John 3:6, "Whosoever sinneth hath not known Him," Charles once again stressed the necessity of being freed from sin on the one hand, but on the other hand he noted that it was a work that would never be completed in this life, that in one sense it was a completed work, yet in another sense it was something that needed to be constantly pursued.

> Lord, unto me the knowledge grant
>   Which, incompatible with sin,
> Supplies my spirit's every want,
>   Brings the celestial nature in,
> My heart renews and purifies,
> And fills with life that never dies.
>
> 2. I want the faith in Jesus blood
>   Which pardon on my conscience seals,
> Imparts the spotless mind of God,
>   The plague original expels,
> Doth all my unbelief remove,
> And sweetly work by perfect love.
>
> 3. I woud be of thy Spirit born,
>   And find, that I can sin no more:
> My soul into thy likeness turn,
>   Wisdom of God, and Truth, and Power
> Fulness of the Divinity,
> Jesus appear, and dwell in me.
>
> 4. Then, only then my God I know,
>   Divinely taught, divinely pure,
> Yet onward to perfection go,
>   And happy to the end endure
> Till faith is swallow'd up in sight
> In glorious, full, eternal Light.[83]

In the first three verses, Charles once again emphasized the possibility of being purified from sin by the blood of Jesus and the work of the Holy Spirit. Once again the "Fullness of the Divinity" dwelling in the believer made the deliverance from sin possible. Charles indicated that this purity was incomplete in the final lines of the last verse. He did this after emphasizing the possibility of being pure in the first three verses and even noted that one could be divinely pure in verse four. However, the last four lines of verse four emphasize the gradual nature of being restored in the image of God. This would only be completed in eternity when "faith is swallowed up in sight / In glorious, full, eternal Light."[84] This poem once again stressed the possibility of being restored in opposition to those with antinomian tendencies, and at the same time stressed the incomplete or progressive nature of that restoration in opposition to those with perfectionistic tendencies.

Charles also addressed the error of antinomianism by focusing on the ability to become spotless and sinless. Part of what was accomplished in Christ's death was that the burden of original sin was destroyed.[85] According to Charles, this allowed a person to overcome the besetting sin and to find complete freedom from sin. Charles continued to emphasize that this was possible only by being attentive to the means of grace and by working out one's salvation. One of the key passages in developing these themes was I John 3:5-6, 8.[86] Reflecting on I John 3:5, "He was manifested, to take away our sins," Charles argued that Jesus' incarnation was in vain unless sin was defeated in the life of the believer:

> O Son of God, in vain
> Wast Thou reveal'd below,
> Unless Thou by thy Spirit again
> Thyself to sinners show:
> Before thy presence here
> Unless my sins depart,
> And Thou the pardning God appear
> To this poor, guilty heart.[87]

This poem focused not on Christ's death but on his incarnation, specifically focusing on the theme of recapitulation, that God became man in order that people could become like God:

> 3. Didst thou not leave thy throne,
> For a mean house of clay,
> And put my feeble nature on,
> To take my sins away?
> Fulfil thy own design,
> The hindring thing remove,
> That God and man in Thee may join,
> And I my Saviour love.[88]

Charles associated the incarnation of Christ with the work of the Spirit. Although the work of restoration began with the incarnation of Christ, it could only be completed in the life of the believer by the presence of the Spirit. Charles associated the presence of the Spirit in the believer with the presence of Jesus. Jesus' presence in the work of the Spirit delivered a person from sin:

> 6. It cannot be thy will
> That I unsav'd shoud live
> Wretched in sin continue still,
> And still thy Spirit grieve;

168 *The Heart of Charles Wesley's Theology*

> But till Thyself I know
> From sin I cannot cease:
> Jesus, appear, thy mercy show,
> And bid me die in peace.[89]

A second poem on this verse argued that sin could not reside in God's presence. In this poem Charles prayed that the presence of the Savior would remove his unbelief and allow him to live in spotless purity like his Savior:

> 2. Come then, O my Saviour, come,
> All this unbelief consume,
> By the Spirit of thy grace
> By the brightness of thy face:
> That I may be clean in heart,
> That I may be as Thou art,
> Live, my spotless Purity,
> Live, my perfect Love, in me.[90]

Charles's reflections on I John 3:6, "Whosoever sinneth hath not known Him," also stressed that the presence of God removed sin. As was shown above, Charles focused on the blood of Christ or the crucifixion instead of the incarnation in this poem. Charles listed several things which resulted from faith "in Jesus blood / which pardon on my conscience seals." A person received "the spotless mind of God," original sin was expelled, unbelief was removed, and the person worked by perfect love. According to verse three this happened when a person was born of the Spirit. As was noted above, although a person could be divinely pure after being born of the Spirit, that person still needed to go on to perfection.[91]

In the last poem from this section in I John, Charles expressed both the seeming impossibility of being freed from sin and his hope that it was true because he saw it as a promise of God. In the first two verses Charles stated his doubts. He asked, "But must my heart, to sin inclin'd, / Inclin'd to sin for ever be?" He also asked if salvation would only come at the very end and that he would be, "saved by fire, if saved at last?"[92] His statement of doubt was stated even stronger in the second verse:

> 2. Most wretched of the fallen race,
>   I must, O Lord, that life abide,
> If all thy blood cannot efface
>   Th' ingrafted filth of self and pride;
> And if the dire original stain
>   In purest saints is always found,
> Thy hallowing blood was shed in vain,
>   And sin doth more than grace abound.[93]

He answered these doubts with a question in verse three. Did God intend to save people from all iniquity here? His answer in verse four was that he would trust in the upmost power of God even if others were willing to accept just a taste of God's love. What is surprising is how Charles concluded this poem. In a poem that stressed the possibility of being restored in the image of God in the face of doubts, Charles confronted those who claimed that they had received or "attain'd a glorious prize." Their error was not that they believed it was possible, but that it was possible in an instant:

> 5. What tho' ten thousand witnesses
>   Deceiving, and deceiv'd, arise,
> Suborn'd by Satan to profess
>   "They *have* attain'd the glorious prize,["]
> Who fancy sin at once destroy'd,
>   Subservient to the fiend's design,
> They cannot make thy promise void,
>   Or falsify the Oath Divine.
>
> 6. Let them who will the truth oppose,
>   The truth of God for ever stands,
> Redeem'd from all, from *all* my foes,
>   I shall perform thy just commands;
> The faithful saying of my Lord
>   I with simplicity receive,
> And saved in deed, and thought, and word
>   Shall soon in all thy image live.[94]

As has already been noted in the poem above, Charles continued to speak against those who claimed that they were already perfect or pure. He argued that those who claimed perfection were a stumbling block for the Church and they were in danger of eternal judgment because of their pride:

> If bold the highest place I claim
>   My own perfection testify,
> Insist, that a pure saint I am
>   And cannot fall, and cannot die
> Is it a great mistake, or small?
> A fault that stumbles none? or all?
>
> 2. I thus the pious Jew offend,
>   Who trembles at a God unknown,
> Darkness I make the heathen blend
>   With light, and all condemn for one,
> The weak I hurt, the lame mislead,
> And grieve the Israelites indeed.
>
> 3. But chiefly thro' my pride of heart,
>   Great God, I vex thy glorious eyes,
> And force thy Spirit to depart,
>   Till cast, like Satan, from the skies,
> I cry to Him that stain'd the tree,
> To save incarnate fiends like me.[95]

170   *The Heart of Charles Wesley's Theology*

He also continued to confront the perfectionists because their becoming perfect in a moment did not leave room for suffering. Charles argued their claim of perfection cut short the work of God and negated the need to grow and suffer in their pursuit of perfection:

> Because his self-deceit I show,
> Am I the self-deceiver's foe,
> When on the pinnacle of pride
> He sits, as wholly sanctified?
> Or woud I rob him of his crown
> Who gently bring the boaster down?
>
> 2. Ye great and good in your own eyes,
> Who instantaneous saints arise,
> Without the Spirit's throes or groans
> Born babes, and full-grown men at once,
> To God's own oracles attend,
> The counsels of your heavenly Friend.
>
> 3. Deny yourselves, the cross embrace
> And walk in all his righteous ways,
> With lawful violence contend,
> Thro' all the means expect the End,
> From strength to strength go on to prove
> The truth of grace is humble love.[96]

So even at the end of his life Charles continued to challenge the beliefs of antinomians and perfectionists. He taught that the antinomians had stopped short of being restored in the image of God because of their beliefs that sin could not be defeated in this life. At the same time he challenged the claims of the perfectionists. Their proclamations of having attained perfection were marked by pride and denied the need for grow and suffering. Charles's commitment to humility was a check to those who claimed to have attained perfection, and his commitment to purity or having a 'single eye' was a check to those who did not act out their faith in Christ through the means of grace.

Conclusion

In the waning years of Charles's life he continued to emphasize the necessity of being restored in the image of God. This emphasis continued to reflect the theology of restoration he discovered while at Oxford. Like Scougal, Charles continued to define restoration and image of God as a dependence upon God marked by purity (or a 'single eye'), humility, and the love of God and neighbor. The major challenge he faced during the last period of his life was how to define having a 'single eye' when it came to raising his children. Although many challenged the way he allowed his sons to pursue music, Charles continued to claim his commitment to having a 'single eye'. This can be seen not only in the way he addressed the issue with the people at Bristol, but also in the way he instructed his children.

Charles also continued to support the Church of England and to fight against those who desired to leave the Church of England. Among the many reasons for his support was his commitment to the means of grace and his perception that the push for a split from the Church of England was motivated by pride. Charles also opposed those who denied the need to work out one's salvation. Charles's support for Fletcher and his writing during the conflict between Calvinistic and Wesleyan Methodism in the early 1770's also illustrated his commitment to the means of grace.

As Charles approached the end of his life, he sometimes expressed doubts. Although he expressed comfort in the face of dying he also feared that he had fallen short of recovering the image of God. His recourse was to express hope in a God who was long-suffering and the probability that he would be saved at the last hour.

Charles's hymns and poems during this time support what has been noted in his writing. Charles continued to emphasize the necessity of having a 'single eye'. This included not only the denial of many worldly things but also the pursuit of God. The presence of God was necessary for a person to fulfill this pursuit. Charles continued to use the images of *theosis* and recapitulation to express this theology.

Charles's poetry also confronted both the antinomians and the perfectionists. He confronted the antinomians with his message of hope and the possibility of being restored in the image of God, even though he seems to have doubts about his own restoration. He confronted the perfectionists because of their pride, and their advocacy for an instantaneous blessing was tantamount to a denial of the need for growth and suffering. Throughout this collection Charles continued to emphasize those things learned at Oxford. Even at the end of his life he presented these ideas as concepts to be wrestled with, ideas which were to be held in tension. Was it possible to be restored in this life? To the antinomian he stressed the possibility, but to those claiming to have been perfected he stressed the difficulty and at times the impossibility of being restored. To the very end of his life Charles continued to confront those ideas which were in conflict with his definition of being restored in the image of God—a faith and reliance on God, which resulted in humility, purity, and a love of both neighbor and God.

Notes

1. Charles Wesley, *Prayers for Condemned Malefactors* (London: Paramore, 1785). See also Joanna Cruickshank, "Singing at the Scaffold: Charles Wesley's Hymns for Condemned Malefactors," *Proceedings of the Wesley Historical Society* 56 (2007): 129–45.

2. Christine Valentine argued that Methodism promoted a "joyful dying" through narratives. The use of narratives can be seen in John Wesley's publication of "exemplary deathbed scenes in the *Arminian* magazine." The Methodist tradition is part of the longer tradition of *ars moriendi*, which "instructed the dying person to make the following

preparations: examine one's life, seek God's forgiveness, forgive others, declare one's faith, place oneself into God's hands, and ensure that one's family was provided for both materially and spiritually." (Christine Valentine, "The 'Moment of Death,'" *OMEGA: The Journal of Death and Dying*, Volume 55, Number 3 (2007): 221-22.

3. Charles Wesley, Letter to Samuel Lloyd (December 21, 1768), Wesleyana from the Collections of Bridwell Library, SMU; Charles Wesley, Letter to Mr. Davis (December 12, 1772), MARC, DDCW 7/60; and Charles Wesley, Letter to to B. B. Collins (Nov 12, 1782), Wesleyana from the Collections of Bridwell Library, SMU.

4. Charles Wesley, Letter to John Langshaw (December 10, 1782), in Charles Wesley et al, *Wesley/Langshaw Correspondence: Charles Wesley, His Sons, and the Lancaster Organists*, ed. Arthur W Wainwright and Don E. Saliers, No. 1, Emory Text and Studies and Ecclesial Life (Atlanta: Scholars Press for Emory University, 1993), 60. Hereafter cited as *Wesley/Langshaw Correspondence*.

5. Charles Wesley, Letter to John Langshaw (November 16, 1778), in *Wesley/Langshaw Correspondence*, 23.

6. Charles Wesley, Letter to John Langshaw (September 25, 1780), in *Wesley/Langshaw Correspondence*, 46.

7. Charles Wesley, Letter to John Langshaw (May 17, 1779), in *Wesley/Langshaw Correspondence*, 35. Charles indicated at the end of this passage that one of the struggles he may have faced when enforcing this principle of rising early with his children was his wife Sarah. Although he noted both of their wives were innocent of keeping their children from rising early, he may have been less than honest in this statement. Why was this practice so important for Charles? On the one hand, Charles never gave the specific reason for rising early as a time of devotion or worship in his letters to John Langshaw. Maybe this was so obvious that it was beyond stating. On the other hand, Charles did link rising early with Jack Langshaw taking lessons with his son Charles. Maybe it was the practice itself, not the actions associated with it that were important for Charles Wesley. It was a sign of a disciplined life. For other passages encouraging Jack Langshaw to rise early see Charles Wesley, Letter to John Langshaw (October 26, 1779), in *Wesley/Langshaw Correspondence*, 40; and Charles Wesley, Letter to John Langshaw (December 4, 1780), in *Wesley/Langshaw Correspondence*, 48.

8. Charles Wesley, Letter to John Langshaw (July 23, [1781]), in *Wesley/Langshaw Correspondence*, 52-53.

9. Charles Wesley, Letter to Elizabeth Briggs (May 26, [1785]), Drew University Methodist Collection.

10. Charles Wesley, Letter to Joseph Cownley (June 9, 1774), in Frank Baker's transcriptions of Charles Wesley's letters, where the item is No. 456.

11. See pp. 131-137.

12. Charles Wesley, Letter to Joseph Benson (January 19, 1773), The Frank Baker Collection of Manuscripts, Duke.

13. L. M. Middleton, "Kelway , Joseph (*c.*1702–1782)," rev. David J. Golby, in *Oxford Dictionary of National Biography*, ed. H. C. G. Matthew and Brian Harrison (Oxford: OUP, 2004); online ed., ed. Lawrence Goldman, *http://www.oxforddnb.com/view/article/15310*.

14. Charles Wesley, Letter to Sarah Gwynne Wesley (March 30, [1771]), MARC, DDCW 7/29.

15. Gareth Lloyd, "Wesley, Charles (1757–1834)," in *Oxford Dictionary of National Biography*, online ed., ed. Lawrence Goldman, Oxford: OUP, , *http://www.oxforddnb.com/view/article/29068*. See CW to Bristol Society, 1769, 0200

16. Ibid.

17. Charles Wesley, Letter to Eleanor Laroche (February 8, 1769), MARC, DDWES 4/73; Charles Wesley, Letter to A Quaker (February 13, 1769), MARC, DDWES 4/72; and Charles Wesley, Letter to The Society at Bristol, (February, 1769), MARC, DDWES 4/83. The first two letters also include a transcript of the letter sent to Charles.

18. Charles Wesley, Letter to Eleanor Laroche (February 8, 1769), MARC, DDWES 4/73.

19. Charles Wesley, Letter to A Quaker (February 13, 1769), MARC, DDWES 4/72.

20. Ibid.

21. Charles Wesley, Letter to The Society at Bristol, (February, 1769), MARC, DDWES 4/83.

22. "Innocent Diversions" in *HSP* (1749), 2:140-41.

23. Ibid.

24. "The true use of musick" in *HSP* (1749), 2:253-54.

25. "Innocent Diversions" in *HSP* (1749), 2:140-41. At the bottom of the page Charles include the following explanation of a grove: "* Ranelagh's Gardens, Vaux-Hall, &c."

26. Charles Wesley, Letter to Eleanor Laroche (February 8, 1769), MARC, DDWES 4/73.

27. Charles Wesley, Letter to The Society at Bristol, (February, 1769), MARC, DDWES 4/83.

28. Ibid.

29. Charles Wesley, Letter to M Bernard, (November 1, 1770), MARC, DDWES 2/69.

30. Charles Wesley, Letter to The Society at Bristol, (February, 1769), MARC, DDWES 4/83.

31. Ibid.

32. Ibid.

33. For instance, see p. 35 above for their acceptance of celibacy.

34. Charles Wesley, Letter to Sally Wesley ([September 21, 1778]) in MARC, DDWES 4/26.

35. See pp. 29-37 above.

36. Charles Wesley, Letter to Sally Wesley ([May 26, 1780]) in MARC, DDWES 4/29.

37. Charles Wesley, Letter to Sally Wesley ([September 21, 1778]) in MARC, DDWES 4/26.

38. Charles Wesley, Letter to Sarah Gwynne Wesley ([Aug 18, 1785]), MARC, DDWES 4/64.

39. Charles Wesley, Letter to John Wesley (Aug 14, 1785), Frank Baker's transcriptions of Charles Wesley's letters, where the item is No. 540.

40. Charles Wesley, Letter to Sarah Gwynne Wesley ([Aug 18, 1785]), MARC, DDWES 4/64.

41. Charles Wesley, Letter to Henry Durbin (October 15, 1785), Frank Baker's transcriptions of Charles Wesley's letters, where the item is No. 543a.

42. Charles Wesley, Letter to Henry Durbin (October 15, 1785), Frank Baker's transcriptions of Charles Wesley's letters, where the item is No. 543a.

43. John Wesley, Letter to Charles Wesley (August 19, 1785), Telford, *Letters of John Wesley*, 7:284.

44. Charles Wesley, Letter to John Wesley (September 8, 1785), Frank Baker's transcriptions of Charles Wesley's letters, where the item is No. 541.

45. Charles Wesley, Letter to Dr. Chandler (Sept 12, 1785), Frank Baker's tran-

scriptions of Charles Wesley's letters, where the item is No. 541b; and John Potter, *A Discourse of Church-Government Wherein the Rights of the Church, and the Supremacy of Christian Princes, Are Vindicated and Adjusted.* (London: printed for Timothy Childe; Robert Knaplock; and Richard Wilkin), 1711.

46. Charles Wesley, Letter to Michael Challender (November 25, 1786), Frank Baker's transcriptions of Charles Wesley's letters, where the item is No.554b.

47. Charles Wesley, Letter to John Wesley (December 6, 1779), DDWES 4/40.

48. Ibid.

49. "O Lord, our strength and righteousness," in "MS Hymns for Preachers Extraordinary," 10-11.

50. Charles Wesley, Letter to John Wesley (November 28, 1779), Frank Baker's transcriptions of Charles Wesley's letters, where the item is No. 497.

51. The cause of this increased division was John Wesley's infamous 1770 Minute. (Heitzenrater, *Wesley and the People Called Methodists*, 246). For a fuller account of the Minute Controversy see Coppedge, *Shaping the Wesleyan Message*, 157-218.

52. Charles Wesley, Letter to Joseph Benson (January 19, 1773), The Frank Baker Collection of Manuscripts, Duke.

53. Ibid.

54. John Fletcher, *Checks to Antinomianism*. (New York: J. Soule and T. Mason, 1820.)

55. Charles Wesley, Letter to John Fletcher [February 22, 1772], Wesley's Chapel. Also in Frank Baker's transcriptions of Charles Wesley's letters, where the item is No. 426.

56. Charles Wesley, Letter to John Wesley (December 8, 1772), MARC, DDWES 4/66.

57. For a description of how Charles taught Calvinism led to antinomianism see pp. 125-28 above.

58. Charles Wesley, Letter to Sally Wesley ([May 27, 1771]), MARC, DDWES 4/30.

59. Charles Wesley, Letter to Joseph Benson (January 19, 1773), The Frank Baker Collection of Manuscripts, Duke.

60. Charles Wesley, Letter to Samuel Lloyd (February 27, 1768), Frank Baker's transcriptions of Charles Wesley's letters, where the item is No. 397.

61. Charles Wesley, Letter to Samuel Lloyd ([December 4, 1769]), Frank Baker's transcriptions of Charles Wesley's letters, where the item is No. 402a.

62. Charles Wesley, Letter to James Hutton (Aug 26, 1772), Frank Baker's transcriptions of Charles Wesley's letters, where the item is No. 1772.

63. Charles Wesley, Letter to Joseph Cownley ([November, 1772]), MARC, DDCW 5/110.

64. Charles Wesley, Letter to Charles Wesley, Jr. (Aug 29, 1987), MARC, DDCW 7/74.

65. Charles Wesley, Letter to John Langshaw (June 5, 1782), *Wesley/Langshaw Correspondence*, 58.

66. Charles Wesley, Letter to Samuel Lloyd (August 28, 1764), The Frank Baker Collection of Manuscripts, Duke.

67. Maddox acknowledged this possibility but seems to favor the idea that these were composed during these two weeks: "The dates apparently refer to the original composition of the hymns, but may indicate instead the time spent copying them into a collected set. In either case, the hymns date from Wesley's later years, and many reflect his growing discomfort since the controversies of the 1760s with those who lightly claimed to have attained Christian Perfection." ("MS Scriptural Hymns").

68. I have accessed this material through the website of The Center for the Studies in the Wesleyan Tradition, Duke Divinity School. I have also checked each of the passages to a copy of the Manuscript. I have adopted the following changes to the text which are used by the website of The Center for the Studies in the Wesleyan Tradition, Duke Divinity School. "For the convenience of current readers, we have adopted three modernizations for scripture references in this volume: excerpts of scripture used as titles have been placed in quotation marks (Wesley typically omits), colons have replaced periods in scripture citations (Wesley's "Gen. 20. 6" becomes "Gen. 20:6"), and "ff" has been used to indicate multiple verses (Wesley uses "&c"). We have maintained the guidelines for the larger collection when transcribing Wesley's actual verse."

"'I am an alien to my mother's children.'—[Ps.] 69:8," in "MS Scriptural Hymns OT," 55.

69. "'Despisest thou the riches of his goodness and forbearance, and long-suffering? not knowing that the goodness of God leadeth thee to repentance?'—[Rom.] 2:4," in "MS Scriptural Hymns NT," 15.

70. See "'Wash thine heart, that thou mayst be saved: how long shall thy vain thoughts lodge within thee?'—[Jer.] 4:14," in "MS Scriptural Hymns OT," 109-10. "'Behold the Lamb of God, who taketh away the sin of the world.'—[John] 1:29," in "MS Scriptural Hymns NT," 5.

71. "'Man walketh in a vain shadow, and disquieteth himself in vain.'—[Ps.] 39:6," in "MS Scriptural Hymns OT," 47-48. See also "'O turn away mine eyes, lest they behold vanity, and quicken then me in thy way.'—[Ps.] 119:37," in "MS Scriptural Hymns OT," 73-74.

72. "['Who can bring a clean *thing* out of an unclean? not one.'—Job 14:4.] IV," in "MS Scriptural Hymns OT," 23-24.

73. "['Who can bring a clean *thing* out of an unclean? not one.'—Job 14:4.] V," in "MS Scriptural Hymns OT," 24.

74. "'Wash thine heart, that thou mayst be saved: how long shall thy vain thoughts lodge within thee?'—[Jer.] 4:14," in "MS Scriptural Hymns OT," 109.

75. Ibid., 110. See also "'Keep thy servant from presumptuous sins.'—[Ps.] 19:13. [I,]" in "MS Scriptural Hymns OT," 34.

76. "['Take away all iniquity.'—Hosea 14:2.] II, in "MS Scriptural Hymns OT," 123.

77. "['God gave them the holy Ghost, purifying their hearts by faith.' Acts 15:8–9,]" II in "MS Scriptural Hymns NT," 13. See also "['God gave them the holy Ghost, purifying their hearts by faith.' Acts 15:8–9,]" I in "MS Scriptural Hymns NT," 12.

78. See "'When wilt Thou come unto me? I will walk in my house with a perfect heart.'—[Ps.] 101:3 [BCP]," in "MS Scriptural Hymns OT," 55.

79. "'Thou, O Lord God, are the thing that I long for.'—[Ps.] 71:4 [BCP]," in "MS Scriptural Hymns OT," 57.

80. "'He that believeth shall not make haste.'—[Isa.] 28:16. [I,]" in "MS Scriptural Hymns OT," 96.

81. Ibid.

82. Ibid., 97.

83. "'Whosoever sinneth hath not known Him.'—[1 John] 3:6," in "MS Scriptural Hymns NT," 130-31.

84. This description of being restored is similar to the Roman Catholic understanding of the Beatific Vision. According to Christian Trottmann most theologians in the fourteenth century "adopted the dispositive role of the light of glory enabling the Intellect to receive the divine essence as form and hence be in bliss." (Christian Trottmann, "Beatific Vision," in *Encyclopedia of the Middle Ages*, Ed. André Vauchez, 2001.)

176 *The Heart of Charles Wesley's Theology*

85. "'Behold the Lamb of God, who taketh away the sin of the world.'—[John] 1:29," in "MS Scriptural Hymns NT," 5.

86. Charles often used I John to present his ideas about being freed from sin. Charles has five poems on these three verses from first John. They fill seven pages and include 22 verses. The amount of space that he devoted to these verses seem to indicate their relative importance to him. ("MS Scriptural Hymns NT," 128-135)

87. "'He was manifested, to take away our sins,'—[I John] 3:5. [I,]" in "MS Scriptural Hymns NT," 128.

88. Ibid., 128-29.

89. Ibid., 129.

90. "'He was manifested, to take away our sins,'—[I John] 3:5. II," in "MS Scriptural Hymns NT," 130.

91. "'Whosoever sinneth hath not known Him.'—[I John] 3:6," in "MS Scriptural Hymns NT," 130-131. Charles also emphasized the role of the crucifixion and Christ's blood in abolishing sin in, "'For this purpose the Son of God was manifested, that he might destroy the works of the devil.'—[1 John] 3:8. [I,] in "MS Scriptural Hymns NT," 131-132.

92. "['For this purpose the Son of God was manifested, that he might destroy the works of the devil.'—1 John 3:8.] II, in "MS Scriptural Hymns NT," 133.

93. Ibid.

94. Ibid., 134-35. Half of these two verses were edited out before the poem was published in Osborn's *Poetical Works,* 13:205-07. The lines which were omitted began with "Who fancy sin at once destroy'd," and end with "I shall perform thy just commands."

95. "'Give none offence, neither to the Jews, nor to the Gentiles, nor to the Church of God.'—[1 Cor.] 10:32," in "MS Scriptural Hymns NT," 39-40.

96. "'Am I therefore become your enemy, because I tell you the truth?'—[Gal.] 4:16," in "MS Scriptural Hymns NT," 62-63.

Conclusion

One of the central themes of Charles Wesley's theology was the goal of being restored in the image of God. This can be seen not only in his hymns, but also in his sermons, letters, and journal. While it may be possible to study the hymns and poems in isolation, looking at the sermons, letters, and journal help provide the context Charles perceived he was dealing with when he was writing the hymns and poems. It is through his letters, and his journal in particular, that one can understand the threats Charles perceived to his theology. Charles seems to overstate his position at times because of the challenges he was addressing. This may explain why his position seems to have contradictions. Many of his hymns and poems were a polemic against groups who had influence within the Methodist movement. One explanation for the contradictions in Charles's poetry is the target audience of the poem. For instance, when he was addressing the problem of antinomianism (both in the Moravians and the predestinarians), he tended to stress the possibility of being restored, but when he was addressing the problem of perfectionism (during the perfectionist controversy), he tended to stress the difficulty of being restored. By understanding the context of Charles's comments, what seem like contradictions can be understood as the same theology presented to different audiences.

Tracing Charles's definition or presentation of being restored in the image of God before his time at Oxford is difficult because of the lack of sources. Charles may have arrived at Oxford with ideas about what it meant to be restored in the image of God, but it was at Oxford that a record of Charles's thought begins, and it was at Oxford that his theology was developed within the context of 'Oxford Methodism'. After a year of diversions, Charles became more serious about his faith. Together with other members of 'Oxford Methodism' Charles followed the pattern laid out in *The Country-Parson's Advice*. The group studied both academic and devotional works and developed a theology of being restored in the image of God. This theology was based primarily on the thought of William Law and Henry Scougal. Like Scougal, Charles defined being restored in the image of God as 'true religion', which was a real participation in God. It included five main characteristics: faith, purity, humility, love of neighbor, and love of God. 'Oxford Methodism' was also marked by an emphasis on asceticism. Charles defined purity as having a 'single eye' to emphasize the necessity of asceticism to being restored in the image of God. Beginning at Oxford this asceticism included the necessity of suffering as a part of being restored in the image of God. The emphasis on suffering continued throughout Charles's life.

The theological model behind these concepts was recapitulation and *theosis*.[1] Charles taught that what was lost in the fall of Adam could be restored in the work of the second Adam—Jesus Christ. The work of Jesus Christ was seen as a means by which a person could be restored to the prelapsarian image and experience union with God. Charles also saw the life of Jesus Christ as an example to be imitated. It was this hope and the optimism of being restored in the image of God that informed Charles's interaction with others who did not emphasize the possibility of being restored in the image of God.

One of the main threats Charles addressed were theologies which intentionally or pragmatically led to antinomianism. Although Charles's ideas of faith were shaped by his interactions with the Moravians, that support was challenged by their doctrine of 'stillness'. Part of the problem at Fetter Lane was the neglect of the means of grace. Charles addressed this neglect by focusing on what he deemed Christian virtues; namely, "a cross, a work of faith, a patience of hope, and a labour of love." This involved having a faith which obeyed God out of love and an imitation of the life of Christ.

Charles and the Moravians or the 'still brethren' defined Christian liberty differently. For the 'still brethren', liberty was a liberty *from* fulfilling the law and for Charles, Christian liberty was "Liberty *from* all Sin, Liberty *to* fulfil the whole Law."[2] For Charles this meant living out God's purpose by observing the means of grace. This had practical consequences and affected the way one lived. Charles confronted the stillness of the Moravians with the lives of the colliers. The Kingswood colliers were an example that belief could and should be accompanied by signs or fruits. These fruits included an active waiting on God in the ordinances and a childlike humility.

Charles also questioned the Moravian denial of the degrees of faith. He felt they had set faith to high; that their denial of a faith that doubts had practical consequences. For instance, because Mr. Stonehouse accepted the Moravian's definition of faith, he believed he "was never justified" and was "going to leave his parish, and transport himself—to Germany!"[3] Charles resisted the Moravians's high definition of faith and argued instead that a believer could experience doubt.

Charles also struggled with the antinomianism of the predestinarians. Charles spoke against their doctrines of reprobation, preservation of the saints, and the "necessity of sinning."[4] He taught that their doctrine of reprobation distorted the image people would have of God, making him a God of hate instead of a God of love. Charles's stress on the love of God was such a prominent part of his ministry that he was seen by some as the primary advocate of universal redemption. One example of this emphasis was the publication of *Hymns on God's Everlasting Love*.[5] Charles responded to the doctrine of reprobation in this pamphlet with a set of polemical hymns and poems. In these hymns and poems, Charles used the word 'all' as a hammer to drive home the point that God's love was not limited to the elect, but universal and available to all.

Charles also challenged the predestinarians' definition of justifying faith as a 'faith of adherence'. He described a 'faith of adherence' as a weak faith which normally kept a person from going on to a stronger faith. It was the struggling faith of Romans 7, not the victorious faith of Romans 8. This contrast can be seen in the predestinarian emphasis of being saved *in* sin which differed from Charles Wesley's emphasis of being saved *from* sin.

Charles's continued rejection of the predestinarian emphasis can be seen in his response to the predestinarian controversy of the 1770's. Charles held up both the lifestyle and the writings of John Fletcher as model of the Christian life. One of his strongest statements against antinomianism during this time was the concern he expressed to his daughter about the Lady Huntington: "A sensible Roman-catholic is above a match for any Calvinist. Her Ladyship approaches too near the Antinomian Extreme."[6]

Charles stressed the possibility of being renewed in the image of God as a check to antinomianism in his hymns and poems. In *HSP* (1749) this included an emphasis on the possibility of being sinless. Sinlessness was defined as a part of what happened in the recapitulation of Christ. It resulted in purity and the removal of inbred sin. To deny that it was possible was to damage the character of God. He presented the high ideal he found in the Scripture reasoning that if a person could not be restored to a sinless state, then God must be deceiving them because God seems to promise this restoration to a sinless state. This would become less prominent in his later writings.

Even in 1762, in the midst of the perfectionist controversies, Charles continued to emphasize the possibility of being restored in the image of God. He used several ideas to express this possibility. He wrote of walking and living in the image of God (which meant becoming "pure in heart" and gaining "that perfect love unknown") and doing the perfect will of God here on earth. Believers could live life as heaven here and experience 'full salvation'. He also noted that the great physician could heal the sin-sick soul. One of the main difficulties the perfectionists posed was that their false claims of absolute and instantaneous perfection were damaging the idea that perfection was truly possible.

Charles also stressed the possibility of being restored in the image of God in MS Scriptural Hymns. The poetry from this collection still stressed the possibility of being restored in opposition to those with antinomian tendencies, but at the same time it stressed the incomplete or progressive nature of that restoration in opposition to those with perfectionistic tendencies.

Charles Wesley's involvement in Methodism was always described by Charles in terms which demonstrated his support for the Church of England. He reminded his wife of these priorities in 1760: "My chief Concern upon earth I said, was the Prosperity of the Church of E[ngland,] my next, That of the Meth[odist]s[,] my 3d that of the Preachers."[7] There were primarily three reasons Charles resisted any split from the Church of England. He argued that those desiring to separate were motivated by pride, which was in opposition to the importance humility played in being restored in the image of God. Second, they had abandoned the ordinances, which Charles argued were a part of the way God restored people. Third, their schismatic tendencies undercut the corporate nature of the Church as the spotless bride of Christ.

The perfectionist controversy of the 1760's provided Charles an opportunity to further explain what he meant by his emphasis on being restored in the image of God. It was during this time that several from the Methodist societies began to emphasize an unqualified perfection which could be attained in an instant. Part of the problem Charles had with this movement was that it was giving Methodists a bad name. and it was putting a strain on an already weakened relationship with Church of England. The perfectionists were accused of antinomianism, enthusiasm, and fanaticism. One of Charles's main difficulties with this group was their lack of humility. While the London society was recovering from the perfectionist controversy Charles wrote, "Another witness fairly confessed herself undeceived, & gave up her perfection, because (as she said) she had never been poor in spirit. It is surprising the readiness of the witnesses to receive my sayings. I don't despair of their all coming right at last."[8] Their lack of humility was demonstrated by their boastful sharing and by their claims of having attained perfection. Charles responded to this controversy by emphasizing some of the major characteristics of being restored in the image of God. In opposition to their claims of instantaneous perfection Charles noted the necessity of patience, suffering, and a 'single eye'. In opposition to their boastful sharing and pride, he taught humility. It was not only the perfectionists that he confronted, he also confronted his brother John. Charles accused John of being engaged in "the work" to immortalize his name:

> 1 And dost thou not thyself suspect,
> Vain founder of the rising sect,
>   Or thine own language see?
> "Is not this Babylon the great,
> 'Stablish'd in her sublime estate,
>   Built up to heaven—by me!"[9]

Charles clarified his theology of the necessity of suffering to being restored in the image of God when faced with persecution, earthquakes, illness, and death. He believed each of these events could be used to refine the character of the person being restored in the image of God. Charles not only indicated that it was possible that suffering could be used, but that it was necessary for a person to suffer in order to be restored in the image of God. When faced with persecution, a person should respond in love. When faced with the threat of an earthquake, Charles seems more uncertain of how to respond. At times he indicated that God would protect his people here, but at other times Charles recognized that the only guaranteed protection was of an eternal nature. Either way, Charles argued that earthquakes were the act of a merciful God. Charles said, "Judgment is MERCY's harbinger."[10] Charles also encouraged people in the midst of their sickness to see it as an opportunity to grow closer to the image of God. In short, Charles saw suffering as a means of grace through which one could experience the God of love and mercy.

One area that changed throughout Charles's life was how he applied his understanding of having a 'single eye'. At Oxford this included a commitment to remaining unmarried. This commitment to remaining single was set aside after a time of intense struggle when Charles decided to marry Sarah Gwynne. Charles had not rejected the necessity of having a 'single eye', only the idea that remaining unmarried was a part of that commitment. Charles would also challenge the Methodist understanding of having a 'single eye' by supporting his sons' pursuit of musical training. The support he showed his sons in the pursuit of music was seen by people both inside and outside of Methodism as an acceptance of diversions. In other words, Charles's application of having a 'single eye' now included activities which were previously labeled as diversions.

Charles referred to a universal restoration in *SHSPS* (1762). This seems to be a development of his emphasis on universal redemption, the major difference being that universal redemption was the offer of redemption, where universal restoration referred to a time when all people would be redeemed. The former was used to argue against the Calvinist, who focused on a select few being offered redemption. The latter focused on the eventual restoration of all of creation by God, a theme echoed by his brother John about 20 years later in the sermon "The General Spread of the Gospel."[11]

What has been shown in this paper is Charles's presentation of what it means to be restored in the image of God. Charles used this concept throughout his life and ministry to define the goal of the Christian life. At times, Charles perceived that others did not take this goal seriously. Many of these have been examined throughout the paper. What is lacking or what requires further research is the accuracy of Charles's perceptions. In what ways has he misrepresented those he has criticized? Charles needs to be seen within the larger context of Methodism. What influence did his ideas have? In what ways was he opposed by others in leadership of the Methodist movement or by the members of the Methodist movement?

Does Charles have anything to say to us today? Is there anything in his emphasis that could be used to question the life of the church or the life of individuals within the church? It seems that Charles's emphasis on universal redemption and the eventual universal restoration of creation could affect the way we interact with others. Believing that God is concerned about all people would lead to a more inclusive approach to ministry and to the way we interact with other people. This would include refusing to write people off just because they disagree with us. Charles's emphasis on love of neighbor is closely related to this. Throughout Charles's life he continued to minister to the poor and to the prisoner. This could serve as a corrective to people who have focused primarily on works of piety (love for God shown by Bible study, prayer, and church attendance). Charles was able to serve and care for people in need because of his focus. Charles continually questioned what it meant to have purity or a 'single eye'. In a world filled with distractions or diversions, questioning what is important, what is our focus could help us to overcome the consumeristic tendencies of our culture. Where those lines are drawn may differ for different people, but it is important that we, like Charles, struggle with what it means to have a 'single eye'. Finally, Charles's emphasis on humility provides a check to those who have a tendency to claim superiority, whether it be spiritually, intellectually, or politically. If we hold our opinions more lightly and focus on loving and caring for others as God cares for them, it may be possible to find more in common than we ever expected. The last part of Charles's definition of being restored in the image of God is faith. Faith is a dependence upon God. This too is a part of the idea of humility. Believing we cannot do it by ourselves, that we need the help of God and others, creates a sense of community. Believing I can do it by myself and I don't need the help of anybody else normally results in isolation and individualism. Although Charles lived in a time which is radically different than ours, his focus on being restored in the image of God could still be helpful in shaping the life of the church and those who are part of that church.

Notes

1. Tyson, *Charles Wesley on Sanctification,* 60-61.
2. Charles Wesley, Letter to the Society at Grimsby (April 27, 1743), MARC, DDCW 6/32. Emphasis mine.
3. Charles Wesley, April 5, 1740, *Manuscript Journal,* 1:233.
4. Charles Wesley, Letter to JW ([March 16-17, 1741]), *Letters* II, in *Works* 26:54.
5. *Hymns on God's Everlasting Love* (1741).
6. Charles Wesley, Letter to Sally Wesley ([May 27, 1771]), MARC, DDWES 4/30.
7. Charles Wesley, Letter to Sarah Gwynne Wesley ([April 13, 1760]), Frank Baker's transcriptions of Charles Wesley's letters, where the item is No. 337.
8. Charles Wesley, Letter to Sarah Gwynne Wesley ([May 27, 1764]), MARC, DDCW 7/31.
9. Charles Wesley, "[Hymn] 1298. 'Is not this great Babylon that I have built?'—[Dan.] iv. 30," in *SHSPS* (1762), 2:60-61.
10. *EqH* (1750), II:21.
11. John Wesley, Sermon 63, "The General Spread of the Gospel," in *Sermons II,* in *Works,* 2:485-99.

Selected Bibliography

I. Primary Sources
A. Manuscripts
Hutton, James, Manuscripts. Moravian Archives, London.
Wesley, Charles, Manuscript. MS Clarke. MARC, MA 1977/561.
⎯⎯⎯⎯, Manuscript. MS Courtship. MARC, MA 1977/583/4.
⎯⎯⎯⎯, Manuscript. MS Death: includes MS Funeral Hymns, MS Hymns for Love, MS Preparation for Death, and MS Death of Mary Horton (draft 3). MARC, MA 1977/578.
⎯⎯⎯⎯, Manuscript. MS Deliberative Hymns. MARC, MA 1977/552.
⎯⎯⎯⎯, Manuscript. MS Family. MARC, MA 1977/564.
⎯⎯⎯⎯, Manuscript. MS Fish. MARC, MA 1977/566.
⎯⎯⎯⎯, Manuscript. MS Friendship I. MARC, MA 1977/558.
⎯⎯⎯⎯, Manuscript. MS Friendship II. MARC, MA 1977/583/8.
⎯⎯⎯⎯, Manuscript. MS Hymns for Preachers Extraordinary. MARC, MA 1977/583/8.
⎯⎯⎯⎯, Manuscript. MS Malefactors. MARC, MA 1977/583/7.
⎯⎯⎯⎯, Manuscript. MS Mark. MARC, MA 1977/574.
⎯⎯⎯⎯, Manuscript. MS Misc. MARC, MA 1977/583/4.
⎯⎯⎯⎯, Manuscript. MS Occasional Hymns. MARC, MA 1977/583/7.
⎯⎯⎯⎯, Manuscript. MS Preachers. MARC, MA 1977/583/10.
⎯⎯⎯⎯, Manuscript. MS Revd.—. MARC, MA 1977/583/9.
⎯⎯⎯⎯, Manuscript. MS Protestant Association. MARC, MA 1977/594/5.
⎯⎯⎯⎯, Manuscript. MS Preachers Extraordinary. MARC, MA 1977/583/8.
⎯⎯⎯⎯, Manuscript. MS Scriptural Hymns (OT & NT). MARC, MA 1977/576.
⎯⎯⎯⎯, Manuscripts. Charles Wesley Papers. MARC, DDCW.
⎯⎯⎯⎯, Manuscripts. Drew University Methodist Collection, ATLA: Digital resources for the study of religion, http://www.atla.com/digitalresources/.
⎯⎯⎯⎯, Manuscripts. Field, Clive. *The People Called Methodists: A Documentary History of the Methodist Church in Great Britain and Ireland on Microfiche: Guide to the Microform Collection.* Leiden [Netherlands]: IDC Publishers, 1998.
⎯⎯⎯⎯, Manuscripts. The Frank Baker Collection of Manuscripts. Rare Book, Manuscript, and Special Collections Library, Duke University.
⎯⎯⎯⎯, Manuscripts. Wesley Family Papers. MARC, DDWES.

_____, Manuscripts. Wesley manuscripts and selected Wesleyana from the Collections of Bridwell Library, Southern Methodist University, ATLA: Digital resources for the study of religion, http://www.atla.com/digitalresources/.

B. Unpublished Primary Sources

Wesley, Charles, Transcriptions. Frank Baker's transcriptions of Charles Wesley's letters, used with permission of the Center for Studies in the Wesleyan Tradition, Duke University Divinity School.

C. Published Primary Sources

Barry, Jonathan, and Kenneth Morgan. *Reformation and Revival in Eighteenth-Century Bristol.* Bristol Record Society's Publications; V. 45. Stroud, Glos.: Printed for the Bristol Record Society, 1994.

Bedford, Arthur. *The Doctrine of Assurance: Or the Case of a Weak and Doubting Conscience.* Second ed. London: Charles Ackers, 1739].

Bengel, Johann Albrecht. *Gnomon Novi Testamenti: in quo ex nativa verborum vi simplicitas, profunditas, concinnitas, salubritas sensuum coelestium indicatur.* Tübingen: H. Philip Schram, 1742.

Briggs, William. "George Bell and Early Methodist Enthusiasm: A New Manuscript Source from the Manchester Archives." Ed. Kenneth G. C. Newport and Gareth Lloyd. *Bulletin John Rylands Library* (1998).

Byrom, John. *The Universal English Short-Hand; or, The Way of Writing English, in the Most Easy, Concise, Regular, and Beautiful Manner, Applicable to Any Other Language, but Particularly Adjusted to Our Own.* Manchester [Eng.]: Printed by J. Harrop, 1767.

Christophilus [*pseud.*]. *A Serious Inquiry Whether a Late Epistle from the Rev. Mr. Charles Wesley to the Rev. Mr. John Wesley Be Not . . . .* [London?]: Printed for the Author, 1755.

Clarke, Adam. *Memoirs of the Wesley Family: Collected Principally from Original Documents.*, 2d ed. New York: Lane & Tippett, for the Methodist Episcopal Church, 1848.

The Country-Parson's Advice to His Parishioners In Two Parts., (London: Printed for Benjamin Tooke, 1680).

Edwards, John. *a doctrine of faith and justification set in a true light.* London: printed for Jonathan Robinson, John Lawrence, and John Wyat, 1708.

Fletcher, John. *Checks to Antinomianism.* New York: J. Soule and T. Mason, 1820.

_____. *Unexampled Labours: Letters of the Revd John Fletcher to leaders in the Evangelical Revival.* Ed. Peter Forsaith. Peterborough: Epworth, 2008.

Gell, Robert. *An Essay towards the Amendment of the English Translation of the Bible; or, A proof, by many instances, that the last translation of the Bible into English may be improved. The first part on the Pentateuch, or five books of Moses.* London: R. Norton, 1659.

Goodwin, Thomas. *The Works of Thomas Goodwin, D. D.*, vol. 8, *The Object and Acts of Justifying Faith.* Edinburgh: James Nichol, 1864.

Halyburton, Thomas. *Memoirs of the Life of the Reverend, Learned and Pious Mr. Thomas Halyburton . . . in Four Parts. Whereof Three Were Drawn Up by Himself, the Fourth Collected by His Friends, . . . The Second Edition. With a Large Recommendatory Epistle by I. Watts.* London: sold by R. Cruttenden, 1718.

Hardy, Richard. *A letter from a clergyman, to one of his parishioners, who was inclined to turn Methodist . . . .* London: Printed for the Author, 1763.

Hastings, Selina. *In the Midst of Early Methodism: Lady Huntingdon and Her Correspondence.* Ed. John R. Tyson and Boyd S. Schlenther. Pietism and Wesleyan Studies.

No. 19: Revitalization: Explorations in World Christian Movements. Lanham, Maryland: The Scarecrow Press, Inc., 2006.

Henry, Matthew. *An Exposition of the Old and New Testament*. 3 vols. London: Stratford, 1706–10.

Herbert, George. *George Herbert: The Country Parson, The Temple*. Ed. John N. Wall Jr. New York: Paulist Press, 1981.

"Holy Communion." In *The Book of Common Prayer*. Cambridge: Printed by John Baskerville, 1662, [24]. http://justus.anglican.org/resources/bcp/1662/baskerville.htm.cf

Impartiality [*pseud.*]. "To the Printer of the London Chronicle." *The London Chronicle*. January 10, 1763, 34.

Ingham, Benjamin. *Diary of an Oxford Methodist, Benjamin Ingham, 1733-1734*, Ed. Richard P. Heitzenrater. Durham: Duke University Press, 1985.

Law, William. *A Practical Treatise Upon Christian Perfection*. London: Printed for William and John Innys, 1726.

⸺. *A Serious Call to a Devout and Holy Life: Adapted to the State and Condition of All Orders of Christians*. London: Printed for William Innys, 1729.

Luther, Martin. *Dr. Martin Luther's Commentary Upon the Epistle to the Galatians: Abridged, Without Any Alterations. Together with Edwin, Bishop of London's License and Commendation of the Work, As Done by the Translators Out of Latin, 28 April, 1575. . . . Together with the Doctor's Own Preface*. London: Printed for J. Brotherton, and J. Oswald, 1734.

Maxfield, Thomas. *Christ the Great Gift of God: and the Nature of Faith in Him*. London: n. p., 1769.

⸺. *A Collection of Psalms and Hymns*. 3rd ed. London: printed and sold at his chapel, 1778.

Norris, John. *Practical Discourses on Several Divine Subjects*. 4 vols. London: 1690.

Philodemas [*pseud.*]. "To the Editor of Lloyd's Evening Post," *Lloyd's Evening Post*. March 2-4, 1763, 210.

Potter, John. *A Discourse of Church-Government Wherein the Rights of the Church, and the Supremacy of Christian Princes, Are Vindicated and Adjusted*. London: printed for Timothy Childe; Robert Knaplock; and Richard Wilkin, 1711.

Scougal, Henry. *The Life of God in the Soul of Man: or, The Nature and Excellency of the Christian Religion: with the Methods of attaining the Happiness it proposes; Also an Account of the Beginnings and Advances of a Spiritual Life. With a preface. By Gilbert Burnet now Lord Bishop of Sarum*. Fourth ed. London: printed for Thomas Bever, 1702.

Wesley, Charles. *Charles Wesley's Earliest Evangelical Sermons: Six Shorthand Manuscript Sermons now for the first time Transcribed from the Original*. Ed. Thomas R. Albin and Oliver A. Beckerlegge. Ilford: Wesley Historical Society, 1987.

⸺. *Charles Wesley: A Reader*. Ed. John Tyson. Oxford: Oxford University Press, 2000.

⸺. *Charles Wesley: As Revealed by His Letters*. Ed. Frank Baker. Rev. ed. Madison, New Jersey: Charles Wesley Society, 1995.

⸺. *A Collection of Hymns for the Use of the People Called Methodists*. Ed. Franz Hildebrandt, Oliver A. Beckerlegge, and James Dale. Vol. 7 of *The Works of John Wesley*. Nashville: Abingdon Press, 1983.

⸺. *An Epistle to the Reverend Mr. John Wesley*. London: [Strahan,] for J. Robinson, 1755. Center for Studies in the Wesleyan Tradition, Duke University, http://www.divinity.duke.edu/initiatives-centers/cswt/wesley-texts/charles-wesley.

⸺. *Hymns and Sacred Poems*, with an editorial introduction by Randy Maddox. Bristol: Felix Farley, 1749. Center for Studies in the Wesleyan Tradition, Duke University. http://www.divinity.duke.edu/initiatives-centers/cswt/wesley-texts/charles-wesley.

_____. *Hymns for the Use of Families*. Bristol: Pine, 1767. The Center for Studies in the Wesleyan Tradition, Duke University. http://www.divinity.duke.edu/initiatives-centers/cswt/wesley-texts/charles-wesley

_____. *The Manuscript Journal of the Rev. Charles Wesley, M.A.* Ed. Kenneth G. C. Newport and S T Kimbrough Jr. 2 vols. Nashville: Kingswood Books, 2007.

_____. *The Poetical Works of John and Charles Wesley: Reprinted from the Originals, with the Last Corrections of the Authors; Together with the Poems of Charles Wesley Not before Published.* Ed. George Osborn. 13 vols. London: Wesleyan-Methodist Conference Office, 1868-1872.

_____. *Prayers for Condemned Malefactors*. London: Paramore, 1785.

_____. *Representative Verse of Charles Wesley*. Ed. Frank Baker. London: Epworth Press, 1962.

_____. *Sermons by the Late Rev. Charles Wesley, A.M. Student of Christ-Church, Oxford. With a Memoir of the Author, by the Editor.* London: Baldwin, Cradock, and Joy, 1816.

_____. *The Sermons of Charles Wesley: A Critical Edition, with Introduction and Notes.* Ed. Kenneth G. C. Newport. Oxford; New York: Oxford University Press, 2001.

_____. *Short Hymns on Select Passages of the Holy Scriptures*. 2 vols., with an editorial introduction by Randy Maddox. Bristol: Farley, 1762. Center for Studies in the Wesleyan Tradition, Duke University, http://www.divinity.duke.edu/initiatives-centers/cswt/wesley-texts/charles-wesley.

_____. *The Unpublished Poetry of Charles Wesley*. Ed. S T Kimbrough Jr., and Oliver A. Beckerlegge. 3 Vol. Nashville, TN: Kingswood Books, 1988.

[Wesley, Charles]. *Hymns for Those to Whom Christ Is All in All*. London, 1761.

_____. *Hymns Occasioned by the Earthquake, March 8, 1750: [Part I]*. London: [Strahan], 1750. Center for Studies in the Wesleyan Tradition, Duke University, http://www.divinity.duke.edu/initiatives-centers/cswt/wesley-texts/charles-wesley.

_____. *Hymns Occasioned by the Earthquake, March 8, 1750: Part II* .London: [Strahan], 1750. Center for Studies in the Wesleyan Tradition, Duke University, http://www.divinity.duke.edu/initiatives-centers/cswt/wesley-texts/charles-wesley.

_____. *Hymns on God's Everlasting Love; To Which is Added the Cry of a Reprobate and the Horrible Decree.* Bristol: Felix Farley, 1741.

_____. *The Means of Grace.* London: Strahan, 1740.

Wesley, Charles et al. *Wesley/Langshaw Correspondence: Charles Wesley, His Sons, and the Lancaster Organists.* Ed. Arthur W Wainwright and Don E. Saliers. No. 1. Emory Text and Studies and Ecclesial Life. Atlanta: Scholars Press for Emory University, 1993.

Wesley, John and Charles Wesley. *Hymns and Sacred Poems: A Facsimile of the First Edition, London: William Strahan, 1739*, with a preface by S T Kimbrough Jr. and a Introduction and Notes by Paul Chilcote. Madison, NJ: The Charles Wesley Society, 2007.

_____. *Hymns and Sacred Poems* (London: Strahan, 1740)

[Wesley, John and Charles Wesley]. *A Short View of the Difference between the Moravian Brethren, lately in England, and the Rev. Mr. John and Charles Wesley.* London: Strahan, 1745.

Wesley, John, Charles Wesley, et al. *Original Letters, by The Rev. John Wesley, and his Friends . . . .* Ed. Joseph Priestley. Birmingham: Printed by Thomas Pearson, and sold by J. Johnson, London, 1791.

Wesley, John. *Cautions and Directions: Given to the Greatest Professors in the Methodist Societies.* London: n. p., 1762.

_____. *John Wesley*. Ed., Albert Cook Outler. New York: Oxford University

Press, 1964.

———. *Journal and Diaries*. Ed. W. Reginald Ward and Richard P. Heitzenrater. Vols. 18-24 of *The Bicentennial Edition of the Works of John Wesley*. Nashville: Abingdon Press, 1988-2003.

———. *Letters*. Ed. Frank Baker. Vols. 25-26 of *The Bicentennial Edition of the Works of John Wesley*. Nashville: Abingdon Press, 1980-1982.

———. *The Letters of the Rev. John Wesley*. Ed. John Telford. 8 vols. London: The Epworth Press, 1931.

———. "A Plain Account of Christian Perfection" (1766). In *The Works of John Wesley*. Ed. Thomas Jackson. Vol. XI. Kansas City: Beacon Hill Press, 1979, reprint.

———. *Sermons*. Ed. Albert C. Outler. Vol. 1-4 of *The Bicentennial Edition of the Works of John Wesley*. Nashville: Abingdon Press, 1984-1987.

———. "A Short History of Methodism" (1765). In *The Methodist Societies: History, Nature, and Design*. Ed. Rupert E. Davis. Vol. 9 of *The Bicentennial Edition of the Works of John Wesley*. Nashville: Abingdon Press, 1989.

———. "A Short History of the People called Methodists (1781)." In *The Methodist Societies: History, Nature, and Design*. Ed. Rupert E. Davis. Vol. 9 of *The Bicentennial Edition of the Works of John Wesley*. Nashville: Abingdon Press, 1989.

———. *Thoughts on Marriage and a Single Life,* 2d ed. Bristol: Printed by Felix Farley, 1743.

———. "To the Editor of the London Chronicle." *The London Chronicle*. January 18, 1763, 63.

———. "To the Printer of the London Chronicle." *The London Chronicle*. February 10, 1763, 143.

Wesley Jr., Samuel. Letter to Charles Wesley (October 11, 1735). In *The Proceedings of the Wesley Historical Society* 11 (1917-8): 151.

Wesley, Susanna. *Susanna Wesley: the Complete Writings*. Ed. Charles Wallace. New York: Oxford University Press, 1997.

Whitefield, George. *George Whitefield's Journals*. London: Banner of Truth Trust, 1960.

Young, Edward. *The Complaint: or Night Thoughts on Life, Death, and Immortality.* 5th ed. [London, 1743].

II. Secondary Sources

Albin, Thomas R. "Charles Wesley's Other Prose Writings." In *Charles Wesley: Poet and Theologian*. Ed. S T Kimbrough Jr. Nashville, TN: Kingswood Books, 1992.

Allchin, A. M. Participation in God: A Forgotten Strand in Anglican Tradition. Wilton, CT: Morehouse-Barlow, 1988.

Baker, Frank. "Charles Wesley to 'Varanese,'" *PWHS* 25 (1945-6): 97-101.

———. "Charles Wesley's Letters." In Charles Wesley: Poet and Theologian. Ed. S T Kimbrough Jr. Nashville, TN: Kingswood Books, 1992.

Bayer, Oswald. *Theology the Lutheran Way*. Trans. Jeffery G. Silcock and Mark C. Mattes. Grand Rapids: William B. Eerdmans, 2007.

Berger, Teresa. Theology in Hymns? A Study of the Relationship of Doxology and Theology According to a Collection of Hymns for the Use of the People Called Methodists (1780). Nashville: Kingswood Books, 1995.

Best, Gary. Charles Wesley: A Biography. London: Epworth, 2006.

Bett, Henry. The Hymns of Methodism in Their Literary Relations. London: Epworth Press, 1920.

Bible, Ken. "The Wesleys' Hymns on Full Redemption and Pentecost: A Brief Comparison." Wesleyan Theological Journal 17, no. 2 (Fall 1982): 79-87.

Brailsford, Mabel Richmond. *A Tale of Two Brothers, John and Charles Wesley.* New York: Oxford University Press, 1954.

Butler, D. *Henry Scougal and the Oxford Methodists: or, The Influence of a Religious Teacher of the Scottish Church.* [London: William Blackwood and Sons, 1899], 112.

Byrum, Roy Delbert. "Theological Implications in the Hymns of Charles Wesley." B.D. thesis, Duke University, 1945.

Campbell, Ted A., and Kenneth G. C. Newport, eds. *Charles Wesley: Life, Literature and Legacy.* London: Epworth Press, 2007.

Clapper, Gregory Scott. "'True Religion' And the Affections: A Study of John Wesley's Abridgment of Jonathan Edward's Treatise on Religious Affections." In *Wesleyan Theology Today: A Bicentennial Theological Consultation.* Ed. Theodore Runyon, 416-423. Nashville: Kingswood Books, 1985.

Coppedge, Allan. *Shaping the Wesleyan Message: John Wesley in Theological Debate.* Nappanee, IN: Evangel Pub., 2003.

Cruickshank, Joanna. "Charles Wesley and the Construction of Suffering in Early English Methodism." Ph.D. diss., The University of Melborne, 2006.

_____. "Singing at the Scaffold: Charles Wesley's Hymns for Condemned Malefactors." *Proceedings of the Wesley Historical Society* 56 (2007): 129–45.

Dale, James. "Theological and Literary Qualities of the Poetry of Charles Wesley in Relation to the Standards of His Age." Ph.D. diss., University of Cambridge 1960.

Downes, J. C. T. "Eschatological Doctrines in the Writings of John and Charles Wesley." Ph.D. diss., University of Edinburgh, 1960.

Dreyer, Frederick A. *The Genesis of Methodism.* Bethlehem, PA: Lehigh University Press, 1999.

Eby, Patrick A. "Reforming the Church: Charles Wesley's Ecclesiology and the Role of Lay Preachers." *Proceedings of the Charles Wesley Society* 11 (2006-2007): 59-68.

Findlay, George Hugo. *Christ's Standard Bearer; a Study in the Hymns of Charles Wesley as They Are Contained in the Last Edition (1876) of a Collection of Hymns for the Use of the People Called Methodists.* London,: Epworth Press, 1956.

Flew, R. Newton. *The Hymns of Charles Wesley, a Study of Their Structure.* London,: Epworth Press, 1953.

Fraser, M. Robert. "Strains in the Understandings of Christian Perfection in Early British Methodism." Ph. D. diss., Vanderbilt University, 1988.

Gallaway, Craig B. "The Presence of Christ with the Worshipping Community: A Study in the Hymns of John and Charles Wesley." Ph. D. diss., Emory University, 1988.

Gill, Frederick C. *Charles Wesley, the First Methodist.* New York,: Abingdon Press, 1964.

Gunter, W. Stephen. *The Limits of 'Love Divine': John Wesley's Response to Antinomianism and Enthusiasm.* Nashville, TN: Kingswood Books, 1989.

Heitzenrater, Richard P. "John Wesley and the Oxford Methodists, 1725-35." Ph.D. diss., Duke University, 1972.

_____. "Purge the Preachers: The Wesleys and Quality Control." In *Charles Wesley: Life, Literature & Legacy.* Ed. Ted A. Campbell and Kenneth G. C. Newport. London: Epworth, 2007.

_____. *Wesley and the People Called Methodists.* Nashville: Abingdon Press, 1995.

Jarboe, Betty. *John and Charles Wesley: A Bibliography.* ATLA Bibliography Series; No. 22. Metuchen, N.J.: American Theological Library Association; Scarecrow Press, 1987.

Jones, Arthur E., Lawrence O. Kline, Richard Green, and Methodist Librarians Fellowship. *A Union Checklist of Editions of the Publications of John and Charles Wesley : (Based Upon the Works of John and Charles Wesley: A Bibliography by Richard Green)*. Madison, N. J.: Drew University, 1959.

Kim, Young Taek. "John Wesley's Anthropology: Restoration of the *Imago Dei* as a Framework for Wesley's Theology." Ph.D. diss., Drew University, 2006.

Kimbrough Jr., S T, ed. *Orthodox and Wesleyan Spirituality*. Crestwood, New York: St Vladimir's Seminary Press, 2002.

_____. *Charles Wesley: Poet and Theologian*. Nashville, TN: Kingswood Books, 1992.

_____. "Charles Wesley and the Journey of Sanctification." *Evangelical Journal* 16, no. 2 (Fall 1986): 49-75.

Kirkham, Donald Henry. "Pamphlet Opposition to the Rise of Methodism: The Eighteenth-Century English Evangelical Revival Under Attack." Ph.D. diss., Duke University, 1973.

Knickerbocker, Waldo E. "Arminian Anglicanism and John and Charles Wesley." *Memphis Theological Seminary Journal* 29 (Fall 1991): 79-97.

Knight, Harold. *The Presence of God in the Christian Life: John Wesley and the Means of Grace*. Pietist and Wesleyan Studies. Ed. David Bundy and J. Steven O'Malley. Lanham, MD: The Scarecrow Press, Inc.,1992.

Lawson, John. "The Conversion of the Wesleys: 1738 Reconsidered." *Asbury Theological Journal* 43 (Fall 1988): 7-44.

Leaver, Robin. "Charles Wesley and Anglicanism." In *Charles Wesley: Poet and Theologian*, ed. S T Kimbrough. (Nashville: Kingswood Books, 1992),

Lee, Hoo-Jung. "The Doctrine of New Creation in the Theology of John Wesley." Ph. D. diss., Emory University, 1991.

Lindström, Harald. *Wesley and Sanctification: A Study in the Doctrine of Salvation.* Grand Rapids: Zondervan Corporation, 1980. Reprint, Nappanee, IN: The Francis Asbury Press, 1996.

Lloyd, Gareth. "Charles Wesley and His Biographers: An Exercise in Methodist Hagiography." *Bulletin of the John Rylands University Library of Manchester* 82, no. 1 (2000): 81-99.

_____. "Charles Wesley and Methodist Religious Life, 1750-1775: The Manuscript Sources." *Proceedings of the Charles Wesley Society* 1 (1994): 33-46.

_____. *Charles Wesley and the Struggle for Methodist Identity.* Oxford: Oxford University Press, 2007.

_____. "The Letters of Charles Wesley." In *Charles Wesley: Life, Literature and Legacy*. Ed. Kenneth G. C. Newport and Ted A. Campbell. Peterborough: Epworth, 2007.

Maddox, Randy L. "A Change of Affections: The Development, Dynamics, and Dethronement of John Wesley's Heart Religion." In *"Heart Religion" in the Methodist Tradition and Related Movements*, ed. Richard B. Steele. Pietist and Wesleyan Studies, no. 12. Lanham, Md: Scarecrow Press, 2001.

_____. "John Wesley and Eastern Orthodoxy: Influences, Convergences and Differences." *The Asbury Theological Journal* 45, no. 2 (1990): 36.

_____. *Responsible Grace: John Wesley's Practical Theology*. Nashville, TN: Kingswood Books, 1994.

Morris, Gilbert. "Imagery in the Hymns of Charles Wesley." Ph.D. diss., University of Arkansas, 1969.

Newport, Kenneth G. C., and Gareth Lloyd. "George Bell and Early Methodist Enthusiasm: A New Manuscript Source from the Manchester Archives." *Bulletin of the John Rylands University Library of Manchester* 80 (Spring 1998): 89-101.

Newport, Kenneth. "Charles Wesley's Sermons." In *Charles Wesley: Life, Literature and Legacy*. Ed. Kenneth G. C. Newport and Ted A. Campbell. Peterborough: Epworth, 2007.

_____. *The Letters of Charles Wesley: A Critical Edition with Introduction and Notes. Vol 1: 1728-1756.* Ed. Kenneth G. C. Newport and Gareth Lloyd. Oxford; New York: Oxford University Press, 2013.

Nicholson, Roy S. "The Holiness Emphasis in the Wesleys' Hymns." *Wesleyan Theological Journal* 5 (Spring 1970): 49-61.

Noll, Mark A. *The Rise of Evangelicalism: The Age of Edwards, Whitefield, and the Wesleys*. A History of Evangelicalism. Vol. 1. Ed. David W. Bebbington and Mark A Noll. Downers Grove, IL: InterVarsity Press, 2003.

Podmore, Colin. *The Moravian Church in England, 1728-1760.* Oxford Historical Monographs. Ed. R. R. Davis, R. J. W. Evans, et. al. New York: Oxford University Press, 1998.

Quantrille, Wilma Jean. "The Triune God in the Hymns of Charles Wesley." Ph. D., Drew University, 1989.

Rattenbury, J. Ernest. *The Conversion of the Wesleys : A Critical Study*. London: Epworth Press, 1938.

_____. *The Evangelical Doctrines of Charles Wesley's Hymns.* London: Epworth Press, 1942.

Rattenbury, J. Ernest, John Wesley, Charles Wesley, and Timothy J. Crouch. *The Eucharistic Hymns of John and Charles Wesley: To Which Is Appended Wesley's Preface Extracted from Brevint's Christian Sacrament and Sacrifice Together with Hymns on the Lord's Supper*. 2nd American ed. Akron, OH: OSL Publications, 1996.

Renshaw, John Rutherford. "The Atonement in the Theology of John and Charles Wesley." Th.D. diss., Boston University, 1965.

Roth, Herbert J. "A Literary Study of the Calvinistic and Deistic Implications in the Hymns of Isaac Watts, Charles Wesley, and William Cowper." Thesis, Texas Christian University., 1978.

Runyon, Theodore. *The New Creation: John Wesley's Theology Today*. Nashville, TN: Abingdon Press, 1998.

_____. "The New Creation: A Wesleyan Distinctive." *Wesleyan Theological Journal* 31, no. 2 (Fall 1996).

Telford, John. *The Treasure House of Charles Wesley: A Short Anthology of the Evangelical Revival*. London: Epworth Press, 1933.

Townsend, James Arthur. "Feelings Related to Assurance in Charles Wesley's Hymns." Ph.D. diss., Fuller Theological Seminary, 1979.

Tyson, John R. "Charles Wesley, Evangelist: The Unpublished New Castle Journal." *Methodist History* 25, no. 1 (October 1986): 41-60.

_____. *Charles Wesley on Sanctification: A Biographical and Theological Study*. Grand Rapids, MI: F. Asbury Press, 1986.

_____. "Charles Wesley's Theology of Redemption: A Study in Structure and Method." *Wesleyan Theological Journal* 20, no. 2 (Fall 1985): 7-28.

_____. "Charles Wesley's Theology of the Cross: An Examination of the Theology and Method of Charles Wesley as Seen in His Doctrine of Atonement." Ph.D. diss., Drew University, 1983.

_____. "God's Everlasting Love: Charles Wesley and the Predestination Controversy." *Evangelical Journal* 3 (1985): 47-62.

Tyson, John R., and Douglas Lister. "Charles Wesley, Pastor: A Glimpse inside His Shorthand Journal." *Quarterly Review* 4 (1984): 9-21.

Valentine, Christine. "The 'Moment of Death.'" *OMEGA: The Journal of Death and Dying* 55, No. 3 (2007): 221-22.

Vallins, George Henry. *The Wesleys and the English Language; Four Essays*. London: Epworth Press, 1957.

Welch, Barbara Ann. "Charles Wesley and the Celebrations of Evangelical Experience." Ph.D. diss., University of Michigan, 1971.

Whitehead, John. *The life of the Rev. John Wesley, M.A. some time Fellow of Lincoln-College, Oxford. Collected from his private papers and printed works; . . . With the life of the Rev. Charles Wesley*. Vol. 1. London: Stephen Couchman, 1793.

Wilder, Franklin. *The Methodist Riots: The Testing of Charles Wesley*. 1st ed. Great Neck, N.Y.: Todd & Honeywell, 1981.

Wiseman, F. L. *Charles Wesley, Evangelist and Poet*. 1st English ed. London: Epworth Press, 1933.

Young, Carlton R. *Music of the Heart: John & Charles Wesley on Music and Musicians: An Anthology*. 1st ed. Carol Stream, IL: Hope Pub. Co., 1995.

www.ingramcontent.com/pod-product-compliance
Lightning Source LLC
Chambersburg PA
CBHW070300230426
43664CB00014B/2592